ANZUS AND THE EARLY COLD WAR

ANZUS and the Early Cold War

Strategy and Diplomacy Between Australia,
New Zealand and the United States,
1945-1956

Andrew Kelly

https://www.openbookpublishers.com

© 2018 Andrew Kelly

This work is licensed under a Creative Commons Attribution 4.0 International license (CC BY 4.0). This license allows you to share, copy, distribute and transmit the work; to adapt the work and to make commercial use of the work providing attribution is made to the authors (but not in any way that suggests that they endorse you or your use of the work). Attribution should include the following information:

Andrew Kelly, *ANZUS and the Early Cold War: Strategy and Diplomacy Between Australia, New Zealand and the United States, 1945-1956*. Cambridge, UK: Open Book Publishers, 2018. https://doi.org/10.11647/OBP.0141

Copyright and permissions for the reuse of many of the images included in this publication differ from the above. Copyright and permissions information for images is provided separately in the List of Illustrations.

Every effort has been made to identify and contact copyright holders and any omission or error will be corrected if notification is made to the publisher.

In order to access detailed and updated information on the license, please visit https://www.openbookpublishers.com/product/781#copyright. Further details about CC BY licenses are available at http://creativecommons.org/licenses/by/4.0/

All external links were active at the time of publication unless otherwise stated and have been archived via the Internet Archive Wayback Machine at https://archive.org/web

Digital material and resources associated with this volume are available at https://www.openbookpublishers.com/product/781#resources

ISBN Paperback: 978-1-78374-494-7
ISBN Hardback: 978-1-78374-495-4
ISBN Digital (PDF): 978-1-78374-496-1
ISBN Digital ebook (epub): 978-1-78374-497-8
ISBN Digital ebook (mobi): 978-1-78374-498-5
DOI: 10.11647/OBP.0141

Cover image: Photo by Lÿvean Imedecis on Unsplash, https://unsplash.com/photos/GhrBhL9kXf4. Cover design: Corin Throsby

All paper used by Open Book Publishers is SFI (Sustainable Forestry Initiative) and PEFC (Programme for the Endorsement of Forest Certification Schemes) Certified.

Printed in the United Kingdom, United States, and Australia by Lightning Source for Open Book Publishers (Cambridge, UK)

Contents

Acknowledgements	vii
List of Abbreviations	ix
Introduction: Disharmonious Allies	1
PART ONE: ORIGINS	11
1. Defence Problems in the Pacific	13
2. Japan, ANZAM, and the Bomb	29
3. Movement Toward an Alliance	51
4. ANZUS Negotiations	71
PART TWO: ANZUS IN FORCE	91
5. Post-Treaty Issues	93
6. Crisis in Southeast Asia	117
7. A Horrible Dilemma in the Taiwan Straits	135
8. Suez	157
Conclusion	179
Bibliography	183
List of Illustrations	197
Index	201

Acknowledgements

I could not have possibly completed a book of this magnitude alone. Firstly, I must thank Peter Mauch, who originally supervised my PhD thesis and encouraged me to revise its findings into this monograph. His guidance in my academic development has been truly invaluable and it is greatly appreciated. I am also thankful to David Walton, for similar assistance as a supervisor and mentor.

Secondly, I have several other people to thank at various research and tertiary institutions. David Jolliffe at the Australian Prime Ministers Centre was helpful in acquainting me with the primary material available at the Australian National Archives and the National Library of Australia. Mary Rickley, Dean Nogle and Michael Johnson at the Eisenhower Foundation were fantastic in their efforts to help me travel around Abilene, especially in very adverse weather conditions. At the Eisenhower Library, Chelsea Millner and Kevin Bailey were very helpful in finding useful material from the Eisenhower Administration. I am in debt to the many archivists I did not know by name at the Australian, New Zealand and United States National Archives who helped guide me through the important archival material. During publication, Lucy Barnes at Open Book Publishers made a time-consuming process feel incredibly easy. She provided great assistance in leading to the creation of this book.

Some of the material in this book was derived in part from two previously published journal articles. In 2014, I published "The Australian-American Alliance, Recognition of China and the 1954-55 Quemoy-Matsu Crisis" with the *Journal of Northeast Asian History*, and in 2017 I published "Discordant Allies: Trans-Tasman Relations in the Aftermath of the ANZUS Treaty, 1951-1955" with the *Journal of Australian Studies*. The latter article is available online at this address: http://www.tandfonline.com/10.1080/14443058.2016.1275744.

Finally, I am thankful to a few people in my personal life. A particular mention must go to Caitlin Holmes, who has been extremely supportive throughout all my professional endeavours. My mother and father, Sharon and Mark, have also been very supportive and deserve recognition for all the help they have given me over the years.

List of Abbreviations

ANZAM   Australian, New Zealand and British arrangement for the joint defence of Malaya and Commonwealth interests in Southeast Asia

ANZUS   Treaty between Australia, New Zealand and the United States

JCS   United States Joint Chiefs of Staff

NATO   North Atlantic Treaty Organisation

NSC   United States National Security Council

PRC   People's Republic of China

ROC   Republic of China

SCAP   Supreme Commander of Allied Forces in Japan

SEATO   Southeast Asia Treaty Organisation

Introduction: Disharmonious Allies

In August 1952, delegates from Australia, New Zealand and the United States met in Honolulu for the first formal round of discussions over how the ANZUS Treaty—a defence alliance signed by these countries in September 1951—would work in practice. The treaty required each signatory to "respond to the common danger" in the Pacific, and these powers indeed saw mutual dangers at the time. The Korean War had been raging for over a year and showed no immediate signs of ending. A Communist government in China appeared to have aggressive intentions. Local revolutionaries in Indochina and Malaya had demanded sovereignty from their colonial governments. Framed in this light, a closer strategic relationship between the ANZUS powers should have been cooperative and rather straightforward.

This was certainly not the case. In advance of Council meetings in Hawaii, Percy Spender—architect of the ANZUS Treaty and then Australian Ambassador in Washington—accused the Pentagon of purposely "diminishing the importance" of the alliance to avoid serious consultation with Australia. According to Spender, even Australia's former enemies—Germany, Italy and Japan—had "the opportunity of consultation on vital matters in a manner which so far has been denied to Australia."[1] Without a doubt, refusing to consult seriously with the Australians was an American objective. The US Joint Chiefs of Staff (JCS) had advised Secretary of State Dean Acheson that joint planning with Australia and New Zealand would mean "serious and far-reaching disadvantages to the present and projected

---

1   Spender to Casey, 18 March 1952, Spender Papers, Box 1, National Library of Australia (hereafter NLA).

© 2018 Andrew Kelly, CC BY 4.0   https://doi.org/10.11647/OBP.0141.10

state of United States planning for a global war."² This position aggravated the Australians, yet the New Zealanders did not share this view, despite their similar geopolitical circumstances. As one adviser told Head of the New Zealand External Affairs Department Alister McIntosh, New Zealand "did not share the long-standing Australian objective of infiltration into the world's policy-making hierarchy" after claiming that the Australian delegation almost demanded this outright at Honolulu.³ McIntosh certainly sympathised with this opinion, and even conceded later that New Zealand "never wanted the damn Pacific Pact in the first place."⁴

How did three allied powers—which shared a common language, similar historical roots and democratic liberal institutions—leave Hawaii with such competing views about the practicality of an alliance signed less than one year earlier? To some extent, disagreements between the ANZUS powers were symbolic of the challenging and divisive time in which the treaty was conceived. While in broad terms these countries shared similar political objectives in combating Soviet-led Communism during the early stages of the Cold War, the underlying purpose of this treaty was unique for each signatory and often created complex diplomatic tensions in the trilateral relationship. Australia, undeniably the most enthusiastic treaty member, viewed ANZUS as a means to rebalance its traditional ties with Britain by fostering a closer strategic relationship with the United States. The treaty limited the likelihood of future existential threats such as those posed by Japan in late 1942, and it provided an additional avenue for Canberra to voice its concerns about world affairs.

Across the Tasman Sea, policymakers in New Zealand were more reluctant to forge a closer political relationship with the United States if it meant damaging relations with Britain. For Wellington, one of the major benefits of ANZUS was that it simply allowed New Zealand to continue its military commitments to the British cause in the Middle East. After all, as Jatinder Mann pointed out about the post-war years,

---

2   Marshall to Acheson, 16 January 1951, Foreign Relations of the United States Series (hereafter FRUS) 1951 Vol. VI, 141.
3   Memorandum for McIntosh, 25 July 1952, Archives NZ, EA, 111/3/3/1 Part 8.
4   McIntosh to Corner, 3 October 1952, in Ian McGibbon ed., *Unofficial Channels: Letters Between Alister McIntosh and Foss Shanahan, George Laking and Frank Corner, 1946-1966* (Wellington: Victoria University Press, 1999), 106.

New Zealand "very much identified itself as a British country and an integral part of a wider British World, which had the UK at its heart."[5] In contradistinction to Australian and New Zealand views on an alliance, the United States refused to consider an ANZUS-style arrangement until the outbreak of the Korean War necessitated trans-Tasman support for a Japanese Peace Treaty. The United States did not want an explicit military commitment to defend critical Australian and New Zealand interests. US eyes were primarily fixated on the situations in Europe and Asia, and did not give much serious thought to strategic issues in the South Pacific. That said, the State Department did recognise the growing importance of the US alliance with Australia and New Zealand as the Cold War began to take shape, especially because they shared similar ways of life and political ideologies.[6]

Looking more broadly, the development of this trilateral relationship from the end of World War II to the 1956 Suez Crisis—two monumental historical events that bookend a period of great change for these countries—provides an interesting and unique case study in alliance diplomacy. Much like the conclusion of the North Atlantic Treaty Organisation (NATO) in 1949 which formalised the collective defence of Western Europe against the Soviet bloc, the ANZUS powers faced significant disunity when responding to mutual defence issues despite similar geopolitical interests in the Pacific. During these years, close Australian and New Zealand ties to Britain caused significant friction in their respective relationships with the United States. Despite Australian and New Zealand policymakers accepting that their post-war security relied upon the United States due to the fleeting nature of the British presence in the Asia-Pacific region, Canberra and Wellington maintained close strategic ties with London. As a result, when British decisions clashed with US policies, the Tasman countries were forced to choose between aligning their policies with one or the other of its two most important allies.

---

5   Jatinder Mann, "The End of the British World and the Redefinition of Citizenship in Aotearoa New Zealand, 1950s–1970s", *National Identities* (2017), 1, https://doi.org/10.1080/14608944.2017.1369019

6   Thomas K. Robb and David James Gill, "The ANZUS Treaty during the Cold War: A Reinterpretation of US Diplomacy in the Southwest Pacific", *Journal of Cold War Studies* 17, no. 4 (2015), 109-157, https://doi.org/10.1162/JCWS_a_00599

Even then, policymakers in Canberra and Wellington did not always agree on how closely to align their respective policies with the United States and Britain. This was due in some measure to mutual distrust, but it also stemmed from trans-Tasman differences over Britain's proper role in the post-war Pacific and Middle East. Canberra continued to cooperate and consult closely with London, yet a global power shift in favour of the US caused Australian diplomats to pursue actively a much closer relationship with the United States to meet their own security requirements. New Zealand also recognised the need for US protection but remained sceptical of American intentions and aimed, wherever possible, to align their policies with Britain to counteract US dominance. In short, while both countries maintained close British ties, active Australian efforts to pursue closer US-Australian strategic cooperation—often at the expense of cooperation within the British Commonwealth—caused significant discord in the trans-Tasman relationship.

Until at least the mid-1950s, the United States also proved unwilling to consult seriously with Australia and New Zealand. This lack of consultation created significant discord in the relationship. In the early years of the Truman Administration, Washington gave little consideration to Australia's and New Zealand's roles in the US containment strategy. Only after the Cold War escalated in Asia during the late 1940s and early 1950s did the United States give far more attention to developments in Asia and the Pacific, and in so doing, began to consider new ways in which to combat the spread of Communism in this region. This in turn drew Washington's gaze to Australian and New Zealand shores. ANZUS became possible because of this shared desire to respond to mutual security threats in the Pacific theatre, even if the three powers disagreed over many strategic issues. As the 1950s progressed, the alliance even offered Australia and New Zealand an unprecedented—albeit still minor—role in global strategy.

Since ANZUS was forged at such a momentous time in world history and subsequently played a significant role in the development of Australian and New Zealand foreign policies, historians have unsurprisingly devoted considerable attention to its conclusion. Early studies were especially critical of the Australian relationship with the United States. This was epitomised by Alan Renouf, former Head of the Australian Department of Foreign Affairs, who characterised the country's general approach to foreign policy as childish because of its marked inclination to stay with "mother" Britain and then the United States.⁷ As more archival records became available, however, it became clear that these views were simplistic and did not properly reflect that the post-war period was one in which Australian foreign policy actually "gained considerable maturity, and its capacity to act independently grew with the professionalism of its diplomatic service."⁸ Recent scholarly developments on Australian foreign policy during the early Cold War highlight this evolution, especially in analyses of individual diplomats and of the complexities that bedevilled the formulation of policy by the Department of External Affairs and the Department of Defence.⁹

Another theme that presented itself was the ongoing struggle Australia faced in managing its relationships with Britain and the United States while simultaneously building its own independent role in foreign affairs. Christine de Matos aptly described this challenge as a "juggling act", which became a common feature of the Australian approach to international crises in the 1940s and 1950s amidst a growing rift in Anglo-American relations.¹⁰ Given Britain's complete inability to protect Australian interests during World War II and afterwards, a post-war strategic shift toward the United States was logical and should have been quite straightforward. Instead, Canberra still maintained a close

---

7   Alan Renouf, *The Frightened Country* (Melbourne: Macmillan, 1979), 3-14. See also Joseph Camilleri, *Australian-American Relations: The Web of Dependence* (Melbourne: Macmillan, 1980).

8   Joan Beaumont, "Making Australian Foreign Policy, 1941-1969", in Joan Beaumont, Christopher Waters, David Lowe, with Gary Woodard eds. *Ministers, Mandarins and Diplomats: Australian Foreign Policy Making 1941-1969* (Melbourne: Melbourne University Press, 2003), 3.

9   Examples include Peter Edwards, *Arthur Tange: Last of the Mandarins* (Sydney: Allen & Unwin, 2006); David Lowe, *Australia Between Empires: The Life of Percy Spender* (London: Pickering & Chatto, 2010); Cotton, James. "R.G. Casey and Australian International Thought: Empire, Nation, Community", *The International History Review* 33, no. 1 (2011), 95-113, https://doi.org/10.1080/07075332.2011.555380; Arthur Tange, *Defence Policy-Making: A Close-Up View, 1950-1980*, Peter Edwards ed. (Canberra: ANU Press, 2008), http://press.anu.edu.au?p=101541

10 Christine de Matos, "Diplomacy Interrupted? Macmahon Ball, Evatt and Labor's Policies in Occupied Japan", *Australian Journal of Politics and History* 52, no. 2 (2006), 193, https://doi.org/10.1111/j.1467-8497.2005.00414.x

relationship with London, and, as a result, often had to walk a tightrope in times of crisis by balancing its relationships with its two great and powerful allies.

An unwillingness to abandon close ties to Britain, then, speaks to something much deeper in the relationship. Australians still saw themselves as inherently British-Australians, so much so that when Prime Minister Ben Chifley visited London in 1948 to discuss a Western Union against the Soviet threat in Europe, he argued that only the United Kingdom, Australia and New Zealand "fully represented the British tradition" despite British insistence on including Southeast Asian countries as part of Commonwealth strategy in the Middle East. This rather embarrassing suggestion, as Neville Meaney argued, points out that being British "meant more to the Australian prime minister than the British themselves."[11] These types of views still persisted through the 1950s, especially as then Prime Minister Robert Menzies—who had once described himself as British to the "bootheels"—strongly supported British actions in the Suez Canal region despite widespread international condemnation, including from the United States.[12] Australia's alliance with the US was indeed important and necessary, yet inclinations to support the British line even after the conclusion of ANZUS demonstrates the strength of pro-British sentiments in Australia as well as the complexities that existed in these relationships.

New Zealand historians have similarly focused on Commonwealth relations, but have also stressed the country's small-power status as a key feature of New Zealand's increasingly the country's growing independent outlook. As W. David McIntyre claimed, "New Zealand began to assert an independent voice in international affairs and not simply in empire affairs" in the post-war years, despite the United States acting as a "more aloof and unpredictable ally" than Britain.[13] To

---

11   Neville Meaney, "Britishness and Australian Identity: The Problem of Nationalism in Australian History and Historiography", *Australian Historical Studies* 32, no. 116 (2001), 80-81, https://doi.org/10.1080/10314610108596148

12   Stuart Ward, "The 'New Nationalism' in Australia, Canada and New Zealand: Civic Culture in the Wake of the British World", in Joan Beaumont and Matthew Jordan eds., *Australia and the World: A Festschrift to Neville Meaney* (Sydney: Sydney University Press, 2013), 191.

13   W. David McIntyre, "From Dual Dependency to Nuclear Free", in Geoffrey Rice, W. H. Oliver and B. R. Williams eds., *The Oxford History of New Zealand* (Melbourne:

be sure, however, Wellington's view of its role in the post-war world was fundamentally shaped by its place in the British Commonwealth. This was because, in the words of Frank Corner, the New Zealand Deputy High Commissioner in London, "New Zealand at heart [had] always been content with a 'colonial' position and had readily accepted the leadership of Britain." Similarly, he suggested in 1954 that "if New Zealand entered the American orbit [...] this would be a great pity."[14] Wellington, in short, wanted US protection but was reluctant to align itself too closely with Washington in case it damaged relations with London. As Australian National University historian T. B. Millar first concluded somewhat derisively in 1968, New Zealand was more inclined to "cling closer than did Australia to the skirts of Mother England." As part of its clinging, "New Zealand have thus from the beginning looked at the world through different eyes, from an increasingly different viewpoint than Australians, and have seen an increasingly different world."[15]

American historians have already extensively analysed almost all aspects of US foreign policy under the first two post-war US Presidents, Harry Truman and Dwight Eisenhower. These studies focus on the attribution of responsibility for the development of the Cold War, the emergence and implementation of global containment strategies, examinations of key individuals and their impact on policymaking decisions, and explanations of the ways in which post-war US foreign policy shaped the international system for the duration of the twentieth century and beyond.[16] This is well-trodden ground; this book's focus

---

    Oxford University Press, 1992), 520-527. Notable works on NZ foreign policy during this period include: Malcolm McKinnon, *Independence and Foreign Policy: New Zealand in the World Since 1935* (Auckland: Auckland University Press, 1993); Ann Trotter, *New Zealand and Japan, 1945-1952: The Occupation and the Peace Treaty* (London: The Athlone Press, 1990); Malcolm Templeton, *Ties of Blood and Empire: New Zealand's Involvement in Middle East Defence and the Suez Crisis, 1947-1957* (Auckland: Auckland University Press, 1994).

14 Frank Corner to Joseph Saville Garner, 27 July 1954, as quoted in James Waite, "Contesting 'the Right of Decision': New Zealand, the Commonwealth, and the New Look", *Diplomatic History* 30, no. 5 (2006), 893, https://doi.org/10.1111/j.1467-7709.2006.00583.x

15 T.B. Millar, *Australia's Foreign Policy* (Sydney: Angus & Robertson, 1968), 182.

16 More recent examples include Wilson Miscamble, *From Roosevelt to Truman: Potsdam, Hiroshima and the Cold War* (New York: Cambridge University Press, 2008); John Lewis Gaddis, *George F. Kennan: An American Life* (New York: Penguin, 2011); William McClenahan, *Eisenhower and the Cold War Economy* (Baltimore: John

lies instead with the roles Australia and New Zealand played in these US strategic and policy decisions. Examinations of US relations with small overlooked countries, such as the Pacific Dominions, offer a new perspective on how Washington managed its alliances as part of the broader East-West struggle. To this end, Tony Smith used the term "pericentrism" to describe the role of junior members of Cold War alliances who "tried to block, moderate, and end the epic contest" but also "played a key role in expanding, intensifying, and prolonging the struggle between East and West."[17] Fitting neatly within Smith's "pericentric" framework, Australia's and New Zealand's small but not insignificant role in influencing US foreign policy during the early Cold War provides a unique insight into such a significant period of international history.

There were certainly many important dimensions to this early trilateral relationship. Some key examples include the impact of these countries' domestic policies on international affairs, increasing trade imports and exports, establishing closer cross-cultural ties, and contrasting ways of approaching the challenges presented by Communism and the post-war international order. This book touches on some of these considerations as they became relevant to the development of ANZUS, yet its principal focus is on the key strategic and foreign policy issues that impacted high-level diplomatic relations. As a secondary theme, it also explores the roles of key individuals who shaped the nature of the relationship. Notable among them are Australian External Affairs Ministers Herbert Evatt, Percy Spender and Richard Casey; New Zealand's Head of External Affairs Alister McIntosh and Minister in the United States Carl Berendsen; Chief US negotiator for ANZUS and US Secretary of State during the Eisenhower Administration John Foster Dulles; and to a lesser extent British prime ministers Winston Churchill and Anthony Eden.

Hopkins University Press, 2011); Hannah Gurman, *The Dissent Papers: The Voices of Diplomats in the Cold War and Beyond* (New York: Columbia University Press, 2012). For a recent historiographical examination of these issues, see Frank Costigliola and Michael Hogan eds. *America in the World: The Historiography of American Foreign Relations since 1941*, 2nd edn. (New York: Cambridge University Press, 2014).

17 Tony Smith, "New Bottles for New Wine: A Pericentric Framework for the Study of the Cold War", *Diplomatic History* 24, no. 4 (2000), 567–591, https://doi.org/10.1111/0145-2096.00237

The book is split into two parts. Part One explores the post-war origins of the ANZUS alliance between 1945 and 1951. In this section, Chapters One and Two analyse mutual security issues such as defence planning after the end of World War II, contestation over control of key Pacific island bases, the Japanese occupation, and trans-Tasman involvement in British defence strategies and nuclear development. By early 1949, trilateral views on these issues left the three countries at odds and with no solid foundation for closer cooperation through a regional defence arrangement. Diplomatic developments during these years also reveal that Australia and New Zealand were not yet prepared to abandon their close political ties to Britain in the face of US dominance.

Despite a somewhat acrimonious start to the post-war relationship, Chapter Three considers some of the international developments in the late 1940s that made concluding a formal defence treaty more viable. These include the outbreak of the Korean War, the establishment of the People's Republic of China (PRC), and the election of new conservative governments in Canberra and Wellington. Following on from these developments, Chapter Four details negotiations over the ANZUS Treaty and highlights the contrasting types of commitment Australia, New Zealand and the United States were aiming to conclude with one another as well as the underlying reasons for these choices. Again, trans-Tasman ties to Britain surfaced as a key factor that complicated closer relations with the United States, especially as policymakers in London saw the conclusion of ANZUS as a significant blow to its international prestige and sought to undermine the treaty's practicality and usefulness.

Part Two explores how ANZUS worked when it came into force between 1952 and 1956. Chapter Five touches on a range of post-treaty issues, including contrasting views surrounding the treaty's actual scope and machinery, dealing with the question of British membership, the development of separate discussions for the joint defence of Southeast Asia, and uncertainty surrounding future of ANZUS after the election of Dwight Eisenhower in January 1953. These initial post-treaty developments provide no clear evidence of an alliance that was practical or even useful for serious consultation or to respond to issues of mutual concern in the Pacific theatre. Then, Chapters Six, Seven, and Eight explore trilateral responses to three international crises: the

1954 Dien Bien Phu Crisis in Indochina, the 1954-55 Quemoy-Matsu Crisis in the Taiwan Straits, and the 1956 Suez Crisis. These case studies provide snapshots of the ways ANZUS worked in practice, as well as illuminating the difficulties that threatened the efforts of the ANZUS powers to agree on a united response. These chapters also highlight that the usefulness of ANZUS often hinged upon British participation when responding to mutual dangers in the Pacific.

Each chapter seeks to answer several pertinent questions about the nature of the early post-war relationship. How did US global leadership impact its post-war relationships with Australia and New Zealand? How and why did Britain complicate relations between the ANZUS partners? Despite shared geopolitical interests, why did Australia and New Zealand disagree so often on fundamental strategic and diplomatic issues? Why did Australia, New Zealand and the United States have different views toward ANZUS but still commit to its conclusion? Was ANZUS ultimately useful in practice? How did the trilateral relationship develop over the first decade of the Cold War period, and what were the factors and who were the individual policymakers that shaped these changes? By including the views, policies and interests of all three countries in its pages, this book addresses these questions about the ANZUS relationship during the early Cold War.

PART ONE: ORIGINS

1. Defence Problems in the Pacific

While the origins of the Australian-New Zealand-American relationship can be traced as far back as the arrival of the US Great White Fleet in Sydney and Auckland in 1908, the pragmatic foundations of ANZUS lie in the aftermath of World War II. This war—which ended officially in September 1945—was the deadliest the world had ever seen, and the threat that the Japanese had posed to Australia and New Zealand during this conflict prompted diplomats in these countries to reconsider how they would safeguard their own security in the post-war world. The Tasman countries were too small to protect themselves, and war-torn Britain was no longer able to provide adequate military support in the Pacific. As Historian C. W. Braddick colourfully described, Britain's wartime experience "cruelly exposed its threadbare imperial clothes", subtly referencing Britain's inability to safeguard Australian and New Zealand interests while it fought against the Axis powers.[1] The only practical solution was pursuing a closer relationship with the United States, the world's most powerful nation that had defeated the Japanese almost single-handedly.

Indeed, this reality was well known to Australians and New Zealanders even before they entered the war against Japan. Soon after the Japanese attack on Pearl Harbour in December 1941, Australian Prime Minister John Curtin had already signalled the future of Australian diplomacy and strategy. "Without any inhibitions of any kind", he declared, "I make it quite clear that Australia looks to America, free of any pangs as to our

---

[1] C.W. Braddick, "Britain, the Commonwealth, and the Post-war Japanese Revival, 1945–70", *The Round Table* 99, no. 409 (2010), 372, https://doi.org/10.1080/00358533.2010.498975

Figure 1. US General Douglas MacArthur signs as Supreme Allied Commander for the formal surrender of Japan during WWII, September 1945. Photo by US Navy (1945), US National Archives Catalog, https://catalog.archives.gov/id/520694, unrestricted use.

traditional links or kinship with the United Kingdom."[2] While not going as far as suggesting a closer US relationship would come at the expense of relations with Britain, New Zealand Prime Minister Peter Fraser made similar comments about the importance of the United States to the future conduct of his country's diplomacy. "New Zealand realises", he said, "that the security and future development of the Pacific can only be satisfactorily achieved in cooperation with the United States."[3] In short, Britain's self-ruling Dominions in the South Pacific had come to the understanding that the United States had replaced Britain as the predominant power in the Pacific, and US officials certainly agreed. The Pearl Harbor attack had utterly discredited the pre-war isolationist movement, and had set the United States on a path toward becoming a global superpower. Nowhere was this more evident than in the Pacific,

---

2   David Day, "27th December 1941: Prime Minister Curtin's New Year Message, Australia Looks to America", in *Turning Points in Australian History*, Martin Crotty and David Andrew Roberts eds. (Sydney: University of New South Wales Press, 2009), 129-142.

3   Fraser Statement, 17 April 1944, in New Zealand Foreign Policy: Statements and Documents, 1943-1957 (hereafter NZFP: SD) (Wellington: New Zealand Ministry of Foreign Affairs, 1972), 65-67.

where the United States maintained an almost complete monopoly of power. As US Secretary of the Navy James Forrestal put it in April 1945, "all discussions of world peace" rested on the assumption that "the United States [would] have the major responsibility for the Pacific."[4]

To that end, the United States moved ahead swiftly with its post-war plans for the Pacific without any serious thought of cooperating closely with Britain or any of the Commonwealth countries. Based on US Joint War Committee plans drafted a year earlier, US Chief of Naval Operations Chester Nimitz and Chief of the Army Dwight Eisenhower agreed that the United States must set up a Pacific Command (stretching from the main Japanese islands through to the Philippines) and a Western Command (covering the "rest of the Pacific") solely under the leadership of American naval officers.[5]

At that time, the United States had no major strategic interest in Australia or New Zealand. As the world's most powerful nation, initial US post-war foreign and defence policies were global in nature. Moreover, all policies (including those in the Pacific) were considered in relation to their impact on the Soviet Union and the global balance of power. As part of these global post-war strategies, relations with Australia and New Zealand were low on the list of US priorities. As US Assistant Secretary of War John McCloy told Secretary of the Navy James Forrestal in November 1945, the "post-war problems are global; that is, the conditions of anarchy, unrest, malnutrition, unemployment [...] the economic dislocations are profound and far-reaching." For the Departments of War and the Navy, the US had to devise and develop broad defence policies to meet these challenges and prepare for war against the most likely post-war enemy, the Soviet Union. The United States had to respond to the "universal fear of the Russian colossus, both in terms of the size of that country and the locust-like effect of their occupation wherever they may be", McCloy reasoned.[6]

---

4   Forrestal Diary Entry, 17 April 1945, in *The Forrestal Diaries*, Walter Mills ed. (New York: The Viking Press, 1951), 45. See also the discussion of forward defence in Melvvn Leffler, *A Preponderance of Power: National Security, the Truman Administration, and the Cold War* (Palo Alto: Stanford University Press, 1994).

5   Meeting between Nimitz and Forrestal, 31 August 1946, in Walter Mills ed. *The Forrestal Diaries* (New York: The Viking Press, 1951), 195.

6   McCloy and Forrestal Meeting, 5 November 1945, in Mills ed. *The Forrestal Diaries*, 105-106.

Reflecting McCloy's global outlook, the US Joint Post-War Committee concluded that in the Pacific, the United States must take a global perspective. This meant the United States must consider Pacific strategy and defence policy in relation to its effect on the Soviet Union and other regions of primary US interest, such as Europe and the Middle East. A report produced by the Committee in July 1945 outlined that in the Pacific theatre, the United States should maintain an island barrier of bases stretching from Japan's northern islands down to the Philippines and the Southwest Pacific. These defence plans aimed to safeguard US territory from again being attacked from Asia, but also to prepare for a global fight against the Soviet Union. Further reports for US global defence policy were drawn up by the Committee in May 1946. These plans were code-named "Pincher." Based on the assumption of war with the Soviet Union, the Pincher Series assessed defence capabilities for the United States and its allies. The plans concluded that the United States must prepare for potential war with Moscow.

In assessing Allied post-war defence capabilities, Australia and New Zealand did not feature in US plans for a future war with the Soviet Union. This was largely due to Australia and New Zealand's respective geographic isolation and limited military potential, but also because Washington thought that their defence plans were largely shaped by British defence priorities. In late 1945, US Envoy in Wellington Kenneth Patton told US Secretary of State James Byrnes that New Zealand was still "strongly inflicted with the Mother Country complex."[7] Similarly, US Ambassador to Canberra Nelson Johnson asserted that "Washington [dealt] with Australia as part of the Empire." Before the war ended, he even went as far as suggesting that post-war discussions between Australia and the United States "would not be settled in Canberra but in consultation at 10 Downing Street."[8]

Unsurprisingly, Australia and New Zealand did look back towards their traditional ally in Europe. The problem these diplomats faced when visiting London, however, was the complete lack of any meaningful Commonwealth regional defence system in the post-war

---

7   Patton to Byrnes, 15 October 1945, United States National Archives and Records Administration (hereafter NARA), Record Group (hereafter RG) 59, 711.47H/10-1545.

8   Johnson Memorandum, 3 February 1945, NARA, RG 59, 711.47/2-345.

world. During the Commonwealth Prime Ministers' Conference in May 1946, Frank Corner, the political affairs officer in the NZ Department of External Affairs, described this dire situation to his colleagues back in Wellington. "What do we do now?" Corner asked rhetorically in a lengthy letter to New Zealand External Affairs Secretary Alister McIntosh during the Conference; "the British stated quite frankly that they are no longer able to defend the whole Commonwealth. Britain is resigning her leadership in the Pacific out of weakness", Corner conceded, and the only "logical development of this trend was to push Australia and New Zealand steadily towards the US."[9] Reporting back from the Prime Ministers' Conference, the Australians made similar observations. In an address to the Australian Parliament on 19 June, Prime Minister Ben Chifley stressed that Australia's post-war relationship with the United States would now form "a cornerstone of our foreign policy."[10]

Figure 2. Australian Prime Minister Ben Chifley (middle), Australian External Affairs Minister Herbert Evatt (left) and British Prime Minister Clement Attlee (right) meet at the 1946 Commonwealth Conference. Photo by unknown (1946), Flickr, https://www.flickr.com/photos/chifleyresearch/14483884882, CC BY 2.0.

---

9   Corner to McIntosh, 27 May 1946, in *Unofficial Channels*, 44-54.

10   Chifley Address to Parliament, 19 June 1946, National Archives of Australia (hereafter NAA), A816, 11/301/586.

The Britons were indeed in dire straits. The Second World War had financially crippled the British economy, so much so that London was the world's greatest debtor by the end of the war and had to borrow over three billion dollars from the US to give it breathing space in which to balance its overseas payments.[11] Even before the war ended officially, British Foreign Secretary Anthony Eden predicted that such severe economic difficulties would limit the influence of its foreign policy and force Whitehall to reassess which foreign strategic interests should be prioritised. At the top of Britain's list of strategic priorities was the post-war reconstruction of Europe and the German occupation, while it simultaneously looked to withdraw from any onerous commitments in the Asia and the Middle East. For instance, British Prime Minister Clement Attlee argued for a withdrawal of British forces in the Middle East, granting independence to India, Ceylon (Sri Lanka) and Pakistan, and later approved plans for Australia to lead the Commonwealth on the advisory Allied Council for Japan during the post-war occupation. These actions all signalled a retreat of British influence in the Asia-Pacific region. It was no longer a major world power, and had to abandon any non-critical commitments lest it further damage its economy or international prestige.

Unlike the United States or even Britain, neither Australia nor New Zealand was a global power and did not possess a sizeable military force or industrialised economy. Much to Australian External Affairs Minister Herbert Evatt's frustration, the United States did not give "countries like Australia and New Zealand" the opportunity to contribute meaningfully to the post-war defence of the Pacific.[12] As far as Australia's defence capabilities were concerned, Australian military personnel were still returning from overseas deployments throughout late 1945. This delayed finalising more concrete objectives for Australian post-war defence policy. As Australian Prime Minister Ben Chifley outlined in November 1945, early defence policy considerations were also affected by:

> The delay in establishing an effective world security organisation, the international difficulties that have arisen in establishing

---

11   George Peden, "Recognising and Responding to Relative Decline: The Case of Post-War Britain", *Diplomacy and Statecraft* 24, no. 1 (2013), 61, https://doi.org/10.1080/09592296.2013.762883

12   Ibid.

cooperation in the immediate post-war world, [and because] any present estimated strength of post-war forces would be very provisional while demobilisation at present leaves a doubt as to the ultimate strengths to which forces can be reduced.[13]

Once Australian personnel returned from overseas and better estimations could be made about Australian military strength, defence policy was first outlined publicly in November 1946. Its rationale revolved around the concept of imperial cooperation. In an address to the Australian Parliament on 2 November, Duke of Gloucester Prince Henry suggested that Australian forces be used in three roles: for UN peace-keeping forces, under old British Empire arrangements and in national defence. It was also announced that Australia would make a larger contribution to Commonwealth defence in the Pacific. This outline was then built upon by Australian military planners in a 1946 proposal titled the "Nature and Function of Post-War Defence Forces", which suggested that the "basic ingredient" of the defence of Australia was "Empire Cooperation."[14] In short, despite the clear decline in British power in the Pacific over the preceding decade, Australia was committed to retaining defence ties with Britain due to personal networks and loyalty to empire.

Australian defence policy did not begin to take a clearer shape until 1947. On 6 March, the Australian Council of Defence (consisting of the Defence Minister, Defence Secretary the Chief of the Australian Defence Forces and other service chiefs) summarised that the post-war security of Australia rested on "cooperation with Empire Defence and the development of regional security with the United States." Australian cooperation with larger powers was crucial, as the Australian Chiefs of Staff concluded that Australia was "an isolated smaller power with limited manpower and resources […] it is not able to defend itself."[15] Later that month, the Joint Intelligence Committee (a sub-organisation of the Department of Defence) approved the Defence Council conclusions

---

13   Chifley Memorandum on Australian Defence Policy, 27 November 1945, NAA, A5954, 2226/6.

14   McIntyre, *Background to the ANZUS Pact*, 173.

15   Notes on the Defence Council Meeting, 6 March 1947, in W. J. Hudson and Wendy Way ed. Documents on Australian Foreign Policy, 1947-1949 Volume XII 1947 (hereafter DAFP) (Canberra: Australian Government Publishing Service, 1995), 299-302; Chiefs of Staff Committee Meeting Minutes, 28 October 1947, DAFP 1947 Vol. XII, 290.

and planned for potential war scenarios that might involve Australian troops. As the Committee could see no immediate threat to Australia "in its own theatre", the most likely threats to Australian security would be in either the Middle East or the Far East. These areas were determined to be the most likely to threaten vital British interests and result in Australia becoming involved because of its ties with the United Kingdom.[16] From these initial reports, it appeared that Australian post-war defence policy was to set to take a similar shape to previous wartime policies insofar as it centred on British cooperation and fighting for Commonwealth interests rather than depending completely on US policy.

Six months later, the Australian Defence Committee (a suborganisation that advised the Defence Minister on matters relating to defence policy) agreed with these recommendations and produced the "Strategic Position of Australia" report. In it, the Australian Chiefs of Staff insisted on preparing Australian troops to be deployed in either the Middle East or the Far East, depending on how desperately British forces needed Australian support and whether such support would serve Australian interests. In each scenario, it was suggested that Australian defence preparations should be orchestrated in cooperation with the British Commonwealth.[17] Again, the Australians appeared to prioritise British cooperation over and above potential cooperation with the United States.

Across the Tasman, New Zealand post-war defence policy rested on two pillars. Firstly, like Australia, New Zealand defence planners recognised that the country was too small to defend itself and wherever possible it would have to coordinate its defence policy with Britain and the United States. The New Zealand Chiefs of Staff explained on 30 October 1945 that local defence would be linked to a system of forward island bases in the Pacific. In short, the Chiefs concluded that the United States would probably take responsibility for the island bases in Northeast Asia, so New Zealand should contribute to the defence of the Southwest Pacific through coordination with British-occupied bases in the Solomon Islands, New Hebrides, and Fiji.[18]

---

16 Joint Intelligence Committee Appreciation, 27 March 1947, DAFP 1947 Vol. XII, 277.
17 The Strategic Position of Australia, September 1947, NAA, 5954, 1628/3.
18 Isitt to Chiefs of Staff, 30 October 1945, Archives New Zealand (hereafter Archives NZ), Registered Secret Subject Files (hereafter RSSF), 022/4/32.

The major problem with adopting this strategy was that Wellington had very little information regarding American post-war policies in the Pacific. Without these plans, New Zealand could not properly coordinate its own defence plans with the United States. As New Zealand Minister in the United States Carl Berendsen told US Representative for the Allied Commission on Japanese Reparations Isador Lubin on 15 October 1945, New Zealand could not support US foreign policy in the Pacific unless the New Zealand Government "knew what American policy was."[19] In response to this lack of information exchange, US Envoy in Wellington Kenneth Patton suggested that New Zealand should be informed of US defence plans. Even while New Zealand generally followed the lead of the United Kingdom, Patton's interpretation of New Zealand's defence policy suggested that New Zealand objectives in the Pacific were "nearly identical" to the United States and that Wellington would support US plans "if they were communicated to the New Zealand Government."[20]

At this stage, however, Washington was not seeking a closer consultative arrangement with Wellington. That being the case, New Zealand Chiefs of Staff concluded that while there was no immediate threat to New Zealand in the Pacific theatre, the second pillar of New Zealand's initial post-war defence policy should be to assist in an Allied victory in the event of war in the Middle East. Under this plan, New Zealand was prepared to send its largest military contribution to the Middle East so that its limited military potential would make the greatest contribution to the outcome of a future war. However, as with the Australians, New Zealand defence policy was tied to British defence planning. It was on the advice of the British Chiefs of Staff that New Zealand Prime Minister Peter Fraser and his Defence Chiefs agreed that New Zealand should make its primary military contribution to the defence of the Middle East. Such a contribution was outlined clearly and with a specific time frame: an army expeditionary force would be deployed within ninety days after the decision to do so was made, and air squadrons within seventy days.[21]

---

19 Patton to Byrnes, 15 October 1945, NARA, RG 59, 711.47H/10-1545.
20 Ibid.
21 Chiefs of Staff Minutes, 24 September 1948, Archives NZ, EA, 85/1/1 Part 3.

Control in the Pacific Islands

American dominance in the Pacific first became a problem for Australia and New Zealand during the post-war settlement of the Pacific Islands. For Australia, New Zealand and the United States, each island held a different strategic value for each country and was considered for different purposes. John Minter, the US chargé in Canberra, relayed to the State Department early in January 1946 that Australian External Affairs Minister Herbert Evatt was "directly interested in security and welfare arrangements in the whole Pacific area" and that the "Australian government [felt] that both countries should participate in any talks which are held on this subject."[22]

Evatt's thoughts were based in part on the Canberra Pact, an Australian-New Zealand agreement reached in January 1944 that formally declared that the two countries have common interests in the South Pacific and that they should have a voice in the settlement of island bases. Evatt's demands reflected his frustration at being left out of the 1943 Cairo Conference (where Allied powers had determined the post-war fate of territories that had been seized by the Japanese in case of Allied victory). Evatt's comments also reflected his determination that Australia's viewpoint should be considered more seriously in Washington. In truth, Australia's realistic Pacific ambitions lay in only a select number of islands. Australia negotiated with Britain the post-war control of Nauru, the Cocos Islands, Christmas Island, the New Hebrides and the British Solomons, all of which have been dealt with extensively elsewhere.[23]

As far as the Australians were concerned, the key island was Manus, the largest island in the Australian-mandated Admiralty Island group just north of modern day Papua New Guinea. In early 1946, the State Department approached Australia to enter discussions over joint-base rights on Manus and the Admiralty Islands. As part of the US proposal, Australia would remain the administering authority of the trust territory and have full legislative control. The United States made it clear that it wanted no obligations or military costs: in a draft agreement sent to the

---

22 Minter to Secretary of State, 26 January 1946, FRUS 1946 Vol. V, 1.

23 David Goldsworthy, *Losing the Blanket: Australia and the End of Britain's Empire* (Melbourne: Melbourne University Press, 2002), 51-72.

Australian Legation, it proposed that the US was "not hereby committed to maintain military forces or facilities in the Admiralty Islands when it judged that military forces or facilities are unnecessary." The US only wanted rights to be able to "import, station, store in or remove from the Islands, personnel, material and supplies."[24] To Australian eyes, it looked as though the United States wanted the right to do whatever it wanted on Manus but without obligating itself to do anything.

Evatt took this approach to pursue his own goals: establish a regional defence arrangement with the United States and strengthen Australia-US defence relations. He was prepared to allow the US Navy to establish a base on the island but in return wanted reciprocal base rights for the Royal Australian Navy in American ports. He also demanded that an agreement over Manus should be concluded as part of a broader settlement over the Pacific Islands and that the US should "develop a regional defence arrangement which would include New Zealand" rather than "discuss individual bases such as the Admiralty Islands." Joint agreement on bases, at least as far as Evatt was concerned, could be reached "more easily" if it was "developed within [a] framework [of] an overall arrangement for the defence of Australia and New Zealand as well as the United States" and give strength in numbers to the defence of the Pacific.[25] US President Harry Truman, in fact, got word that Evatt "refused" to consider a joint-base solution unless it was part of an overall defence arrangement. Evatt was also "very keen", according to US Secretary of State James Byrnes, for an international conference on the settlement of the Pacific Islands rather than pursuing these negotiations privately.[26]

The United States strongly opposed Evatt's counter-terms. According to Byrnes, the only reason the United States was interested in Manus was because they had spent 156 million US dollars on the Manus Island base during the war and did not want to do "anything more than is absolutely essential for defence purposes." As Manus was not a high US priority, Byrnes thought that it was better not to have a

---

24 State Department to Australian Legation, 14 March 1946, FRUS 1946 Vol. V, 16-17.
25 Minter to Byrnes, 13 April 1946, FRUS 1946 Vol. V, 27-28; Gallman to Byrnes, 25 April 1946, FRUS 1946 Vol. V, 33.
26 Acheson to Truman, 7 May 1946, FRUS 1946 Vol. V, 41-42; Byrnes Memorandum, 28 February 1946, FRUS 1946 Vol. V, 6-8.

formal meeting because "it would only serve to create a lot of talk." For its part, New Zealand was likewise uninterested in partaking in Manus Island discussions or a formal conference over the settlement of islands in the South Pacific. "This question of bases has to be dealt with very discreetly", New Zealand Minister in the United States Carl Berendsen told New Zealand External Affairs Secretary Alister McIntosh on 4 June 1946, "the worst possible thing we could do [...] would be to embark on a course of public polemics."[27]

A formal conference also proved unnecessary because the State Department rejected categorically Evatt's suggestion that the settlement of the Pacific Islands should be undertaken as part of broader discussions toward a regional defence arrangement. On 25 April 1946, Under Secretary of State Dean Acheson advised that any regional defence arrangement was "premature" and "inadvisable." The US military agreed wholeheartedly with Acheson. Assistant Chief of Naval Operations Robert Dennison thought that since the United States was "not discussing the larger question of reciprocal use of bases", the "present negotiations have no relation whatsoever to a mutual defence arrangement or a regional security pact. Such a plan would be artificial and impossible under present conditions."[28] George Lincoln, US Military Adviser to the Secretary of State, added that Evatt's Pacific plan was "strategically unsound and contrary to the accepted military concept of the Joint Chiefs of Staff" to avoid binding military obligations in the Pacific.[29] Instead of pursuing a joint base on Manus further, the US preferred ultimately to abandon the project and leave the island in Australian hands. "At the suggestion of the Joint Chiefs of Staff", US Under Secretary of State Robert Lovett later advised President Truman, the United States "has no further interest in having bases in territory under Australian jurisdiction."[30]

---

27 Berendsen to McIntosh, 4 June 1946, in Ian McGibbon ed. *Undiplomatic Dialogue: Letters Between Carl Berendsen and Alister McIntosh, 1943-1952* (Auckland: Auckland University Press, 1993), 109.

28 Dennison to Hickerson, 22 April 1946, FRUS 1946 Vol. V, 32; Acheson to Harriman, 27 April 1946, FRUS 1946 Vol. V, 34.

29 Lincoln to Byrnes, 1 May 1946, FRUS 1946 Vol. V, 35-36.

30 Lovett to Truman, 7 October 1947, NARA, RG 59, 711.47/10-747.

The reality was that the United States had little interest in the entire Southwest Pacific. While there was "undoubtedly some strategic interest" in the Southwest Pacific for defensive purposes and civil aviation, the United States only made serious claims for exclusive rights to three islands: Canton, Christmas and Funafuti. The United States staked a claim to twenty-five islands, but Washington was prepared to abandon these claims if it could acquire exclusive rights over these three islands.[31] The US Joint Chiefs of Staff thought that "these islands were somewhat more important from a purely strategic and military standpoint than the others." Outside of these islands, the United States pursued joint rights for territory under the administrative authority of other countries.

At the same time the United States approached Australia for joint-base rights to Manus, the State Department was in advanced negotiations with New Zealand over a joint trusteeship for Western Samoa. These negotiations progressed more smoothly than with the Australians over Manus, but were not without their share of disagreement. Like Manus, Western Samoa was a New Zealand mandate and the only New Zealand territory to which the United States wanted rights. The United States had built an airfield there during the war and spent several million dollars on defence installations. The US Joint Chiefs of Staff asked for joint operating rights but wanted New Zealand to cover airfield operation at its own expense and demanded that any defence installations fall under a "strategic area trusteeship."[32]

New Zealand did not respond favourably to this US proposal. Prime Minister Peter Fraser was "not too happy" about the proposal for Western Samoa to become a US "strategic area", nor did External Affairs Secretary Alister McIntosh agree that the settlement of a United Nations Trusteeship Agreement should go ahead before negotiations for military bases were settled. "While it was perfectly apparent that we all wanted to achieve the same ends", McIntosh told Deputy Director of the Office of European Affairs John Hickerson, "[I] do not feel that we were in agreement." McIntosh suggested that a military base agreement

---

31 Lovett to Forrestal, 23 September 1948, NARA, RG 59, 811.014/9-2048. See also Hickerson Memorandum, 19 March 1946, FRUS 1946 Vol. V, 15; Furber Memorandum, 22 March 1946, NARA, RG 59, 811.24590/3-2246.

32 Hickerson to Acheson, 11 July 1946, FRUS 1946 Vol. V, 47.

should be settled before a trusteeship was put into effect in Western Samoa because he was concerned about what might happen if the joint US-NZ trusteeship failed to be approved by the UN.[33] McIntosh, in other words, was concerned that New Zealand's views would be ignored.

After raising these concerns with Hickerson, McIntosh and Fraser were eventually able to work out an acceptable solution and the UN approved the New Zealand-Western Samoa Trusteeship Agreement on 13 December 1946. The Australians, for their part, were "extremely angry" with New Zealand for not reaching the Western Samoa trusteeship solution jointly with their Manus Island problem.[34] Before the General Assembly, the Australian government cabled New Zealand Prime Minister Peter Fraser on 26 August, stating that Australia was "anxious to ensure mutual full support at the next General Assembly." The cablegram continued to stress that it was "desirable to [Australia] to attempt to attempt to remove without delay any point of substantial difference between us" over the settlement of trusteeships in the Pacific Islands, and hoped for an "early expression of [New Zealand] views."[35]

No reply from New Zealand was sent to Australia. Although this lack of a response was unusual and difficult to explain, it is plausible that at least part of New Zealand's unwillingness to cooperate with Australia in the UN was its recent frustration that Australia appeared only to cooperate with New Zealand when it suited Australian interests. "I am getting very fed up with Australia", Minister in the United States Carl Berendsen told McIntosh in April 1946 after supporting Australia's bid for a UN Security Council seat. "I don't remember any single instance where Australia has supported any action that I have taken […] I am bound to say that [Australia-New Zealand consultation] appears to be a validity [sic] only when it involves the support of Australian policy, and I am getting a little tired of it."[36] Berendsen—who, incidentally, was Australian by birth—recorded similar comments about this abrasive and non-consultative style of Australian diplomacy in his memoirs.[37]

---

33 Hickerson Memorandum, 27 February 1946, FRUS 1946 Vol. V, 8-10.
34 Warren to Acheson, 24 July 1946, FRUS 1946 Vol. V, 48-49.
35 Australian Government to Fraser, 26 August 1946, NAA 1838/238, 306/1/1 part II.
36 Berendsen to McIntosh, 2 April 1946, in *Undiplomatic Dialogue*, 106-107.
37 Hugh Templeton ed. *Mr. Ambassador: Memoirs of Carl Berendsen* (Wellington: Victoria University Press, 2009), 152-153, 171-183.

McIntosh shared Berendsen's frustrations with Australian diplomacy toward settling the post-war control of South Pacific islands. In this instance, New Zealand's unwillingness to cooperate undercut Evatt's diplomatic efforts to work towards a broader regional defence arrangement. It also highlighted that Australia and New Zealand were not working together in the Southwest Pacific but at cross-purposes. "I get more and more fed up with Australia", McIntosh replied to Berendsen later in May 1947 over Australian diplomacy in the UN and the Pacific Islands, "you simply don't know where they are except that they will be following their own interests in every case."[38]

Irrespective of differences between Australia and New Zealand, the latter was eventually able to come to an agreement with the United States over Western Samoa, even though many politicians in the Fraser Cabinet were uneasy about US activity in the South Pacific. The New Zealand government "strongly opposed" the transfer of sovereignty of Canton, Christmas and Funafuti to the United States for exclusive rights, believing that this was "unnecessary" for the strategic and civil aviation reasons the State Department offered.[39] In the end, there was clearly no mutually acceptable solution to all Australian, New Zealand and American ambitions in the Southwest Pacific. Each country's primary interests lay in different islands, and when these interests overlapped, agreement was not easy to come by. Although Evatt tried desperately to secure a broader American commitment through the settlement of Manus, the island remained in Australian hands. New Zealand was eventually able to conclude UN trusteeship agreement concerning Western Samoa. The US ultimately secured access to the three islands (Canton, Christmas and Funafuti) it considered to be most valuable for strategic purposes through negotiations with Britain.

Even though control over these island bases had been largely settled by 1946-1947, tensions simmered during negotiations between Australia, New Zealand and the United States. This friction only increased throughout the remainder of the 1940s. Occupation policies in Japan and greater trans-Tasman involvement in British defence plans were set to divide these powers further.

---

38 Berendsen to McIntosh, 21 May 1947, in *Undiplomatic Dialogue*, 125.
39 Acheson Memorandum, 11 July 1946, FRUS 1946 Vol. V, 48.

2. Japan, ANZAM, and the Bomb

Outside of the South Pacific, Australia, New Zealand and the United States also shared a keen interest in the post-war treatment and occupation of Japan. The United States led the occupation and dominated the organisations put in place to oversee the terms of Japanese surrender (which were the Allied Council and the Far Eastern Commission). This American preeminence caused considerable indignation in Australia and New Zealand. Once the US abandoned its initial occupation policies and began planning for a Japanese peace settlement in mid to late 1947, Australian and New Zealand protestations grew louder. The treatment of Japan quickly became one of the major divisive issues in the early Australian-New Zealand-American post-war relationship.

The United States took charge of the post-war occupation of Japan in part because they bore the overwhelming brunt of the war effort against them during World War II. Australia and New Zealand did form part of the British Commonwealth Occupation Force and were assigned their own districts; however, the United States assumed what diplomat George Kennan later termed a "totality of responsibility" in Japan.[1] US Secretary of State James Byrnes made it clear that unlike Germany, Japan would be an American-led occupation and they retained the right to make final decisions on post-war policy. As Assistant Secretary of State Charles Dunn told Byrnes, under no circumstances would Washington allow a "control Council in Japan" to diminish American influence.[2]

Initially, the United States pursued two basic objectives in the occupation of Japan: demilitarisation and democratisation. These policies ensured that "Japan [would] not again become a menace to the peace and security

---

[1] George Kennan, *Memoirs, 1925-1950* (New York: Bantam Books, 1967), 388.
[2] Dunn to Byrnes, 30 August 1945, FRUS 1945 Vol. VI, 697.

of the world."³ As far as war reparations were concerned, President Truman's Personal Representative Edwin Pauley asserted in late 1945 that the United States would seek a complete industrial disarmament of Japan and pass on much of Japanese industrial equipment and plants to countries entitled to reparations. Japan, in turn, would be left only with access to industries that were essential, such as food production.⁴ Australia and New Zealand had no objections to these plans. They ensured that Japan was completely unable to threaten Australia and New Zealand in the short-term future.

The major objections Australia and New Zealand raised during the occupation's early stages related to the Allied Council and the Far Eastern Commission. The Council acted as an advisory body intended to ensure that Japan's surrender, occupation and control plans were met, whereas the Commission was an organisation based in Washington that oversaw the Council. Both Canberra and Wellington argued that their voices were silenced by the Americans, who were unwilling to consult seriously with their allies about occupation policy. Indeed, whilst it appeared that these committees might offer the Allied powers a shared voice in the Japanese occupation, the United States refused to consider seriously any views that differed from or criticised US policy.

In Wellington, New Zealand policymakers were initially pleased with their position on the Far Eastern Commission. A place on the Commission offered New Zealand diplomats an opportunity to ensure that Japan's capacity for aggressive expansion would be completely removed, and so to protect New Zealand from the possibility that Japan would again come close to threatening its borders as it did in 1942. After the first Commission meetings were held in early 1946, Counsellor in the New Zealand Legation Guy Powles reported to Prime Minister Peter Fraser that "there seemed to be a general feeling of pleasure" that New Zealand was "able to do something" in regards to overseeing the Japanese occupation.⁵ New Zealand's position on the Commission also offered its senior diplomat, Minister to the United States Carl Berendsen, a unique opportunity to discuss New Zealand's post-war

---

3   US Initial Post-Defeat Policy Relating to Japan, 12 August 1945, FRUS 1945 Vol. VI, 609.

4   Statement by Edwin Pauley, 31 October 1945, FRUS 1945 Vol. VI, 997-998.

5   Powles to Fraser, 20 March 1946, Documents on New Zealand's External Relations (hereafter DNZER) Vol. II, 347-349.

security interests as they related to Japan with all the great powers. Berendsen was even appointed Chairman of the Steering Committee, an organisation that aimed to organise the Commission into various sub-committees and make recommendations about each aspect of the Occupation (including reparations, economic problems, legal reforms and war criminals). At this early stage, policymakers in New Zealand were likely unaware about the powerlessness of the Commission and these sub-organisations.

The Australians, in contrast, were not satisfied with a position on the Far Eastern Commission. Japanese attacks on Australian soil had spurred a strong sense of hatred towards Japan and its people. As both a punishment for wartime misdeeds and to prevent future Japanese aggression, the Australian people urged their leaders to demand a tough peace with Japan. Australian External Affairs Minister Herbert Evatt stated that Australia could not address these issues if it was not awarded a significant voice on Allied post-war policy towards Japan. More specifically, Evatt believed that the British government was at fault for not pressing upon the Americans that Canberra should be involved more closely in occupation plans because of its primary strategic interest in preventing a resurgence of Japanese militarism. Evatt simply did not think Britain fully understood Australian concerns about Japan. "Japan is an enemy who tried to destroy us", Evatt told British Prime Minister Clement Attlee and Foreign Minister Ernest Bevin bluntly in May 1946.[6]

Canberra did secure one concession from the great powers. It was agreed in Moscow that a fourth member of the Allied Council would jointly represent Britain, Australia, New Zealand and India. Responding to Evatt's claims to Attlee and Bevin, London conceded that Australia should be this Commonwealth representative. The Chifley Government appointed William Macmahon Ball as the British Commonwealth member of the Allied Council of Japan in January 1946. With Ball's appointment, Australia hoped it might influence Japanese policy, establish its status as a Pacific power and strengthen its claim to be "Britain's representative" in the region. The Americans, however, were unwilling to offer Australia (or any other power) a chance to meaningfully influence the policymaking process for the

---

6   Corner to McIntosh, 27 May 1946, in *Unofficial Channels*, 50.

Japanese occupation. In short, the United States was not pleased with Ball's appointment. Chairman of the Allied Council George Atcheson even complained that Ball's early criticisms of occupation policy were "palpably designed to cause embarrassment" to the United States.[7]

Indeed, Ball had immense difficulty in getting Australian views—and, by extension, Commonwealth views—considered seriously by the Americans. When he proposed slight alterations to the policies in mid-July, Ball noted with frustration that "during most of the time I was talking Atcheson paid no attention but was turning over papers and talking with his State Department assistant." When Ball finished, he complained to Evatt that Atcheson "looked up and said that he could not understand my line of argument and expressed disappointment that 'no specific and concrete' proposals had been made." Ball concluded that the US intended to "bog" the Council with a series of routine administrative matters to limit its influence in shaping occupation policy.[8]

As the weeks progressed, Ball grew further frustrated at American attempts to sideline the Allied Council. "I am sure there is a quiet and effective campaign to minimise in Japanese eyes the influence and prestige of all Allied Powers but the American", Ball complained again to Evatt on 23 July 1946. Because of this reality, Ball even recommended that the Allied Council be abolished. "If [the Council] is to be exclusively American", Ball continued to Evatt, "I regard it advisable to remove the pretence of an Allied Council."[9]

Ball's inability to get Commonwealth views considered in Japan began to cause serious repercussions for Anglo-Australian relations. As the Australian Government urged Britain to support Australian efforts to find appropriate resolutions on the Allied Council, London stressed that it simply had more pressing matters and needed US support elsewhere. As British Secretary of State for Dominion Affairs Viscount Addison told Canberra,

---

7   Eiji Takemae, *Inside GHQ: The Allied Occupation of Japan and its Legacy* (New York: Continuum, 2002), 102.

8   Ball to Evatt, 12 July 1946, NAA, A1838, 482/1/7.

9   Ball to Evatt, 23 July 1946, NAA, A1838, 482/1/7. For a recent detailed examination of Ball's time in Japan, see Ai Kobayashi, *W. MacMahon Ball: Politics for the People* (Melbourne: Australian Scholarly Publishing, 2013).

> Our collaboration with the Americans in other parts of the world (e.g. at this juncture in the Middle East and the forthcoming meeting of Foreign Ministers) is of such outstanding importance that we are not prepared to be committed in advance to a general policy of mediation in Japan. This might well fail to achieve its purpose in Japan and at the same time cause friction with the United States Government.[10]

In other words, even though Australia was tasked with representing British interests as well as Indian and New Zealand interests, Canberra was unable to find any support from London for its views on the Council in Japan. Annoyed that the Americans were ignoring every proposal he made, in July 1947 Ball resigned as the British Commonwealth Representative on the Allied Council. Even with Ball's resignation, however, there was no fundamental change in the main elements of Australian foreign policy towards Japan.[11]

New Zealand came to share Australian concerns with the US disinclination to consult its allies in Japan. "There is resistance to any proposed course of action which will involve the slightest deviation from the line that has been adopted" by the Supreme Commander of the Allied Forces in Japan Douglas MacArthur, Berendsen told McIntosh on 31 May. He added that "I cannot over-emphasise the degree of exasperation and frustration which this attitude presents to New Zealand and other members of the Far Eastern Commission." Adding to Berendsen's frustration was the evidence that his efforts to change this US dominance were unsuccessful. In late May, Berendsen candidly told Chairman of the Far Eastern Commission Frank McCoy about his "extreme dissatisfaction with the lack of progress" on the Commission but doubted whether even sharing this view "served any useful purpose."[12] As a result, Berendsen concluded that the Commission was "nothing but a joke." The Commission was not "allowed to decide on any questions of policy at all", Berendsen later told McIntosh, but rather

---

10 Addison to Department of External Affairs, 16 April 1946, NAA, A3317, 1/46 Part 2; Christopher Waters, *The Empire Fractures: Anglo-Australian Conflict in the 1940s* (Melbourne: Australian Scholarly Publishing, 1995).

11 De Matos, "Diplomacy Interrupted?", 196.

12 Berendsen to McIntosh, 31 May 1946, DNZER Vol. II, 409-412; Berendsen to McIntosh, 2 April 1946, in *Undiplomatic Dialogue*, 107; Berendsen to McIntosh, 4 June 1946, in *Undiplomatic Dialogue*, 110-111.

it "follow[ed] behind [MacArthur] in every step, and merely applauded him."

Berendsen was equally annoyed that Australia did not support New Zealand and instead opposed all its proposals. Even after speaking with Evatt and agreeing that Australia and New Zealand had similar concerns about the futility of the Commission, there was no subsequent trans-Tasman cooperation on these issues. "On the Far Eastern Commission, [the Australians] seem to go out of their way to oppose our views", he complained to McIntosh on 2 April 1946, citing protestations about the timing of Japanese elections and the proposed wording of the Japanese Constitution.[13] Taking these concerns one step further, McIntosh thought that Australia aimed to be the Commonwealth representative for all matters relating to the American occupation and the Japanese peace settlement.

Revising Policies in Japan

By 1947, growing Cold War tensions with the Soviet Union and fears over the global threat of Communism forced Washington to reconsider its policies in Japan. The United States abandoned its twin demilitarisation and democratisation objectives and instead planned to rebuild Japan's economy so that it might become a powerful American ally in Northeast Asia. In August 1947, the Policy Planning Staff (PPS) expert on Asian affairs John Davies told Kennan that they should propose to the National Security Council that the US encourage a "stable Japan, integrated into the Pacific economy, friendly to the US, and in case of need, a ready and dependable ally of the US."[14] As a result, the US began an intensive economic recovery program in Japan to revive the war-ravaged nation as a powerful American ally and ultimately push the balance of power further in America's favour.

Among other US allies and partners, Australia was concerned by the US revision of Japanese occupation policies. As the future of Japan was vital to Australian security interests, any movement towards an economic recovery could put Australia at risk. At least as far as the

---

13 Berendsen to McIntosh, 31 May 1946, DNZER Vol. II, 411-412.
14 Davies to Kennan, 11 August 1947, FRUS 1947 Vol. VI, 485-486.

Australian military were concerned, its own interests were best served by a continued American presence in Japan. Therefore, they believed the occupation should continue under the existing conditions. As the Australian Defence Committee concluded in June 1947, the "most important single strategic question affecting Australia's security in the Pacific is the continuance of the present favourable balance of power in the Pacific brought about by the United States participation in the occupation of Japan." The Australian military believed that US should continue the Allied occupation of Japan "until such time as Japan is considered unlikely to endanger the peaceful aims of the United Nations." As part of this hope for a continued Allied occupation, it was also concluded that there should also be a continued "destruction of Japanese war potential."[15]

In the External Affairs Department, Australian policymakers argued similarly that a change of policy afforded Tokyo the possibility of returning to its imperialistic ways and threatened the security of Australia. Even after his position somewhat softened after visiting Japan in late 1947, Evatt reported that

> The first principle of our policy has always been the safety and security of the Pacific, including our own country [...] Australia has called for the disarmament and demilitarisation of Japan, destruction of its capacity to wage war, and a sufficient degree of supervision under the peace treaty to prevent the regrowth of war-making capacity. The second principle has been the encouragement of democracy in Japan, which involves the gradual growth of the social, political and economic system.[16]

In other words, Evatt's public position appeared to match closely America's original post-war Japanese policy insofar as it urged complete disarmament and demilitarisation, but was reluctant to accept any immediate change to policies for Japan.

On top of Evatt's outline of Australian policy for Japan, the Chifley Government also demanded that Japan award reparations to Canberra for its war waged against Australia during World War II. These demands became especially urgent considering potential revisions to US policy in

---

15 Australian Defence Committee Minutes, 24 June 1947, NAA, A1838, 539/1/2.
16 Evatt Statement, 17 August 1947, Current Notes on International Affairs (hereafter CNIA) 1947 Vol. 28, 470.

Japan that focused on economic development, as Australian diplomats feared that any delay might mean that Australia would not get fairly compensated. "The Australian Government feels that [the] total amount and distribution of reparations from Japan should be settled urgently", a Department memorandum to New Zealand Prime Minister Peter Fraser specified. The message warned that "it is possible that the United States may go ahead now and issue an interim directive on reparations" which might entail that there would be "no reparations at all from Japan."[17]

Australian pronouncements against an immediate revision to Japanese economic and reparation policies were causing considerable headaches for the United States. While the US began redrafting its Japanese occupation plans, US Political Adviser in Japan George Atcheson Jr. complained on 5 July 1947 to US Secretary of State George Marshall that Australia's "distorted pronouncements and unwarranted criticisms have been so violent and so widely publicised" that they threatened US prestige in Japan and throughout the Far East. He also warned Marshall that "any appeasement of [the] Australians will without question seriously undermine American prestige in this part of the world."[18]

Complicating problems further was Evatt himself, whose abrasive and demanding personality grated on the Americans. Under Secretary of State Robert Lovett was particularly scathing of Evatt, telling Truman in October about

> [Evatt's] aggressive, egocentric manner [...] He has been accused of self-seeking, and it is not always clear whether he is motivated by true patriotism or simply by egotism. He has great self-confidence and determination, is anxious to have a finger in every pie, is slow in giving his confidence, and insists on receiving full credit for his achievements.[19]

While Lovett was indeed concerned by the way in which Evatt acted, there remained hope in the State Department that his egocentrism could benefit the United States if properly cultivated. This was especially true in relation to Evatt's efforts to purposely champion the voices of smaller

---

17   Australian Government to Fraser, 20 April 1948, NAA, A1838/2, 479/10 Part V.

18   Atcheson to Marshall, 5 July 1947, FRUS 1947 Vol. VI, 531.

19   Lovett to Truman, 7 October 1947, President's Secretary's Files, Truman Papers, Harry S. Truman Presidential Library (hereafter TL).

powers in the United Nations rather than always support US policies. In the instances when Evatt's views and American views aligned, the State Department later concluded that "Evatt's egotism [should] be turned into constructive channels [...] When we are satisfied that the Australians will follow our line of thinking he, as Australia's spokesman, should be encouraged to take the initiative."[20]

New Zealand had similar problems with Evatt, who all too often spoke on New Zealand's behalf or ignored their point of view entirely. "If [Evatt] ever stops to think", McIntosh once told one of his External Affairs Officers Frank Corner, he would sometimes "go out of his way to consider New Zealand's viewpoints." The problem was that Evatt's list of concerns were "so large that he sometimes forgets our irons amongst the others he has in the fire", McIntosh added, mixing his metaphors.[21] So far as the revision of Japanese policies was concerned, the Americans found New Zealand diplomats much easier to deal with than Evatt and the Australians. Although Wellington also feared that a soft peace treaty and an economic revival might reignite Japanese aggression, New Zealand policymakers realised that Evatt's antics were doing little to advance their cause with the Americans. It would be better, so far as Wellington were concerned, to keep quiet on the issue.

At the time, there were few Australians with enough expertise in international affairs to mitigate the detrimental effect Evatt's diplomatic style appeared to have on Australia's allies. John Beasley and Norman Makin, Australian High Commissioner in London and Australian Ambassador in Washington respectively, were two notable exceptions and they helped to decrease the tensions that arose when Australia's allies grew increasingly frustrated with Evatt, at least in part. The former, Beasley, was a rather softly-spoken and shy person who arrived in London in August 1946. He did, however, argue assertively for Australia's right to be consulted on international issues and took a strongly anti-Communist stance on most matters pertaining to the Soviet Union, a position that neatly aligned with British Foreign Secretary Ernest Bevin's views on the global communist threat. At times when the British Foreign Office saw Evatt's behaviour as "sinister" and

---

20 Policy Statement of the Department of State, 18 August 1948, NARA, RG 59, 711.47/8-1848.

21 McIntosh to Corner, 14 June 1946, in *Unofficial Channels*, 58.

"nonsensical", Beasley was often able to smooth over these differences and provided a channel for continued discussions about critical matters affecting Anglo-American relations such as Commonwealth policy in Japan and later discussions about joint defence arrangements.[22] He could not offset every clash Evatt had with Bevin and other policymakers in London, nor could he always consistently articulate Australian views relating to the United Nations or post-war international order due to Evatt's predisposition for ad hoc and non-consultative policymaking. That said, Beasley navigated his position quite well during a difficult period in world affairs, in which individuals such as Evatt complicated the efficacy of Anglo-Australian relations in dealing with matters of mutual strategic interest.

Across the Atlantic, Makin was another simple but more direct type of diplomat. Historian Frank Bongiorno described the British-Australian as a "small, bespectacled and tidy man that was a Labor-type more common in Britain than in Australia [...] an earnest, abstaining, self-improving Methodist layman."[23] Before moving to Washington, Makin earned his diplomatic stripes through representing Australia in London at the UN General Assembly and the first meeting of the UN Security Council in 1946. While some historians and politicians have suggested Makin did not make the most of his opportunity to improve Australian-American relations in the late 1940s and early 1950s (Makin, for instance, abstained from drinking alcohol and found social gatherings with diplomats in Washington a rather frivolous and tiresome affair), he earned praise from his colleagues by providing a much friendlier and more courteous face to US policymakers than Evatt did. Paul Hasluck, the Australian counsellor in charge of the Australian mission to the UN and acting representative on the Atomic Energy Commission, described Makin as someone with "unfailing courtesy

---

22 Frank Bongiorno, "John Beasley and the Postwar World", in Carl Bridge, Frank Biongiorno and David Lee eds., *The High Commissioners: Australia's Representatives in the United Kingdom, 1910-2010* (Canberra: Australian Department of Foreign Affairs and Trade, 2010), 124, https://dfat.gov.au/about-us/publications/historical-documents/Documents/high-commissioners.pdf

23 Frank Bongiorno, "Norman Makin and Post-War Diplomacy, 1946-1951", in David Lower, David Lee and Carl Bridge eds., *Australia Goes to Washington: 75 Years of Australian Representation in the United States, 1940-2015* (Canberra: ANU Press, 2016), 39, https://press.anu.edu.au/publications/australia-goes-washington

and dignity."[24] These character traits were precious commodities in the Department of External Affairs while Evatt was still serving as Minister. By most accounts, Makin was well-liked in Washington despite having to try to defuse tense situations between the United States and Australia on policy issues such as the Japanese occupation.

Despite their knack for mitigating some of the difficulties that Evatt created in Australia's external relations, neither Beasley nor Makin could exercise enough influence in their respective posts to convince policymakers in Washington and London of the necessity for a continued hard-line policy on Japan. Reaching a common position about this became urgent after the United States issued invitations to the eleven countries on the Far Eastern Commission to attend preliminary talks for the Japanese settlement in July 1947. In an effort to find some degree of policy agreement between Australia, New Zealand and other Commonwealth countries in the face of revised US Japanese occupation policies, a Commonwealth Conference was held in Canberra from 26 August to 2 September 1947. Although Australian policymakers had been very vocal in their support for long-term demilitarisation and democratisation policies in Japan, it was agreed that a peace treaty could be finalised so long as Japan remained demilitarised. It was also agreed that there should be strict controls over Japanese imports and exports and that there should be some form of supervisory commission established to implement the terms of the treaty.[25] In other words, the Commonwealth delegates hoped for a virtual continuation of strict early occupation-era controls.

Overall, the communiqué that was issued after the Conference urged support for an early yet hard-line demilitarised peace treaty for Japan. In Wellington, the agreements reached at the Conference were "commended" by the New Zealand External Affairs Department. A report by the External Affairs Committee on the Japanese Peace Settlement concluded that as far as a potential peace treaty was concerned, Japan "must be completely disarmed and demilitarised for an indefinite period." The report also concluded that "post-treaty

---

24 Ibid., 45.

25 Department of External Affairs to Mission in Tokyo, 8 September 1947, NAA, A1068, P47/10/61 Part IV. For an agenda list of the Commonwealth Conference, see Preliminary Notes on Provisional Agenda by Evatt, August 1947, DAFP 1947 Vol. XII, 578-591.

Figure 3. Delegates to the British Commonwealth Conference on the Japanese Peace Treaty in Canberra, August 1947. *Back row, left to right*: R.T. Pollard (Australia), Sir Raghanath Paranjpye (India), U. Shwe Baw, Thakin Lun Baw (Burma); *Middle row, left to right*: J.J. Dedman (Australia), J.G. Barclay (NZ), Hector McNeill (UK), E.J. Williams (UK), Sir B. Rama Rau (India), M.M. Rafi (Pakistan), K.A. Greene (Canada); *Front row, left to right*: Peter Fraser (NZ), Lord Addison (UK), J.B. Chifley, H.V. Evatt (Australia), Brooke Claxton (Canada), H.G. Lawrence (South Africa). Photo by unknown (1947), Flickr, https://www.flickr.com/photos/archivesnz/28950147372, CC BY 2.0.

economic controls will be required" so that a peace conference could be held at an early date.[26] In other words, if an early peace settlement was reached, New Zealand made it clear that it favoured a hard-line settlement with Japan.

This sentiment was shared in Australia. As Evatt said to US Secretary of State George Marshall after the Conference, if the Commonwealth was to support a peace treaty, special provisions must be made to ensure that Japan could not access "certain industries with obvious war potential" such as steel and iron ore.[27] External Affairs Advisor to the Australian Delegation at the Commonwealth Conference Frederic

---

26 Report by the External Affairs Committee on the Japanese Peace Settlement, 20 November 1947, DNZER Vol. III, 195-107.

27 Evatt to Marshall, 2 September 1947, NAA, A1838, 538/1 Part II.

Eggleston went one step further, arguing that the Conference did not properly demonstrate how important it was for Australia that Japan remained demilitarised if it was to agree to any Japanese peace settlement. "Conferences of this kind do not approach the crucial issues", he told Assistant Secretary of External Affairs Alan Watt in September, "to agree on negatives is a waste of time."[28]

Eggleston warned Evatt directly against reaching a speedy settlement in Japan and doubted the possibility of the country becoming truly democratic. "I feel somewhat disturbed at the views which appeared to predominate at the British Commonwealth Conference", he told Evatt, adding that "there seems to be a feeling that nothing could be done except to demilitarise [Japan] and that the democratisation of Japan was desirable, but the Allies could not impose it and it was futile to try." According to Eggleston,

> If these views prevail, a position of instability will develop in the Pacific which will be very disappointing to the Australian people. Japan will be free to resume her superiority in East Asia and will then be available to move with all her economic and strategic power into the orbit of the highest bidder [...] under these circumstances, I strongly urge that we ask for a prolonged occupation or control of Japan.[29]

Evatt had no serious problems with Eggleston's claims about the risks associated with a militarised Japan. The crucial issue, especially in Australia, was Japanese remilitarisation. At the time, Australia and the Commonwealth was only open to a peace settlement if Japan's war potential was completely denied or strictly controlled. Evatt, assuming that no movement had yet been made towards remilitarising Japan, told US Secretary of State George Marshall and MacArthur that the Commonwealth agreed with US policy in Japan and supported movement towards a peace settlement. However, the State Department was in the middle of reconsidering the idea of a demilitarised Japan. In September 1947, the Policy Planning Staff drafted a top-secret paper titled "US Policy Toward a Peace Settlement with Japan" which outlined that "a major shift in US policy toward Japan [was] being talked about under cover." The paper suggested that the "idea of eliminating Japan

---

28 Eggleston to Watt, 3 September 1947, DAFP 1947 Vol. XII, 613-615.
29 Eggleston to Evatt, 1 October 1947, DAFP 1947 Vol. XII, 617-621.

as a military power for all time [was] changing" and that a peace treaty "would have to allow for this changed attitude."[30] This drastic alteration in US policy would have serious ramifications for the movement towards a peace settlement, as Australia and New Zealand vehemently opposed the idea of post-occupied Japan having its own military power without assurances from the United States that their countries would be protected. This critical issue between Australia, New Zealand and the United States subsequently formed one basis for future treaty negotiations.

Under these policy changes, Australia would still not be afforded the opportunity to influence the decision-making process. The United States, in short, remained intent on dominating the Japanese occupation without seriously consulting with its allies in the Pacific. Even while it was highly desirable to procure Australian support for its policies in Japan, the State Department advised that the United States should do little more than explain the reasons for these new policies to its allies rather than involve them in the decision-making process. "Whenever possible", the State Department suggested on 18 August 1948, "announcements of new policy decisions should be preceded by [a] frank explanation of our motives to the Australians both here and in Canberra" in order to avoid any measures being "misunderstood by the Australian Government." Since the Australian public took a "lively interest" in Japan, the Department advised that "every effort should be made to brief Australian correspondents both [in Washington] and in Japan on reasons for SCAP policies."[31]

Similarly, the State Department recognised that efforts should also be made to explain American policies to New Zealand diplomats and journalists. As a State Department policy statement claimed on 24 September 1948, "New Zealand shares Australia's certain dissatisfaction with present relations between the Far Eastern Commission and SCAP and has been critical of many of General MacArthur's policies." The United States, in turn, should "be careful to prepare the ground through diplomatic channels before new measures are adopted in Japan" and "unheralded interim directives by SCAP should be avoided wherever

---

30 Kennan Memorandum, 14 October 1947, FRUS 1947 Vol. VI, 536-537.
31 Policy Statement of the Department of State, 18 August 1948, NARA, RG 59, 711.47/8-1848.

possible."[32] Again, these conclusions concisely demonstrated US disinclination to consult with Australia and New Zealand in Japan. US policymakers aimed to explain American policies as clearly as possible to Australian and New Zealand policymakers after decisions were made in Washington and Tokyo, yet these diplomats would not be accommodated a place in the decision-making process.

ANZAM and the Bomb

As discussions over the Japanese occupation and a potential peace treaty progressed, Australia hoped to secure a regional defence pact with the United States to safeguard against the possibility that it might be attacked by Japan or elsewhere. "What [Australia] needs is an appropriate regional instrumentality in Southeast Asia and the Western Pacific", Evatt announced in Parliament on 26 February 1947 as part of his endeavours to conclude a regional pact with the United States over the settlement of Manus Island. He also suggested Australia needed access to US military planning so that it might better prepare for its own defence in the event of another world war. "The proposed regional instrumentality", Evatt announced, "will at least facilitate the free and rapid exchange of basic information [...] and plans for regional cooperation."[33] The United States, however, was unwilling to consider a formal pact during negotiations over Manus Island and refused to share military information. As a result, Australia's attention turned to coordinating defence planning more closely with Britain. This manifested itself in two ways: the formation of ANZAM and the Anglo-Australian Joint Rocket Project.[34]

Britain's dire post-war economic situation forced London to look for allied assistance in regions that were not in its primary interests. Against this backdrop, it became wholly practical for Britain to work more closely with Australia and New Zealand in the defence of bases in

---

32 Policy Statement of the Department of State, 24 September 1948, NARA, RG 59, 711.47H/9-2448.

33 Evatt Statement, 26 February 1947, Commonwealth of Australia House of Representatives Debates, no. 9 1947, 166.

34 ANZAM refers to the Australian, New Zealand and British arrangement for the joint defence of Malaya and Commonwealth interests in Southeast Asia.

Southeast Asia. In the Pacific, Britain's major post-war concerns centred on Hong Kong, Singapore and security issues resulting from Communist insurgencies in Malaya. The Foreign Office and British Chiefs of Staff realised that in the event of a global war the defence of the Far East and Southeast Asia would be a low priority. That being the case, London was open to the possibility of coordinating strategic planning more closely with Australia and New Zealand. As Communistt activity in Southeast Asia became one of the most immediate post-war threats to Australia and New Zealand, both Canberra and Wellington welcomed closer strategic coordination with Britain. Australian, New Zealand and British security interests in Southeast Asia coincided and the informal agreement known as ANZAM was established.

On 1 April 1947, the Australian Defence Committee considered reports from the Joint Planning Committee about plans for cooperation with Britain for Commonwealth Defence in Southeast Asia. These reports were based on discussions about a Joint Australian-New Zealand-British Liaison Staff to deal with mutual defence problems, which took place during the Prime Ministers' Conference in May 1946. The Australian Defence Committee report suggested that the Australian government should undertake greater responsibility in strategic planning relating to regional security matters in the Pacific. Such planning would have to be derived, the Committee concluded, from a broader worldwide strategic plan in which the British Commonwealth would participate.[35] One month later, a memorandum on "Commonwealth Defence Cooperation" was produced on 23 May that outlined the larger contribution Australia was prepared to make to Commonwealth defence in the Pacific in coordination with Britain. The report advised that a Joint Defence Committee with British and New Zealand representatives would be established to achieve this goal.[36] This Committee also formed the basis for trilateral discussions relating to the activities of Commonwealth forces stationed in Occupied Japan.

Five days later, Australian Prime Minister Ben Chifley sent a letter to British Prime Minister Clement Attlee that explained his government's plans for this Committee. At a meeting chaired by Attlee in June, the

---

35 Defence Committee Memorandum, 1 April 1947, NAA, A2031, 119/1947.
36 Memorandum by the Australian Defence Committee, 23 May 1947, NAA, A5954, 1850/1.

British agreed to appoint three lower-rank representatives of their Chiefs of Staff to attend Australian Defence Committee meetings. Attlee then replied formally to Chifley's offer on 17 August, welcoming Australia's willingness to chair defence council meetings and take primary responsibility for strategic planning in Malaya.[37]

After Britain indicated it was agreeable to the Australian proposal, Chifley contacted Wellington in October to enquire whether New Zealand would also accept its joint strategic plan. New Zealand Prime Minister Peter Fraser responded on 13 November, saying that his government was also agreeable to Australia's proposals for cooperation in British Commonwealth Defence. "I have no doubt that the arrangements will prove satisfactory", Fraser noted after he told Chifley that New Zealand was appointing Chief of Staff Colonel Duff as the NZ Joint Service Representative.[38] With Britain and New Zealand accepting Australian plans, the revised system of defence cooperation for Malaya and Southeast Asia (which was later termed the ANZAM area) began on 1 January 1948.

Once joint planning began in 1948, the Australians raised the perennial question of the relationship between Commonwealth planning and American planning. Australian Prime Minister Ben Chifley argued that Australia needed concrete information from the British Chiefs of Staff about US plans in the Pacific. Australia would need to know, as a minimum, about American plans for the Pacific in relation to Australian security, the southern boundaries of the US zone of responsibility and the extent to which any assistance might be required from Australia in the Pacific. The British joint planners appreciated Australian concerns, but also realised that sharing American information involved confidentiality issues.

British reluctance to share American military information stemmed from issues arising during the Anglo-Australian Rocket Project, in which Australia hosted and assisted British efforts to acquire its own nuclear arsenal. Australia was eager to take part in a British-led nuclear weapons project. As an Australian Defence Appreciation Report

---

37 Chifley to Attlee, 28 May 1947, DAFP 1947 Vol. XII, 322-324; McIntyre, Background to the ANZUS Pact, 213.
38 Fraser to Chifley, 13 November 1947, Archives NZ, EA, 156/10/2 Part 2.

concluded, "the advent of the atomic bomb [...] may revolutionise the organisation, equipment and employment of armed forces."[39] With these benefits in mind, Chifley accepted the British plan for a joint rocket project and began working on the project in mid-1947. The Australian Defence Committee even began contemplating a proposal for an Australian atomic stockpile. Defence officials argued that Australia should develop "atomic energy from the viewpoint of Defence." Australian atomic energy development would also have advantages for "industrialisation, scientific and technological development."[40]

While New Zealand tended to be an ardent supporter of British foreign and defence policy, New Zealand External Affairs Department officials were particularly apprehensive about the joint rocket project and the proliferation of atomic weapons. At the same time Chifley and Evatt were negotiating with Britain over this possible joint project, New Zealand Ambassador in Washington Carl Berendsen expressed to New Zealand External Affairs Secretary McIntosh that he "heartily dislike[d] the look of the world" which was especially grim because of America's recent discovery of the atomic bomb. The atomic bomb's "completely destructive power", Berendsen said, "just completes my cup of doom." "[The bomb] will certainly be discovered very quickly by others" including Britain, Berendsen added, and he "did not see anything to be gained, and perhaps a good deal to be lost, by such a course." McIntosh shared Berendsen's concerns and was fearful of Attlee's determined pursuit of the bomb. "This damned atomic bomb is certainly the worst thing that has ever happened", he wrote in reply to Berendsen, suggesting almost jokingly that Attlee's talks with Truman and the Australians were about "nice and friendly [...] ways and means of devising bigger and better slaughters by atomic methods in the future."[41]

---

39   Appreciation for the Strategical Position of Australia, February 1946, NAA, A5954/1, 1664/4.

40   Report by New Weapons and Equipment Development Committee, 7 May 1948, in *Documents on Australian Foreign Policy: Australia and the Nuclear Non-Proliferation Treaty, 1945-1974*, Wayne Reynolds and David Lee ed. (Canberra: Australian Department of Foreign Affairs and Trade, 2013), 10-11, https://dfat.gov.au/about-us/publications/historical-documents/Documents/australia-and-the-nuclear-non-proliferation-treaty.pdf

41   Berendsen to McIntosh, 1 October 1945, in *Undiplomatic Dialogue*, 100; McIntosh to Berendsen, 1 November 1945, in *Undiplomatic Dialogue*, 103.

The State Department and Pentagon were also anxious about closer Anglo-Australian defence relations, especially when they involved the production of atomic weapons outside of American control. Recent US relations with Australia were chilly, not least because of Evatt's abrasive diplomatic style and his demands for closer US-Australian cooperation and exchange of military information. Relations with respect to the joint rocket project took a further hit once the Australian media found out about present and planned military projects through a series of leaks to the press. Australian Defence Minister John Dedman was particularly fearful as to what these leaks would mean for Australia's relations with the United States and Britain. The leaks will "increase the distrust in the safeguarding of secret information in Australia, and may have a serious effect on the readiness of the United Kingdom and the United States to furnish information to Australia", Dedman told a fellow minister.[42] His fear soon materialised after the US, which became convinced these leaks confirmed Australia could not be trusted with its own military secrets, banned Australia from receiving classified information from the United States. Although its motives were not entirely clear, the Central Intelligence Agency concluded that there was an "unsatisfactory security situation" in Australia and demoted the country to a "Category E" recipient of US military information. This was the lowest category among all nations with diplomatic representation in Washington.

The US ban on classified information to Australia was an embarrassment for the Chifley government, which had argued both publicly and privately in Washington that Australia and the United States shared a lot of common ground and that both countries should work together in tackling mutual threats in the Asia-Pacific region. Australian Ambassador to the United States Norman Makin speculated that it "placed [Australia] on a basis little better than the USSR." Although Makin was briefed on 3 July 1948 that the ban was temporary, he was concerned that there was no certainty when the United States might reverse this decision. "In [the] United States", Makin told Chifley apprehensively, "'temporary' arrangements frequently extend over an indefinite period." In any case, Makin was certain that the ban would

---

42 Peter Morton, *Fire across the Desert: Woomera and the Anglo-Australian Joint Project, 1946-1980* (Canberra: Australian Government Publishing Service, 1989), 104.

"seriously hinder" the joint rocket project and Australia's relationship with the United States.[43]

Determined to upgrade Australia's reliability in the eyes of the Americans, Chifley realised that although Australia wanted to play a greater role in world affairs, it could not do so effectively unless this ban was reversed. "Australia should assume a large share of defence responsibilities", according to Chifley, especially because Australia's defence expenditures were large in comparison to its small population. His Defence Secretary, Frederick Shedden, reiterated this point later to the State Department, pointing to the difficulties that occurred during the launch of the joint UK-Australian rocket projects because of a ban on classified information. "In addition to the difficulties in connection with the rocket range project, defence planning in the Pacific was being hampered by the lack of exchange of information", Shedden remarked. So far as he was concerned, all Australia needed to fix these difficulties was "information which would enable her to shape her plans for Australia's role in Pacific defence" that the State Department and US Department of Defense was refusing to pass over.[44]

The US position on the exchange of military information with Australia highlighted its overall reluctance to treat Australia as an equal and trustworthy partner. Australia did not even receive information on US atomic projects first hand. Evatt, after telling the State Department in February 1949 that it was his "understanding that information on rocket projects at the present time passed through a third country" (presumably Britain), argued that this arrangement was unsatisfactory and hoped that the "mutually beneficial cooperation between the two countries which had obtained during the recent war might be continued."[45] Even after these protestations, State Department officials

---

43   Makin to Chifley, 3 July 1948, NAA, A3300, 750.

44   Memorandum of Conversation, 20 April 1949, Secretary of State File, Acheson Papers, TL, https://www.trumanlibrary.org/whistlestop/study_collections/achesonmemos/view.php?documentVersion=both&documentid=65-3_34&documentYear=1949&pagenumber=1

45   Memorandum of Conversation, 17 February 1949, Secretary of State File, Acheson Papers, TL, https://www.trumanlibrary.org/whistlestop/study_collections/achesonmemos/view.php?documentVersion=both&documentid=65-01_54&documentYear=1949&pagenumber=1

did little to re-evaluate US security ties with Australia, preferring instead to pass information through other countries which was then relayed to Canberra. The United States simply did not trust Australia with classified military information.

By early 1949, there was little agreement between Australia, New Zealand and the United States on mutual post-war security issues. Australia and New Zealand bitterly opposed efforts to soften Japanese occupation policies. These countries also pursued closer strategic cooperation with Britain in Southeast Asia, an effort that undercut US primacy in the region. Further distrust between the three countries manifested during the Anglo-Australian rocket project. New Zealand was seriously concerned by potential Anglo-Australian access to nuclear weapons and the United States simply refused to share military information with Australia once secrets about the project was leaked in the Australian media. How, then, did these countries manage to agree on forming an alliance less than two years after Washington demoted Canberra to the lowest category recipient of US military information? The following chapter explores the unique international and domestic circumstances that facilitated speedy movement toward the ANZUS Treaty.

3. Movement Toward an Alliance

The early years of the post-war Australian-New Zealand-American relationship were often frostier than cordial. Yet, after several rapid international changes during 1949 and 1950—such as the Soviet Blockade of Berlin and its first successful test of an atomic bomb; Mao's Zedong Communist victory in the Chinese Civil War; and the outbreak of the Korean War—Australian, New Zealand and American interests began to coincide more closely. Against this backdrop the United States began seriously to consider the idea of a defence pact with Australia and New Zealand, an idea first proposed by Australian diplomats. Under a new Australian External Affairs Minister, Percy Spender, Canberra pushed for a binding commitment with the United States. Spender's New Zealand counterpart Frederick Doidge initially thought along similar lines, although this was a minority view in Wellington. Most other New Zealand diplomats and military officers did not want a formal commitment with the United States. Across the Pacific, policymakers in Washington refused to consider the idea of a Pacific Pact until the outbreak of the Korean War, which made obtaining Australian and New Zealand support for a speedy peace settlement in Japan highly valuable, and the State Department reasoned that concluding a defence pact with the Australia and New Zealand was a practical trade-off.

Under the Ben Chifley Government (1945-1949), one of Australia's primary foreign policy objectives was to secure a formal defence pact with the United States. This plan was spearheaded by Australian External Affairs Minister Herbert Evatt. A regional defence scheme had always been Evatt's "pet plan", as John Minter, the US Chargé in Canberra, commented as far back as 1946. He wanted to "keep the United States and Australia in the closest association", Minter noted, adding that Evatt proposed a regional pact not once but "many times."[1] Across the Tasman, New Zealand policymakers did not share Evatt's views on a formal defence arrangement with the United States. On 6 July 1948, New Zealand Prime Minister Peter Fraser thought that a regional pact would only "effectively contribute to our security" if Britain was a member. A pact would only develop "if the need arose" for New Zealand, Fraser announced in January 1949. In his view, that need "had not yet arisen."[2]

In any case, the State Department was unconvinced by Australian arguments for any kind of regional defence scheme. In a bid both to reassure Western Europe that the US remained committed to NATO and to deter unwanted pressure for a pact in the Asia-Pacific region, Secretary of State Dean Acheson dismissed a NATO-type pact in the Pacific. "While [NATO] does not mean any lessening of our interest in the security of other areas", Acheson announced at a press conference on 18 May 1949, "the United States is not currently considering participation in any further special collective defence arrangements." In his view, NATO was the product of a "solid foundation" of defence collaboration with Western Europe, whereas no such foundation existed in Asia and the Pacific. Yet beyond any foundation for a defence partnership in the region, Acheson feared that if the United States committed to a defence treaty in Asia and the Pacific it might overextend US forces into areas that were not primary interests (such as the long-simmering conflicts in Indochina, Malaya and Indonesia). "A Pacific Pact could not take shape until present internal conflicts in Asia were resolved", Acheson said. He simply thought that "the time was not ripe for a pact."[3]

The time for a regional defence arrangement with Australia and New Zealand might not have seemed "ripe" for Acheson in May, but by late 1949 to mid-1950, several events drastically changed the situation for the three countries in Asia and the Pacific. The declarations of Indonesian and Vietnamese independence from Dutch and French colonial control presented two uncertain security challenges to Australia, New Zealand and the United States in Southeast Asia. However, the most concerning development in Asia was the establishment of a Communist government

---

1   Minter to Byrnes, 9 April 1946, FRUS 1946 Vol. V, 28.

2   Fraser to Duff, 6 July 1948, DNZER Vol. III, 477-478; Fraser Memorandum, 11 January 1949, Archives NZ, EA, 10/4/7.

3   Cablegram to Canberra, 18 May 1949, NAA, A1838, 383/1/2/8, Part I.

in Beijing. After a protracted civil war between the People's Republic of China (PRC) and the Republic of China (ROC), PRC Chairman Mao Zedong announced the establishment of the People's Republic of China on 1 October 1949. The defeated Nationalists, led by Chiang Kai-shek, fled to the island of Taiwan (also known as Formosa). As Cold War tensions continued to rise between the United States and the Soviet Union, the emergence of a major Communist government in Northeast Asia was an uncertain and disruptive situation that challenged the West. Mao's victory especially provoked extensive debate in Australia, New Zealand and the United States over whether to continue supporting Chiang's government, or instead recognise the PRC by opening diplomatic relations in Beijing and supporting its claim to hold China's seat in the United Nations. On the one hand, the ROC appeared fragile and corrupt, and struggled to justify its claim to represent all of China while its government only controlled the island of Taiwan. On the other hand, Western governments feared that awarding recognition to the PRC would strengthen the Soviet bloc and encourage further aggression from mainland China.

Figure 4. Chairman Mao Zedong proclaiming the founding of the People's Republic of China (PRC), 1 October 1949. Photo by Hou Bo (1949), Wikimedia, https://commons.wikimedia.org/wiki/File:PRCFounding.jpg, public domain.

For the United States, peaceful co-existence with the PRC and eventual formal recognition of its status as China's governing party remained a possibility due to a lingering hope that Mao might avoid aligning China with the Soviet Union. However, in the immediate aftermath of Mao's announcement, the State Department shaped its policies toward the PRC on the premise that mainland China was entrenched firmly in the Soviet bloc and should not yet be awarded recognition. In an address to the Senate Foreign Relations Committee on 12 October, Secretary of State Dean Acheson stated that the "Chinese Government is really a tool of Russian Imperialism in China. That gives us our fundamental starting point in regards to our relations with China."[4]

Australia and New Zealand held their own bilateral talks over whether to recognise the PRC in November 1949. During these discussions, New Zealand Secretary of External Affairs McIntosh noted with frustration that the trans-Tasman talks appeared aimed only to increase Australia's international prestige and to encourage New Zealand to support Australian views on China. "It was a typical Australian show", McIntosh wrote to Berendsen on 18 November, "the object was publicity for Evatt, External Affairs and Australia in that order." According to McIntosh, Australian Secretary of External Affairs John Burton organised the talks as a "publicity stunt." Burton, convinced recognition was "necessary and inevitable", continually pressed McIntosh and the New Zealanders about supporting the Australian position.[5]

Indeed, the Australians appeared entirely ready and willing to abandon the Nationalists and instead recognise Mao's government on mainland China. Even before the Australian-New Zealand talks began in November, Canberra recalled its diplomatic mission in Nanking. Some of the Australian staff returned to Canberra, while other staff members established a temporary post in Hong Kong that could be quickly moved to Beijing once recognition was granted. "Personally", Australian External Affairs Minister Evatt wrote to British Foreign Minister Ernest Bevin only three days after Mao's announcement, "I do not see why [mainland China] should not be recognised." In Evatt's view, Australia and the rest of the Commonwealth could take the lead

---

4   Supplemental Notes on the Senate Foreign Relations Committee, 12 October 1949, Harry Truman Papers, President's Secretary's Files, Box 140, TL.

5   McIntosh to Berendsen, 18 November 1949, in *Undiplomatic Dialogue*, 186-187.

in recognising Beijing. He told Bevin that Mao's government could be recognised as the legitimate government of mainland China, whereas the Nationalists could similarly retain recognition of their government in Taiwan.[6] For New Zealand, McIntosh did not think that the Tasman countries should take the lead in recognising the PRC. He did, however, think that there might be substantial benefits of recognition. He thought that doing so would prevent the PRC from acting aggressively and counter Russian influence in China. Moreover, if for no other reason, McIntosh concluded that on legal grounds the PRC should be awarded recognition because it already controlled mainland China.

Irrespective of these early views, Australia, New Zealand and the United States all opposed recognising the PRC even after Britain did so in early 1950. In both Australia and New Zealand, responding to the threat of Communism in China and elsewhere was a hotly debated topic and became a pertinent election issue. In New Zealand, after fourteen years in power, the Labour government was defeated at the polls in November 1949. Sidney Holland led the newly-formed conservative National government, with Frederick Doidge as his External Affairs Minister. Holland turned out to "dominate the NZ Cabinet", as "one man or two men" often do, Berendsen complained. Yet, in contrast to his predecessor Peter Fraser, Holland had "almost no interest in foreign affairs."[7] Revealingly he took the Finance rather than the External Affairs portfolio in addition to the prime ministership, and when he did intervene in foreign affairs, he "frequently made gaffes."

The new External Affairs Minister, Frederick Doidge, was better equipped to handle New Zealand's foreign relations than was Holland. In contrast to the long-standing convictions of many in New Zealand that a US guarantee for New Zealand's security was undesirable, Doidge, at least in the early stages of his time as External Affairs Minister, was one of the strongest advocates for a Pacific Pact with the United States. Doidge was "very pact-minded" and was convinced that the United States had to be a signatory to any regional arrangement. In January 1950 Doidge raised the idea of a pact at the Colombo Conference, an international meeting held in Sri Lanka to discuss how the living

---

6 Evatt to Bevin, 4 October 1949, NAA, A1838/278, 494/2/10 Part I.

7 Berendsen to McIntosh, 28 March 1950, in *Undiplomatic Dialogue*, 222; McKinnon, *Independence and Foreign Policy*, 114.

Figure 5. New Zealand Prime Minister Sidney Holland (1949-1957), 1951. Photo taken by Crown Studies of Wellington (1951), Wikimedia, https://commons.wikimedia.org/wiki/File:Sidney_George_Holland_(1951).jpg, public domain.

standards of people in the Asia-Pacific region could be improved. At the conference, he suggested that a pact would be useless without the inclusion of the United States, Canada and India. According to Doidge, the security of Australia and New Zealand could not be ensured without the United States to "wall in the tide of Communism."[8]

In Australia, the Liberal Country Coalition led by Robert Menzies won the 1949 election. Menzies's victory ended Evatt's term as External Affairs Minister. He was replaced by Percy Spender, a move that signalled a new era of Australia's external relations with the United States. The new Menzies Government recognised that Australian security interests in the region rested squarely with the US, and as part

---

8   Doidge to Berendsen, 9 May 1950, DNZER Vol. III, 546; Doidge Statement, 9 May 1950, DNZER, Vol. III, 547.

of this assessment, External Affairs Minister Percy Spender continued Australia's push for a formal defence pact. US policymakers certainly recognised early on that Spender was determined to secure a closer relationship. After "differences of opinion rising from dissimilar views of the Japanese occupation policy [...] and by the difficult personality of Evatt", the State Department concluded, "Spender is desirous of establishing the closest and most cooperative relations with the United States and has in effect made this a cardinal point in his foreign policy."⁹

Figure 6. Australian Prime Minister Robert Menzies (1939-1941, 1949-1966), 1950. Photo by unknown (1950), National Library of Australia, https://catalogue.nla.gov.au/Record/3307904, copyright expired.

The Holland Government clearly recognised that a close relationship with the United States was important to New Zealand, yet policymakers in Wellington still described the relationship as less fundamental to its security interests in the Pacific compared to their Australian counterparts. While the American-Australian relationship was described as a "cardinal point" of Australian foreign policy by the State Department, Counselor of the New Zealand Embassy in Washington George Laking told US

---

9 Department of State Policy Statement, 21 April 1950, NARA, RG 59, 611.43/4-2150.

Assistant Secretary of State William Butterworth that it was simply "very sensible" for New Zealand to have a "close association between the United States [and] New Zealand."[10]

As for Spender, New Zealand responses to his appointment and its impact on trans-Tasman relations were mixed. Berendsen was concerned that Spender might be a mere successor to Australia's "irresponsible" and "hoodlum" behaviour in international affairs that he witnessed with Evatt. When it came to Spender, he was afraid that, like most Australians, either by nature or by upbringing, they seemed to him to be "impossible people."[11] McIntosh and Doidge were even less complimentary about Australia's new External Affairs Minister, fearing that he would be just as difficult as Evatt. Spender was an "absolute little tick", McIntosh told Berendsen, complaining that he was just as "great an exhibitionist as Evatt" and that "Doidge took an instant dislike to him." Spender and Doidge's relationship—and, consequently, Australia and New Zealand's relationship—did not improve in the immediate future. Less than four months later, McIntosh noted that not only do Spender and Doidge "not get on", but that there is "no common link" between the Australian and New Zealand Cabinet.

This lack of a common link between the Australian and New Zealand Cabinets stemmed in part from Spender's relentless pursuit of a regional defence arrangement with the United States as well as his ambitious Colombo Plan (a multinational initiative to assist in the economic recovery of South and Southeast Asia), which he introduced at the Colombo Conference in January 1950. He might not have been the ideal man to improve Australian-New Zealand relations, yet as far as the pursuit of Australia's foreign policy objectives were concerned, Spender was more than a capable replacement for Evatt. He was, as Berendsen pointed out, a man of "intellectual gifts" and was blessed with an "incomparably more attractive personality" than Evatt. On first glance, he also seemed more likely to succeed where Evatt could not in securing a US guarantee. He was headstrong, experienced, and more than willing to stand up to Menzies—or anyone in Washington for that

---

10 Meeting between Laking and Butterworth, 18 November 1949, DNZER Vol. III, 291-297.

11 Berendsen to McIntosh, 14 February 1950, in *Undiplomatic Dialogue*, 212; Berendsen to McIntosh, 15 December 1949, in *Undiplomatic Dialogue*, 194-195.

matter, should he think it was in Australia's interest—to ensure that Australia's post-war protection was secured; namely, through a pact with the United States. The "future peace of the whole Pacific rested, almost entirely, upon the United States", Spender had argued shortly before his appointment.[12]

Spender also recognised that Communist insurgencies in Southeast Asia presented just as clear a threat to Australia as did a potential resurgence of Japanese imperialism and aggression. Upon being handed the External Affairs portfolio, Spender's primary task remained clear: enlist the United States as a guarantor of Australian security to repel these threats. His first job was to ensure that all his officers, diplomats and staff members understood his vision for Australia's relations with the world as revolving around a closer relationship with the United States. Because of their "common British heritage" and "greater technical and industrial development", Australia and the United States were the "two countries which can, in cooperation one with the other, make the greatest contribution to stability." In Spender's view, it was only by "concerted action" that this was possible. Later, during a comprehensive speech in the Australian House of Representatives, Spender made his vision for Australia's external relations clear to both the Parliament and public. As part of Spender's outlook, maintaining Australia's peace and security rested on four pillars: the Pacific, in Western Europe through cooperation with the British Commonwealth, the United Nations, and the United States. In outlining this last pillar, Spender said

> I have emphasised how essential it is for Australia to maintain the closest links with the United States for vital security reasons [...] we propose actively to maintain the official and personal contacts and interchanges which resulted from the urgent needs of a common military effort.

To maintain these links at the highest level possible, Spender had a clear idea in mind:

> What I envisage is a defensive military arrangement having as its basis a firm agreement between countries that have a vital interest in the stability of Asia and the Pacific, and which are at the same time capable of undertaking military commitments [...] I fervently hope other

---

12 Spender Statement, 16 February 1949, Commonwealth Debates, House of Representatives, Vol. 201, 358.

Commonwealth countries might form a nucleus [...] [but] I also have in mind particularly the United States of America, whose participation would give such a pact a substance that it would otherwise lack. Indeed, it would be rather meaningless without her.[13]

On top of convincing the Americans, Spender had to persuade his own Prime Minister, Robert Menzies, that Australia needed a formal pact with the United States. Such a task was perhaps surprising, as during Menzies's first term as Prime Minister (1939-1941) he had hoped for some form of US security guarantee and appealed to US President Franklin Roosevelt for American aid during World War II. However, Menzies believed that such a pact might compromise Australia's close relationship with the United Kingdom and the British Commonwealth and Australia simply "did not need a pact with America", as Menzies told his Deputy Prime Minister Arthur Fadden in August 1950, because "they are already overwhelmingly friendly to us."[14] Menzies was sceptical about the pact until it was nearly completed. At one stage, while Spender was straining every effort to conclude the alliance, Menzies remarked provocatively that "Percy is trying to build a castle on a foundation of jelly", much to the annoyance of Spender and his wife Jean.[15]

New Zealand Minister to the United States Carl Berendsen shared Menzies's misgivings about the proposed pact. For Berendsen, a Pacific Pact as it had been spoken about so far was "superficially attractive" and "ambiguous, imprecise and completely impracticable." He feared the result might be Australia and New Zealand having to "defend the indefensible" in areas outside of their primary strategic interests. The New Zealand military was equally unconvinced. The Chiefs of Staff in Wellington produced a defence report in April 1950 which outlined their

---

13 Spender Statement, 9 March 1950, *Current Notes on International Affairs* (hereafter CNIA), Vol. 21, 1950, 153-172; See also Roger Holdich, Vivianne Johnson and Pamela Andre ed. *Documents on Australian Foreign Policy: The ANZUS Treaty, 1951* (hereafter DAFP: ANZUS) (Canberra: Department of Foreign Affairs and Trade, 2001), 9-10.

14 Menzies to Fadden, 3 August 1950, NAA, A11782, 1950/1.

15 Bell, Coral. *Dependent Ally: A Study in Australian Foreign Policy* (Melbourne: Oxford University Press, 1988), 45. See also Jean Spender, *Ambassador's Wife: A Woman's View of Life in Politics, Diplomacy and International Law* (Sydney: Angus & Robertson, 1968), 23.

strategic thinking from a purely military perspective. It concluded that there were "no reasons on military grounds" to approach the United States for a Pacific Pact because Washington would see no direct threat to New Zealand. From a US perspective, any New Zealand deployment would in fact be more useful in the Middle East than in the Pacific or Far East. The United States, the Chiefs of Staff maintained, would certainly "prefer to see a New Zealand Division and RNZAF (Royal New Zealand Air Force) tactical forces employed in the Middle East rather than tied down in the Far East in operations which would have no decisive effect on the ultimate outcome of the war."[16]

Berendsen, however, thought there was some merit to the narrow arrangement that the New Zealand Defence Chiefs proposed. He recognised, for instance, that Australia and New Zealand's limited defence capabilities and the grim realities of the world in the early 1950s left these countries little choice other than to secure a formal guarantee with the major sea power in the Pacific, the United States. Convinced that society was moving toward a third world war that would be brought about by the "thugs and gangsters" of the Soviet Union, Berendsen thought that Asia was a "boiling cauldron" that was "vibrant with resurgent nationalism." In this cauldron, the situation seemed ideal for Soviet "fishing in muddy waters." Since the dangers were so great and a world system of collective security so distant, he was "entirely ready" to accept a regional system as the best compromise available. To this end, Berendsen recognised that Spender and Doidge's efforts to reach some sort of pact with the United States were perhaps in Australia and New Zealand's best interests. "We are forced to look for something more real, more actual, more practical", Berendsen told Doidge. "From our point of view", he went on to suggest, "the logical conclusion which is so simple and obvious that it is present in everybody's mind, and has been frequently advanced by Spender, is that what we essentially need in our defence is the assistance of the United States."[17]

To strike a compromise between his reservations about a complete defence arrangement and his desire to meet New Zealand's security requirements, Berendsen proposed a limited pact. Under this pact, the

---

16 The Assistant Secretary of the Chiefs of Staff Committee to the Secretary of External Affairs, 28 April 1950, DNZER Vol. III, 537.

17 Ibid., 531.

United States would commit to the defence of Australia and New Zealand in return for their support in defending Japan and the US position in Northeast Asia. The response in Wellington was disappointing. Doidge had not discussed the idea for over a month after Berendsen's proposal was sent. When Doidge finally replied, he said he would be "very happy to consider it" because he regarded an American guarantee of New Zealand's security as "the richest prize of New Zealand diplomacy."[18]

Doidge did not give much more consideration to this proposal. Instead, he remained convinced that New Zealand needed a full commitment from the United States. McIntosh informed Berendsen on 12 April that Doidge had not given his idea any deliberation, writing that "[Doidge] had not thought the thing out, indeed none of them (the Cabinet) will."[19] McIntosh himself was reluctant to pursue Berendsen's limited pact proposal. He was particularly dismayed by the prospect that New Zealand would have to take part in a guarantee of Japanese integrity so soon after fighting a major war against them.

In any event, up until mid-1950, there was no sign that the talk of concluding a defence agreement with Australia and New Zealand, either limited or full-scale, had been considered seriously in the United States. As Second Secretary of the East Asia Section in the Australian Department of External Affairs David Dexter noted, "between the end of 1947 and mid-1950 the Americans showed little inclination to be involved in […] a Pacific pact."[20] In Far Eastern matters, the Japanese Peace Treaty and its impact on the US-Soviet balance of power in East Asia had been the major subject of deliberation between the State Department and the Joint Chiefs of Staff (JCS). The former favoured moving toward a peace treaty, whereas the latter wanted no diminution of its control in Japan. Given the deadlock between restoring normal political and economic relations with Japan and a continued occupation—neither of which were "wholly desirable" for the United States—US Secretary of State Dean Acheson appointed John Foster Dulles as a special advisor for reaching a suitable peace settlement.

Dulles's appointment was crucial for three reasons. Since he was a Republican, Truman and Acheson could fend off criticism that the

---

18 Doidge to Berendsen, 9 May 1950, DNZER Vol. III, 546.
19 McIntosh to Berendsen, 12 April 1950, in *Undiplomatic Dialogue*, 225.
20 Dexter to Shaw, 27 October 1950, NAA, A1838, 535/6 part i.

Democrats were failing in Asia and were unwilling to take a bipartisan approach to meet their objectives. As a specialist in international affairs—he was a legal counsel with the US delegation at the Versailles Peace Conference in 1918, an adviser at the San Francisco Conference in 1945, and helped draft the preamble for the United Nations Charter— Dulles brought considerable experience to the role and was able to reach a settlement with Japan in little over a year. From a historian's vantage point, it is also possible to see that as a future US Secretary of State from 1953 to 1959, his relationship with Australian and New Zealand policymakers would be pivotal in shaping the contours of the relationship for most of the decade. Dulles's first task was to visit Tokyo to discuss a Japanese peace settlement with SCAP Commander Douglas MacArthur, as well as members of the Far Eastern Commission. His second task was to get Australia and New Zealand, the two most outspoken opponents of a soft peace treaty, to agree to a settlement that was also acceptable to the United States. Although their support was not essential, the State Department believed that Australian and New Zealand support for American policy in Japan was still "highly desirable."[21]

Obtaining Australian and New Zealand support for the Japanese Peace Treaty as quickly as possible became even more urgent after mid-1950. In the early morning of 25 June, North Korean (DPRK) forces crossed the 38th parallel on the Korean Peninsula and began a full-scale invasion of South Korea with the support of the Soviet Union. The United States, believing that the North Korean advance was Soviet-inspired aggression, was quick to commit US ground forces which were readily available in Japan. With an American need for an increased war effort, Australia and New Zealand were uniquely placed to provide much needed military support to the United States. It was the perfect opportunity to demonstrate that Canberra and Wellington were prepared to support the US bid for UN intervention in Korea, which was approved shortly after the North Korean invasion (The Soviet Union could not veto the resolution because at the time it was boycotting the UN over the non-recognition of Communist China). Both Acheson and MacArthur urged Canberra to supply material aid and battalions

---

21 Department of State Policy Statement, 21 April 1950, NARA, RG 59, 611.43/4-2150.

to Korea.[22] Menzies was in London where he argued that Australian troops should not be sent to Korea due to their small number and that deploying these forces would prevent an Australian contribution to the Commonwealth defence in the Middle East.

Figure 7. A Soviet-made North Korean T-34 tank knocked out during the UN led intervention on the Korean Peninsula. Photo by Curtis A. Ulz (1950), Wikimedia, https://commons.wikimedia.org/wiki/File:T-34_knocked_out_September_1950.jpg, public domain.

Spender, however, saw Korea as a blessing in disguise with respect to his Pacific Pact ambitions and pushed for a speedy Australian response. Spender cabled Menzies in early July, warning that the "heat may be put on us for further aid" after UN Secretary General Trygve Lie urged over fifty UN members to supply more ground forces in Korea. Receiving no response and growing agitated, Spender wrote to Menzies again on 17 July arguing that from "Australia's long-term point of view, any additional aid we can give to the US now, small though it may be, will [be repaid] in the future one hundred fold." Spender added that "if we refrain from giving any further aid, we may lose an opportunity of cementing friendship with the US which may not easily present itself again."[23]

Menzies, who was abroad at the time and unable to take direct part in policy decisions, was unconvinced by Spender's push for Australian

---

22 Acheson to UK Embassy, 28 June 1950, FRUS Vol. VII 1950, 223; Watt to Spender, 15 November 1952, Spender Papers, Box 1, National Library of Australia (hereafter NLA).

23 Spender to Menzies, 17 July 1950, NAA, A462/2, 443/1/8 part i.

support in Korea. After attending a British Cabinet meeting, he pointed out that for Australia there was a "great danger in allowing the Korean affair to disturb our strategic planning based on the importance of the Middle East and on our national service scheme."[24] Menzies's stance on Korea became increasingly isolated, especially after the Australian Embassy in Washington suggested "the Korea attack has given fresh impetus to the consideration of Spender's initiative and ideas." Embassy staff also suggested that "prior consultation between Australia and the United States would have been helpful in meeting the sudden crisis" and that "some machinery for automatic consultation would be helpful in meeting future crises." Determined not to let this opportunity slide, Spender phoned Acting Prime Minister Arthur Fadden to issue a statement that Australia had decided to send troops to Korea, who agreed reluctantly. Even without their Prime Minister at home to object, Spender was able to push for an Australian contribution to Korea in the hope that it might encourage the State Department to better see the benefits of a Pacific Pact with Australia. It was certainly an audacious move by Spender, so much so that external affairs officer Arthur Tange commented later that it left his colleagues "somewhat bewildered" that he would push so quickly and without the support of the Australian Prime Minister.[25]

Spender's swiftness, however, made a strong mark on policymakers in Washington. There was "genuine gratification at Australia's prompt response" in the United States, the Australian Embassy in Washington cabled to Canberra. After observing US sentiments starting to shift on Australia's strategic value in the Asian region, Spender certainly felt encouraged and motivated to keep pushing at home for a closer defence relationship with the United States. More specifically, he stressed again to Menzies that Australia should capitalise on this response and seek a formal defence pact. "This immediate action by Australia made a strong impression on official and unofficial American opinion which has resulted in the closest of friendly relationships", Spender argued. He added that in order for Washington to realise the benefits

---

24 Robert O'Neill, *Australia in the Korean War: Volume 1, Strategy and Diplomacy, 1950-1953* (Canberra: Australian Government Publishing Service, 1981), 66.

25 Arthur Tange, *Defence Policy-Making: A Close-Up View, 1950-1980*, Peter Edwards ed. (Canberra: ANU Press, 2008), 4, http://press.anu.edu.au?p=101541

of a pact, Australia should demonstrate to the United States that it was wholeheartedly prepared to support US policy in the Pacific. Otherwise, the "Australian attitude might be misunderstood and the genuine warmth of [the] present relationship since the opening of the Korean conflict may be diminished."[26] In this regard Spender's persistence on such an important matter is commendable, particularly given Menzies' reluctance to accept that the United States had to replace Britain as the new bulwark of Australian security.

Across the Tasman, New Zealand preempted the Australian response by announcing first that it would support the US and UN to repel the North Korean advance. On 1 July, Holland declared that two warships, Pukaki and Tutira, would be sent to the Korea area. He later committed a special combat unit to the fighting. In so doing, Wellington demonstrated that New Zealand was likewise willing to support the global fight against Communism and that it was a reliable ally in the Pacific theatre. Carl Berendsen, New Zealand Ambassador in Washington, was particularly happy with this quick response: "we have got kudos and widespread appreciation [in the United States] for this immediate indication that we are one of those who do not confine our support of the principles of freedom to words alone."[27]

Yet over and above any benefit this move had in Washington, New Zealand's hasty response was primarily due to British consultation and consideration of London's attitudes. Wellington's decision to make a naval deployment into Korean waters and its subsequent land-force contributions were made because New Zealand was "unprepared to undertake a military, and through it a political commitment which required it to act independently of a familiar and secure British-led Commonwealth."[28] After incessant pressing by the Australian Government, the New Zealand military response was likewise not part of a combined ANZAC Brigade. "That is the very thing we do not want to do", McIntosh told Berendsen on 7 August, "we can supply artillery,

---

26 Spender to Menzies, 21 July 1950, NAA, A11537 [1].

27 Berendsen to McIntosh, 14 July 1950, in *Undiplomatic Dialogue*, 234; NZ Ambassador in Washington to Doidge, 20 July 1950, DNZER Vol. III, 390.

28 McKinnon, *Independence and Foreign Policy*, 118. See also Ian McGibbon, "New Zealand's Intervention in the Korean War: June-July 1950", *International History Review* 11, no. 1 (1989), 272-290.

[and] we would feel safer in having this particular type of unit and my own view is that we should stick to it." Berendsen agreed and thought such a plan would be "disastrous." If New Zealand cooperated with Australia militarily in Korea, "there [was] no doubt at all about it that the Australians would shove us right into the background and we will get no credit whatsoever for this force which will be represented as, and certainly accepted as, Australian."[29] Despite these concerns both Australia and New Zealand later contributed soldiers to the creation of the 1st Commonwealth Division, a unit that formed part of the British military presence in Korea. This division was made up primarily of British and Canadian forces, but also included troops from India and South Korea. At least with this type of multinational military arrangement, McIntosh and Berendsen could be assured that it would be quite difficult for Australia to claim credit for any contributions made by New Zealand.

As for China, American-Australian-New Zealand views against recognition hardened considerably after the PRC intervened in Korea in November 1950. US President Harry Truman responded by completely rejecting any possibility of recognition and instead approved a National Security Council (NSC) recommendation to impose strict political and economic sanctions on the PRC. In addition, the Truman Administration threw its support behind Chiang Kai-shek as the legitimate head of the government of China. Fighting alongside American forces in Korea, respective Australian and New Zealand Prime Ministers Robert Menzies and Sidney Holland enforced similar sanctions and publicly declared their support for Chiang's embattled regime.

The possibility of recognising Beijing in the short-term future was dismissed. In Australia, Spender feared that recognising the PRC after its intervention in Korea would encourage Beijing to act aggressively elsewhere. "If Communist Chinese demands for Taiwan and recognition are accepted", Spender asked fellow Australian diplomat Keith Officer rhetorically on 11 December, "what guarantee is there that she [China] will not press in Indochina or elsewhere?" Despite these concerns, Spender thought that recognition should not be completely ruled out. He told Officer that "on the question of ultimate recognition of Communist

---

29 McIntosh to Berendsen, 7 August 1950, in *Undiplomatic Dialogue*, 238; Berendsen to McIntosh, 15 August 1950, in *Undiplomatic Dialogue*, 242.

China, the door should not be barred." In other words, Spender thought that "if a reasonable settlement can be arranged regarding Korea, the question of recognition will be reconsidered."[30]

Meanwhile, as the Korean situation worsened, several UN countries introduced a draft resolution in the First Committee of the General Assembly on 12 December to form a separate committee that would work towards reaching a ceasefire. This committee also decided to vote upon whether the PRC should be admitted as a temporary UN member to assist in reaching an immediate ceasefire. During these negotiations, another tussle broke out between Australian and New Zealand representatives after Australia tried to pressure New Zealand into abstaining from voting. Berendsen, who was representing New Zealand, was "infuriated" when Australian delegate Keith Officer told him that "he (Officer) intended to vote for [Beijing's] admission" temporarily to work towards reaching a ceasefire, and "hoped that I (Berendsen) would abstain." "I could scarcely believe my ears", Berendsen told McIntosh after hearing that Australia wanted New Zealand to simply step aside and not get in the way of its own decisions. "The long and short of it is I don't understand the Australians any more than I understand the British" on Chinese matters, Berendsen complained.[31]

Although his reasons for wanting to New Zealand to abstain while he voted for Beijing's temporary seating are unclear, it is evident that Officer questioned whether hardline US policies were a prudent means of calming hostilities in Korea and subduing Chinese aggression. "My own view is that the attitude of the United States at the moment is quite unreal", he wrote to Spender, "I can see few practical arguments against a ceasefire."[32] It is possible that Officer's demands on the committee issue were part of a broader Australian concern that New Zealand, with strong British ties and a demonstrated propensity to consider PRC recognition, saw the committee as a partial step toward potential recognition without consultation with Australia. Any such move would

---

30 Spender to Officer, 11 December 1950, NAA, A11537 Part I.
31 Berendsen to McIntosh, 25 November 1950, in *Undiplomatic Dialogue*, 250.
32 Officer to Spender, 12 December 1950, in Stuart Doran and David Lee ed. Documents on Australian Foreign Policy: Australia and Recognition of the People's Republic of China, 1949-1972 (hereafter DAFP: China) (Canberra: Department of Foreign Affairs and Trade, 2002), 33.

be disastrous for Australia, especially because, at the time, Spender was working hard towards reaching a formal defence arrangement with the United States.

The Korean War, the PRC and new conservative governments in Canberra and Wellington meant that concluding some form of a defence arrangement became more practical for Australia, New Zealand and the United States. American policymakers began to view a treaty with Australia and New Zealand as a means to reach a speedy settlement regarding the Japanese Peace Treaty. In Australia, Spender accepted this trade off and hoped to conclude as binding an arrangement as possible with the United States. New Zealand, however, continued to favour a limited understanding through a Presidential Declaration. There was in fact significant apprehension amongst New Zealand diplomats and military officers about concluding a binding arrangement with the United States. Negotiations for some form of alliance nonetheless played out in late 1950 and early 1951, and had a decisive impact on the future of the relationship.

4. ANZUS Negotiations

The outbreak of the Korean War signalled to American policymakers that Communism was a growing danger in the Asia-Pacific region and stronger efforts must be made to prevent its spread. It could not, however, continue to do so alone. The US was bearing the overwhelming brunt of the war effort through both the financial cost of funding military equipment and the loss of lives. In consideration of this heavy burden, the State Department lauded Australia's quick response to the Korean War. "The prompt reaction of Australia to the invasion of Korea and the unanimous vote of approval given by the Australian parliament to the military measures taken by the Government", a State Department memorandum noted on 24 July, "afforded a good indication of the close identity of views between the United States and Australia on matters of fundamental importance."[1] It is interesting to note that little mention was made of New Zealand, suggesting that perhaps Berendsen was correct in his previous concerns that Wellington's contributions in Korea would be overshadowed by the Australian contribution.

In any event, the State Department quickly began manoeuvring for discussions to conclude a formal defence treaty. Allen Brown, Australian Secretary for the Prime Minister's Department, reported this change in US policy in early August 1950. While visiting Washington, he cabled Spender on 3 August to say that in a meeting with Assistant Secretary for Far Eastern Affairs Dean Rusk and other members of the US Far Eastern Bureau, Rusk told him that the State Department's views toward a pact were now "very

---

[1] State Department Policy Background Memorandum, 24 July 1950, NARA, RG 59, 743.13/7-2450.

fluid" and they were "willing to exchange ideas."[2] This willingness stemmed from an increasing need to finalise a suitable peace settlement in Japan as the situation in Korea worsened.

Australia and New Zealand were outspoken opponents of a soft peace treaty without suitable assurances that Japan would not again be a menace in Asia. In September 1950, the United States entered discussions with other governments in the Far Eastern Committee about the Japanese Peace Treaty. Dulles, charged with the primary responsibility of reaching an agreement over Japan, made it clear that the basic American aim was a treaty that restored Japanese sovereignty and kept Japan as an American ally. American desire for a multilateral peace treaty with Japan offered Australia an opportunity to achieve its own objectives; namely, an American guarantee of its security in exchange for Australian acquiescence to the Japanese Peace Treaty.

Spender was excited by the prospect that the United States was now more open to discussions about a Pacific Pact. As a result, he worked harder than ever to "sow the seeds" for a formal defence commitment from the United States.[3] Spender undoubtedly saw such a commitment as vital to Australian security interests, but in his discussions with American policymakers after the Korean War had begun, Spender also stressed that Australia desperately needed a pact in order to be more closely involved in the global planning and international decision-making processes among Western powers. Meeting with President Truman on 15 September, Spender stressed that in the Japanese war Australia had "thrown all she had into that conflict." He added that its recent commitment to Korea demonstrated further that Australia "could be counted upon in an emergency to give the utmost of her manpower and equipment to meet all new crises." This, according to Spender, "should merit a greater degree of consideration in matters of consultation among the great powers." "Australia did not have any say in most of the important international decisions now being made by the friendly powers", Spender told Truman, suggesting that it was a "great handicap to his country."[4]

---

2   Cablegram from Embassy in Washington to Spender, 3 August 1950, NAA, A1838, 250/7/10 part I.

3   Jean Spender, *Ambassador's Wife*, 21.

4   Notes of Meeting between Spender and Truman, 15 September 1950, NARA, RG 59, 611.43/9-1550.

Truman sympathised with Spender and the Australian position, but suggested that this was a matter that he should take up with Secretary of State Dean Acheson. Disappointed by this response from the President, Spender commented publicly at a UN General Assembly in New York that Australia was keen for a regional defence pact and had clear ideas about what scope it should take. He told Alan Watt on 15 September that a Pacific Pact should be as wide as possible, "including the countries of the Indian Ocean capable of entering into firm commitments, but that if that were not possible, then an area generally including Australia, New Zealand, the Philippines, North America and Great Britain."[5] He also had no objection to including South American countries.

Figure 8. President Truman (second left) meeting with US Secretary of Defense George Marshall (left), Secretary of State Dean Acheson (second from right) and Secretary of the Treasury John Snyder (right), October 1950. Photo by Abbie Rowe (1950), US National Archives Catalog, https://catalog.archives.gov/id/200235, unrestricted use.

---

5   Spender Cablegram, 15 September 1950, DAFP: ANZUS, 21-22. Spender's ideas for a Pacific Pact can be found in Percy Spender, *Exercises in Diplomacy: The ANZUS Treaty and the Colombo Plan* (Sydney: Sydney University Press, 1969).

Spender soon received a clearer idea of US thinking towards Japan and a regional pact. On 22 September, Dulles pulled Spender aside during US negotiations with Far Eastern Commission nations for the peace settlement in Japan. Dulles presented a seven-point memorandum which outlined that the United States had plans to revitalise Japan as a military power that was friendly to the United States. According to Dulles, this was because Japan was no longer an isolated problem but part of a broader struggle against Communism. It was in America's self-interest that "Japan should be denied to [Russia] and attracted to the side of the Western democracies." Spender was not pleased by this memorandum. Recalling the meeting, John Allison, Director of Northeast Asian Affairs in the State Department, penned that "[Spender's] face grew more and more suffused with colour. At one point, I thought he would burst a vessel."[6] Spender told Dulles that Australia could not subscribe to a Japanese treaty unless there were adequate assurances for Australia's protection. In other words, to "allay Australia's fears", he wanted a "formal commitment by the United States." In response, Dulles told Spender that Australia's security was assured through a continued US presence in Japan. Nevertheless, he recognised Australian trepidations and suggested "some compromise might have to be found."[7]

At the same time, New Zealand Minister for External Affairs Frederick Doidge surprisingly cooled towards the idea. Although Doidge had initially been a strong supporter of a Pacific Pact, his enthusiasm dropped once the war in Korea began. Again, unlike Spender, he also had no clear idea of what form a pact should take. In September 1950 Doidge proclaimed in the New Zealand Parliament

> My own view now, and I think the view of the government, is the pact is not as necessary as we thought it was six months ago. It is unnecessary now because of what is happening in Korea. Today the United States of America is in the Pacific. I think she is there now as a permanent partner in the policing of the Pacific.[8]

---

6   John Allison, *Ambassador from the Prairie or Allison Wonderland* (Boston: Houghton Miffin, 1973), 151.

7   Australian Mission to the United Nations to External Affairs, 22 September 1950, NAA, A816, 19/304/451; Cablegram to the Department of External Affairs, 22 September 1950, NAA, A1838, 532/11 part i.

8   Doidge Statement, 5 September 1950, NZ Parliamentary Debates, Vol. 291, 2142-2143.

There was equally little enthusiasm from the New Zealand Department of External Affairs to collaborate with Australia on the matter. It was not a surprise that Spender complained that "even New Zealand displayed little active interest" in the pact proposals he made in late 1950.[9]

Doidge, nevertheless, left for Washington in October to discuss a regional defence pact with the United States. While in Washington, New Zealand-American talks appeared to reignite Doidge's interest in a pact but it did not take the shape he had advocated previously. Doidge recalled that after the discussions in Washington, the US was still a crucial signatory to any regional agreement but suggested different treaty signatories than did Spender. He told Parliament on 2 November that there can be "no satisfactory pact without the United States, Canada and India", and that the "Pacific pact should be the natural corollary to an Atlantic Pact."[10] This was not the same view he had had several months earlier when he thought such a pact was unnecessary. A pact similar in scope to the Atlantic Pact would most likely entail a direct New Zealand military commitment to defend US interests in the region.

This was also not the pact Spender was suggesting. A month earlier, Spender had stressed to US Assistant Secretary of State John Hickerson in a meeting on 12 October that Indian inclusion was "unlikely" and that the United States, Britain, Australia, New Zealand and possibly the Philippines were the only "essential" potential treaty signatories. Spender also dismissed Canada because it had "heavy obligations in Europe" and was "not deeply interested in the Pacific."[11] Disagreement over the scope of membership aside, Spender's desire to pursue a regional pact had an additional layer that Doidge was not considering. As well as seeking reassurance of support in the event of future Japanese aggression, Spender wanted a Pacific Pact because Australia was not associated with any "body of nations dealing with global strategy or similar questions." If there were a Pacific Pact with Australia as a member, it could be "brought into consultation" with US military planning that the Pentagon was currently unwilling to share with Canberra.[12]

---

9 Spender, *Exercises in Diplomacy*, 35.

10 Doidge Statement, 2 November 1950, NZ Parliamentary Debates, Vol. 292, 3942.

11 Spender, *Exercises in Diplomacy*, 33. See also Meeting Between Spender and Truman, 1 September 1950, NARA, RG 59, 611.43/9-150.

12 Note by Officer, 13 October 1950, NAA, A1838, 532/11 part I; NZ High Commissioner in Canberra to McIntosh, 27 October 1950, DNZER Vol. III, 548-550.

Dulles's task to find a solution in Japan became even more urgent once Chinese forces intervened in the Korean War in late November 1950. With Chinese involvement in Korea and the situation fast deteriorating, Dulles informed New Zealand that he hoped to devise "some satisfactory means of assuring the government and people of New Zealand" as soon as possible. At the same time, the State Department told Spender that they were giving "active consideration" to his proposals for a Pacific Pact.[13] Further interest came from Undersecretary Dean Rusk, who appeared more sympathetic to Australia's and New Zealand's desire to secure US protection. As a means of enlisting Australian and New Zealand support for the Japanese Peace Treaty, Rusk proposed a plan for a Presidential Declaration that announced that both countries were defensively tied to the United States. "There is merit in tightening our relationship with Australia and New Zealand", Rusk told Deputy Under Secretary of Political Affairs Elbert Matthews on 9 October, and the US should consider "a more formal statement of mutual security commitments."

This statement, Rusk thought, would be welcomed by Spender and the Australian government. "It is unlikely that the Australians would press for more than this", Rusk added, "[Australia and New Zealand] appear to be interested not so much in written assurances of military protection as in an opportunity to participate more closely in military and political planning."[14] Doidge and New Zealand would have been content with such a statement, but Spender wanted a more binding commitment. He later told Rusk that while he appreciated Rusk's sincerity in his desire to establish a closer Australian-American relationship, a Presidential Statement was "not sufficient at all." Australia, in Spender's view, required "something of more substance."[15]

After Spender rejected a Presidential Statement, Allison suggested to Dulles in early December that he and the US should consider a formal

---

13 New Zealand Embassy in Washington to the Secretary of External Affairs, 5 January 1951, DNZER Vol. III, 424-425; O'Neill, *Australia in the Korean War*, 177.

14 Rusk to Matthews, 9 October 1950, NARA, RG 59, 790.5/10-950; McNicol to Officer; 31 October 1950, NAA, A1838, 532/11 part i; Spender to Watt, 1 November 1950, A6768, EATS 77 part i.

15 Spender, *Exercises in Diplomacy*, 65; McNicol to Officer; 31 October 1950, NAA, A1838, 532/11 part i; Spender to Watt, 1 November 1950, A6768, EATS 77 part i; Spender to Watt, 3 November 1950, A1838, 535/6 part i.

defence arrangement with Australia and New Zealand. For Allison, a security treaty was a worthwhile commitment to ensure a speedy Japanese settlement after the recent intervention of Chinese forces in the Korean War. "In my opinion", Allison told Dulles, the United States should consider concluding "mutual defence arrangements with New Zealand, Australia and the Philippines."[16] Five days later, Allison again raised the pact idea with Dulles. Allison's general proposal for a Pacific collective security pact would "have the dual purpose of defending Japan from Communist aggression and assuring our friends that Japan would be on their side and not a menace to them." After these discussions, Dulles wrote to Acheson and stressed that the US must consider all measures that might hasten an acceptable settlement. In other words, Dulles thought that a Pacific Pact with Australia and New Zealand might be necessary.

Figure 9. John Foster Dulles, US Negotiator to the ANZUS Treaty and US Secretary of State (1953-1959). Photo by US Department of State (n. d.), Flickr, https://www.flickr.com/photos/statephotos/2358513061/, unrestricted use.

---

16 Allison to Dulles, 2 December 1950, FRUS 1950 Vol. VI, 1354-1355.

Allison also told David McNicol, Australia's Second Secretary in its Washington Embassy, that discussions for a formal defence arrangement were now being given greater consideration in the State Department. "There was now considerably more support in the State Department for a Pacific Island Pact", he told McNicol confidentially on 9 December, adding that Dulles had "come around to the support of a Pacific Pact."[17] In response, Spender and the Australian government increased their demands for a pact with the United States in exchange for agreeing to the Japanese Peace Treaty and remilitarisation plans. After Spender was informed of Allison's briefing, he announced publicly that the need for a regional pact has become "more urgent." Australia was "not satisfied that Japan [could] be trusted with military power", Spender said on 11 January 1951, because it was "too great a gamble for Australia to be asked to take [without] effective regional security."[18]

At the 1951 Commonwealth Prime Ministers' Conference in January, Australia continued to take a noticeably hard line toward the Japanese Peace Treaty. Australia was alarmed at the "tendency to slip into an easy treaty" as Australian High Commissioner in London Eric Harrison said. Australia objected to the possibility of Japan's military resurgence and distrusted Japan to remain a loyal ally. Australia, Harrison said, needed security against future Japanese aggression.[19] In London, New Zealand Prime Minister Sidney Holland took a similar line but was more flexible than the Australians. While he conceded that New Zealand interests were "much the same" as Australia's, its fear of Japanese aggression was "slightly less." In terms of opposing a soft peace treaty for Japan, Holland was "not prepared to push this point too far."[20]

Holland's reluctance to follow the Australian line in London and press hard for a comprehensive Pacific Pact reflected a growing belief in the External Affairs Department that New Zealand's political and military interests would be best served by concluding an arrangement with the United States that was as informal as possible. Shortly after

---

17   Makin to Spender, 9 December 1950, NAA, A6768, EATS 77 part iv.
18   Spender Statement, 11 January 1951, NAA, A4534, 46/2/4 Part II.
19   Paper by the United Kingdom Government on the Japanese Peace Treaty, 2 January 1951, DNZER Vol. III, 425-431.
20   Report of the Commonwealth Prime Ministers' Meeting in London, 9 January 1951, DNZER Vol. III, 433-434.

the Prime Ministers' Conference, an External Affairs Department memorandum that was prepared for the New Zealand Chiefs of Staff in late January considered three possible types of arrangement that might be struck with the United States in exchange for agreeing to the Japanese Peace Treaty. The report concluded that the disadvantages of the comprehensive NATO-type pact that the Australians were pursuing would outweigh any advantages for Wellington, citing that it would "provide little reassurance against the long-term threat from Asia […] and impair the ability of Australia and New Zealand to meet that threat."[21] Alternatively, the usefulness of a "limited" pact similar to the idea Berendsen proposed could not yet be determined because New Zealand's military capacity needed to be studied further, while its commitments continued in the Middle East. Dismissing these two possibilities, the report concluded that the best outcome was a declaration from President Truman that the United States would defend New Zealand, even though the Australian attitude to such an arrangement would be unfavourable. "Such an undertaking", the report conceded, "would be insufficiently precise to afford Australia real assurance of American assistance in the event of hostilities in the Pacific."[22]

Meanwhile, the State Department proposed to the Australian and New Zealand External Affairs Departments that Dulles visit in mid-February to discuss the Japanese Peace Treaty and the question of a Pacific security arrangement. Holland and his External Affairs Department were unsure of whether Dulles would also stop in Wellington or whether there would be joint talks in Canberra. When his visit was first proposed, New Zealand got word that Dulles thought combined talks in Canberra would be better in case "time did not allow him to visit both countries."[23] As the weaker party, New Zealand thought joint talks were best and proposed that Doidge and the New Zealand delegation would meet Spender and Dulles in Canberra. From a New Zealand perspective, joint talks potentially disposed of the possibility that major policy differences between Australia and New Zealand would be noticeable to Dulles. There was also a danger that if Dulles met with Doidge after he

---

21 External Affairs Notes on a Pacific Pact, 30 January 1951, Archives NZ, EA, 111/3/3.
22 Ibid.
23 External Affairs Minister to the NZ High Commissioner in Canberra, 27 January 1951, DNZER Vol. III, 555.

had seen Spender, Australia would make "impossible demands" and it would be difficult for Doidge or anyone else in New Zealand to argue against them.[24] If the discussions proceeded independently in Canberra and Wellington, New Zealand could be faced with an agreement it did not like and one it would find difficult to change.[25]

For their part, the Australians feared that having Doidge at the talks with Dulles would be inhibiting. While his presence might project solidarity between Australia and New Zealand, it could also prevent Spender from putting forward his point of view as forcefully. New Zealand had not, after all, shown the same level of opposition to Japanese rearmament at the recent Prime Ministers' Conference in London. In other words, New Zealand and Australia did not approach the Dulles talks with the sense of solidarity and confidence in one another that might have been expected from two neighbouring countries importuning the United States.[26]

Allison drew up US plans for Dulles's visit. These drafts were then forwarded from Dulles to US Ambassador at Large Philip Jessup. So far as membership of a pact was concerned, the draft proposed six signatories: the United States, Japan, the Philippines, Indonesia, Australia and New Zealand. Dulles explained in early January that one major consideration was to "give significant reassurance to Australia, New Zealand and the Philippines so that they will consent to a peace treaty with Japan which will not contain limitations upon rearmament." To alleviate these fears, Dulles raised the possibility of a defence council, where Australia and New Zealand could be afforded a "voice in how Japan's defence forces progressed." Above all else, however, Dulles stressed that it was essential that the US "should not become committed to the Pact unless it is assured that the other Parties will agree to the kind of Japanese Peace Treaty the United States feels is necessary."[27]

Allison forwarded Dulles's plans to Australian Second Secretary in Washington David McNicol on 21 January. The confidential brief

---

24 Trotter, *New Zealand and Japan*, 152.
25 Shanahan to McIntosh, 26 January 1951, Archives NZ, EA 102/9/4.
26 Trotter, *New Zealand and Japan*, 152.
27 Allison to Jessup, 4 January 1951, FRUS 1951 Vol. VI, 132-134; Dulles to Jessup, 4 January 1951, FRUS 1951 Vol. VI, 134-137; Allison Memorandum, 11 January 1951, FRUS 1951 Vol. VI, 790-792.

emphasised strong US support for a Pacific Pact. The Department of Defense "favoured" a pact and some of the Joint Chiefs of Staff (JCS) were "very keen." The Far Eastern sub-committees of the House and Senate Foreign Relations Committee also both approved of the idea. Allison stressed that Dulles had in mind "an arrangement not quite as formal as [NATO]." In other words, US thinking did not necessarily contemplate an "attack upon one, attack upon all provision" and an "organic link" with NATO.[28]

Meanwhile, the New Zealand military reconsidered its preferred structure and scope of a defence arrangement with Australia and the United States. The New Zealand Defence Chiefs concluded that an informal guarantee of New Zealand's security in the form of a Presidential announcement seemed to best suit its interests. In reaching this conclusion, it was decided that a formal pact could never be confined to the Southwest Pacific. Rather, a pact would only serve US interests in Northeast Asia and commit Australian and New Zealand forces there. "The United States cannot give a direct and precise guarantee to New Zealand and Australia which are in any case remote from the centre of the danger", the Chiefs concluded, adding that it was "only in connection with [American] arrangements in the Philippines and Japan that sufficient Congressional and public support could be given for an extension of American commitments to Australia and New Zealand."[29]

As New Zealand policymakers decided that a formal defence arrangement with the United States did not meet their strategic interests, the External Affairs Department agreed that a Presidential declaration announcing a US commitment to the defence of Australia and New Zealand was the best course of action. The Department suggested that Doidge should keep this possibility in mind during talks with Dulles later in February. Since Wellington did not see "any immediate threat to New Zealand or the Pacific", no formal pact was required. Instead, a "Presidential Statement would be useful."[30] Doidge left for Canberra with the proposal for a Presidential guarantee as his first preference.

---

28   Makin to Spender, 21 January 1951, NAA, A1838, TS250/7/10.
29   Notes on the Defence Aspects of the Japanese Peace Settlement, 30 January 1951, DNZER Vol. III, 558-563.
30   Memorandum for Doidge, 8 February 1951, Archives NZ, EA, 111/3/3 part 3.

Australia wanted no part in the Presidential Statement, nor could it accept any arrangement other than a formal commitment from the United States. In Spender's view, any agreement short of a formal guarantee of US protection in Asia and the Pacific would be worthless to meet Australia's security needs. Spender argued that the preferred arrangement was a "treaty in solemn form." Dulles's visit might be the "last opportunity" Australia and New Zealand had to secure an American guarantee, he told Doidge, so it was imperative that they cooperated and did not squander the opportunity.[31] In the end, it was agreed that it would be counterproductive to propose different things to Dulles. Spender and Doidge finally agreed to push for the same tripartite pact, after which Spender commented that New Zealand had finally "seen the light."[32]

After meeting with Japanese representatives in Tokyo to finalise the arrangements for a peace treaty, Dulles flew to Canberra where official talks began on 15 February. Dulles stressed immediately to both Spender and Doidge the US plans for post-occupied Japan and unlimited rearmament. He stated that a continued US military presence in Japan should quell Australian and New Zealand concerns over revived Japanese aggression. Moreover, any restrictions on Japanese rearmament were counterproductive for American efforts to prevent the spread of Communism. As he was concerned by the perception of a "White Man's Club" in Asia, Dulles also pushed for a broader security treaty that included the Philippines. This echoed Acheson's original instructions to Dulles, which specified that the US was willing to enter some sort of "mutual assistance arrangement" with countries including Australia and New Zealand but also Japan, the Philippines and possibly even Indonesia. The condition attached to these types of arrangement was that these countries must support US objectives regarding the peace settlement in Japan.[33]

For his part, Spender seemed unconvinced. Whether he truly disagreed with Dulles or was cunningly using "the negotiating value of Australia's agreement to sign a peace treaty as a lever to obtain an

---

31 Note on Discussion between the New Zealand and Australian Ministers of External Affairs, 13 February 1951, DNZER Vol. III, 590-591.

32 Spender, *Exercises in Diplomacy*, 124.

33 Acheson to Dulles, 9 January 1951, FRUS 1951, Vol. VI, 789.

effective security guarantee", he told Dulles that Australia could not so easily accept a soft policy toward Japan. He argued that Australia needed adequate assurances that it was safe from any future Japanese aggression. "[Australia] is not satisfied that in the long-run, it was wholly unlikely that [Japan] would not [...] present any menace to peace" Spender replied.[34] As for including the Philippines, Spender and Doidge successfully resisted Dulles's efforts even though Spender later admitted he would have been prepared to accept the Philippines if the alternative was no form of defence arrangement.

As Thomas K. Robb and David James Gill concluded, the reasons for this resistance reflected a range of geopolitical, security, and racial motivations.[35] That said, there is certainly enough evidence from these meetings to praise Spender's and Doidge's diplomacy, particularly because it was likely they would have begrudgingly accepted the Philippines into ANZUS if there was no other option. It is also worth noting that these efforts were well received in London. The British were keen to ensure that the Philippines were not included in ANZUS, because such an inclusion would completely undermine British influence in the region.

With respect to the Japanese Peace Treaty, New Zealand had always been more pessimistic about Australia's and New Zealand's chances of influencing its conclusion. For example, regarding Japan, McIntosh had long thought "all [New Zealand] could do is to plug the old line and see what, if anything can be salvaged." For McIntosh, it seemed unrealistic to hope for the demilitarisation of Japan based purely on Australian and New Zealand objections. The only acceptable compromise was a "guarantee against Japanese aggression."[36] In a similar spirit, Doidge expressed New Zealand's reservations about the long-term possibility of revived Japanese aggression. Doidge told Dulles that his explanation for the US plan for Japan in the short term was "highly convincing", but it "did not seem to cover the long term possibilities."[37] Australia and

---

34 Spender to Harrison, 21 February 1951, NAA, A6768, EATS 77 Annex A.
35 Robb and Gill, "The ANZUS Treaty during the Cold War", 139.
36 McIntosh to Berendsen, 12 April 1950, in *Undiplomatic Dialogue*, 225.
37 Notes on the Australian-New Zealand-United States Talks in Canberra, 15-17 February 1951, DNZER Vol. III, 599-606.

New Zealand needed some other guarantee to cover themselves against the long-term prospects in Japan.

Doidge also raised concerns about New Zealand military commitments elsewhere. Holland had told him that he was concerned about what a Pacific Pact might mean for its obligations in the Middle East if its provisions did not adequately protect New Zealand's security concerns closer to home. "We cannot do both", Doidge said to Dulles, passing on Holland's reservations, "a Pacific Pact [cannot] lead us into obligations which would conflict with those we undertook to fulfil in the Middle East." Doidge also pointed out the "folly of securing the front door and leaving the back door open." New Zealand's military commitment to global strategy could only be met, as Doidge stressed, with a "guarantee from the United States" in New Zealand's "back door."[38]

As a possible compromise, talks moved towards a trilateral regional security pact. When Spender and Doidge argued for a pact on 16 February, Dulles spoke about the difficulties it would cause for the Philippines, which only had an informal US guarantee. He also raised Britain's clear objections to a pact, as the British Foreign Office did not want to see a US treaty with two Commonwealth nations that excluded Britain as a signatory. Spender, who was unaware Britain had pressed the United States to reconsider discussions for a pact with Australia and New Zealand, protested vehemently. He pointed out that Britain was no longer a major Pacific power and its objections were not relevant.

After lengthy discussions, Dulles agreed to examine possible draft tripartite pacts. Ralph Harry, part of the Australian delegation during the talks, prepared a possible treaty. Harry had studied the NATO treaty and hoped to model his draft on its provisions, suggesting that Dulles was more likely to accept its clauses if "every point [...] [had a] precedent in some other treaty to which the US was a party."[39] Harry's draft, although amended to meet Dulles's more specific demands about the scope of any commitment, provided a solid base for discussions between Spender, Doidge and Dulles on 17 February. After the meeting,

---

38 Ibid., 599.

39 The Dulles Visit to Canberra, DAFP: ANZUS, 78.

the three representatives agreed that the draft should be presented to their respective governments for further consideration.

Even after a draft treaty was agreed upon, there were still three potential issues that threatened to derail the entire project. The first was getting the treaty through the US Senate. In the lead up to its presentation to the Senate, Spender and Berendsen were still discussing changes to the wording with Dulles. Berendsen was particularly apprehensive about what these discussions might entail. "Here we have been offered on a platter the greatest gift that the most powerful country in the world could offer to a small and comparatively helpless group of people and we persist in niggling and naggling about what seems to me to be the most ridiculous trifles", Berendsen told McIntosh on 25 June. He added that this sort of "stupid pin-pricking" could "cost us very dearly." Berendsen feared that late objections to the treaty's provisions would prevent getting it through the Senate. "It is not Acheson, Rusk, Dulles, the President and the State Department that we need to worry about", Berendsen suggested, "it is the Senate, and my mind is on the Senate all the time." Senate approval, according to Berendsen, was the "most difficult hurdle", and trying to get further assurances from Dulles could "ruin the whole thing."[40] It certainly appeared that Berendsen had come around to the idea of a more binding commitment with the United States.

The second issue was British objections to the conclusion of the ANZUS Treaty. From London's perspective, ANZUS demonstrated to the world that Britain was incapable of protecting Commonwealth countries in the Pacific and potentially threatened its positions in Hong Kong, Singapore and Malaya. While Whitehall was pleased that the Philippines was not ultimately included in the draft treaty and British Minister of State for Foreign Affairs Kenneth Younger acknowledged publicly that ANZUS was "a most useful contribution to Commonwealth strategy", the British Government deeply resented the conclusion of ANZUS without being included as a signatory. "We are most certainly a Pacific power", British Foreign Secretary Herbert Morrison argued,

---

40 Berendsen to McIntosh, 25 June 1951, in *Undiplomatic Dialogue*, 265-266; Berendsen to McIntosh, 13 July 1951, in *Undiplomatic Dialogue*, 267.

and "it would not have been unwelcome to us if we were included in the proposed pact."[41]

British efforts to stifle and undermine ANZUS came well before the treaty's presentation to the Senate. While Dulles was in Tokyo finalising the peace treaty and post-occupation plans, Political Representative of the British Liaison Mission Sir Alvary Gascoigne told him that the UK Chiefs of Staff were reluctant to accept the US as Australia's and New Zealand's chief protector. "From the standpoint of the United Kingdom's position as a world power", he told Dulles on 2 February, the proposed Pacific Pact "would be interpreted in the Pacific and elsewhere as a renunciation of [Britain's] responsibilities and possibly as evidence of [a] rift in policy between Britain and the United States."[42] He also argued that excluding Asian countries would encourage aggression in areas where Communist activity was highest.

Then, during ANZUS negotiations, Britain went to great lengths to prevent the US signing a formal agreement with Australia and New Zealand by voicing its strong discontent in Washington. London "hated" the idea of the ANZUS Treaty and had been doing its best to "head the Americans off and get them to substitute a Presidential Declaration", McIntosh suggested in March 1951. The British also played on Dulles's concerns over the inclusion of the Philippines. As McIntosh described shortly after Dulles's visit to Canberra,

> The British are obviously doing their best to torpedo the whole thing and they want to represent to the Americans the undesirability of including the Philippines because of the adverse effect it would have on United Kingdom prestige, more particularly in United Kingdom territories like Borneo, Malaya, Hong Kong and so forth. The Australians are ropeable about the British. They say they have been doing everything they can before Dulles arrived and since he arrived to stop the treaty.[43]

Although New Zealand still considered itself tied firmly to the Commonwealth and the British Empire, even the New Zealand External Affairs Department was upset by British efforts to stifle conclusion of the pact. Along with Britain's sudden recognition of Communist China

---

41 Spender Memorandum, 19 April 1951, Spender Papers, Box 1, NLA.
42 Dulles to Rusk, 2 February 1951, FRUS 1951 Vol VI Part I, 143-144.
43 McIntosh to Berendsen, 16 March 1951, in *Undiplomatic Dialogue*, 255.

in January 1950, which caused a noticeable rift in Anglo-American relations, Berendsen argued to McIntosh in early April that Britain were "behaving like stupid children" and had done a "great deal of harm."[44]

Another distraction was the development of a Middle East Command, which was already being discussed in depth by US and British officials to protect Western interests in the region. Britain contacted Australia and New Zealand about the possibility of forming a Middle East Command in mid-1951. Australia and New Zealand shared similar post-war interests in the security of the Middle East. For both countries, the Suez Canal was the major shipping route to Britain and the rest of Europe. Access to the region's oil reserves was also especially important for the post-war industrial development schemes of both countries. However, it was only after New Zealand protestations over how little opportunity it had to influence policy and defence decisions that it accepted a formal British invitation to participate in the Middle East Defence Command.

Australia, on the other hand, was far less forthcoming in its support for a defence commitment to the Middle East. While Canberra "agreed in principle" to the Command and was willing to participate in discussions, the Australian External Affairs Department stressed that its agreement "[did] not involve any commitment to provide forces to the Middle East." Its final position on the Command would be "substantially affected by arrangements for higher political direction and by views which are worked out as to the place of Southeast Asia in those elements of strategy which are relevant to Australia."[45] For Australian policymakers, ANZUS had to remain the priority.

Lastly, the final version and scope of the ANZUS Treaty had to be approved by the US military. Spender was particularly anxious about the military reaction to the ANZUS Treaty, as he hoped that it might provide a means for Australia to access US strategic plans and influence global strategy. After Dulles left Canberra in February, Spender wrote to him on 8 March and said, "I know you won't mind me saying directly that we in this country are a metropolitan power in the Pacific and we hope that our view will be predominate." He also hoped that closer ties with the United States might become a pretext for further US assistance

---

44 Berendsen to McIntosh, 2 April 1951, in *Undiplomatic Dialogue*, 257-259.
45 Middle East Command Report, 11 October 1951, NAA, A4462, 439/1/10 Part 1.

in meeting Australia's own defence production needs. In the same letter to Dulles, Spender wrote that "our objective is to get into full production, to increase our military forces and to take steps necessary to ensure that defence needs have priority. The lead which the United States has given on these matters is an inspiration", Spender added, but urged that Australia needed more assistance to deal with "serious industrial troubles."[46]

While the Department of Defense had already indicated in January that the conclusion of the treaty was a favourable outcome for the United States, many top-ranking US military officials now argued that the scope of American military and strategic consultation obligations should be as narrow as possible. In a combined State Department-Joint Chiefs of Staff meeting on 11 April, Chief of Naval Operations Forrest Sherman stressed the "value of informality in establishing joint planning" and indicated his preference for "leaving such arrangements out of the treaty." Chairman of the Joint Chiefs of Staff Omar Bradley agreed with Sherman's conclusions. In Bradley's estimation, combined planning was "theoretically all right but practically objectionable" because too many countries would have access to US strategic plans and could thereby complicate the policymaking process.[47]

Two days after this meeting, Secretary of Defense George Marshall suggested even at this late stage that, from a military perspective, any formal commitment to Australia and New Zealand's defence was not an ideal outcome for the United States. "Any trilateral agreement with Australia and New Zealand should be made a simple understanding or public declaration rather than a formal pact." Marshall wrote to Acheson on 13 April. At the very least, Marshall argued that "if political considerations are so overriding that a formal pact must be made, the Joint Chiefs of Staff oppose the inclusion in the pact of any reference to military plans, planning or organisations." Recognising that a formal treaty was necessary for Australian and New Zealand acquiescence to the Japanese Peace Treaty, Dulles and Acheson refused to make a public declaration rather than a formal commitment. However, they accepted these military views and made sure to omit any reference to secret

---

46 Spender to Dulles, 8 March 1951, Spender Papers, Box 1, NLA.
47 Department of State-Joint Chiefs of Staff Meeting, 11 April 1951, NARA, RG 59, Lot 64, D 563.

military planning under the ANZUS Treaty. "In the case of the trilateral arrangement with Australia and New Zealand", Dulles told Acheson, "we can, I think, make it clear that any organisation thereunder will not have the right to demand knowledge of and to participate in planning."[48]

Figure 10. ANZUS logo. Archives New Zealand (n. d.), Flickr, https://www.flickr.com/photos/archivesnz/20921987801/, CC BY 2.0.

Despite these uncertainties, the US Senate approved the ANZUS Treaty. Several days before the Japanese Peace Treaty was signed formally, Acheson, along with Australian and New Zealand representatives Percy Spender and Carl Berendsen, signed the ANZUS Treaty at a ceremony at The Presidio in San Francisco on 1 September 1951. The treaty was planned to enter into force on 29 April 1952. Australia, New Zealand and the United States were now allied formally and agreed to respond to mutual dangers in the Asia-Pacific region. After securing the agreement with the Americans, Spender declared that ANZUS was a momentous landmark in Australian history. In his view, ANZUS did more than express formally the close ties of comradeship between the parties; it

---

48 Marshall to Acheson, 13 April 1951, FRUS 1951 Vol. VI Part I, 202; Dulles to Acheson, 13 April 1951, FRUS 1951 Vol. VI Part I, 203.

also marked "the first step in building of the ramparts of freedom in the vast and increasingly important area of the Pacific Ocean." He added that the treaty was "directed to regional security in the Pacific" and took the "first step towards what we hope will prove to be an ever widening system of peaceful security in the vital area."[49]

Spender's New Zealand counterpart, Frederick Doidge, also welcomed the conclusion of the treaty but appeared less convinced about its significance. The treaty represented "nothing new in the relationship of the three countries", Doidge announced to the New Zealand House of Representatives on 13 July, as there was already "a deep and firm understanding on security between the United States and ourselves." Unlike the other ANZUS powers, Doidge also alluded to the possibility of future British membership or consultation. In the same address, Doidge announced that "the New Zealand Government looks forward, in giving effect to the provisions of this treaty, to the closest consultation with the United Kingdom and other powers concerned with the security of the Pacific [...] both New Zealand and Australia have special obligations in defence as members of the British Commonwealth of Nations."[50] The issue of British membership of ANZUS surfaced later once the treaty came into effect.

Doidge's comments aside, the ANZUS Treaty undoubtedly signalled a crucial new era of Australian-New Zealand-American relations. In finalising its conclusion, Spender achieved what most people thought might be impossible. Given the circumstances, he could not have secured a more binding commitment from the United States at the time. Dulles certainly meant what he said when he told Spender's wife Jean that "there would have been no ANZUS without Percy." Achieved in the face of active opposition within the United States, Britain and most of the Commonwealth, it was one of the most impressive achievements by any Australian foreign affairs minister. If the ANZUS Treaty would be effective in practice, however, remained to be seen.

---

49 US Department of State Bulletin, 24 September 1951, reproduced in ANZUS Council Preparations, 24 July 1952, Acheson Papers, TL.

50 Doidge Statement, 13 July 1951, New Zealand Parliamentary Debates Vol. 294, 1951, 318-319.

PART TWO: ANZUS IN FORCE

5. Post-Treaty Issues

Conclusion of the ANZUS Treaty was a watershed moment in Australian and New Zealand history. After the 1944 Australia-New Zealand Agreement, ANZUS was the first major international treaty that Australia and New Zealand signed that did not include Britain as a member. While policymakers in Canberra and Wellington stressed that its conclusion would not weaken their country's ties to the British Commonwealth, ANZUS testified to Australia's and New Zealand's newfound security reliance on the United States during the early Cold War. Although it was a far less historic event in Washington, ANZUS enabled the United States to finalise the Japanese Peace Treaty and provide further support to its defence structure along the Pacific Rim. Even allowing for this difference in significance, ANZUS was important for all three countries.

Once ANZUS came into effect, however, there were still four key post-treaty issues that the signatories needed to address. Firstly, opinions were divided over the proposed machinery of the treaty. While New Zealand had no issues with the ANZUS consultation and discussion process, Australia wanted greater access to strategic and military planning undertaken by NATO and the Pentagon. The Americans, however, were unwilling to provide such access. Secondly, opinions were also divided over the question of British membership. New Zealand wanted Britain to be included as a member of ANZUS, the United States opposed British inclusion, and Australia remained ambivalent. Thirdly, once it was clear that Britain would not become a treaty member, planning began for a separate defence arrangement for Southeast Asia through the Five Power Staff Agency. Again, hoping to include Britain, New Zealand thought that this new mechanism might be a means to merge ANZUS with Commonwealth defence planning in Southeast Asia. Australia, on the other hand, remained aloof until its diplomats received confirmation from Washington that ANZUS would not be superseded by these new defence arrangements. Washington did not intend to replace ANZUS with a broader defence mechanism in Southeast Asia, but major US commitments were put on hold until after the 1952 elections. Finally, uncertainty over the future of ANZUS ensued after Dwight Eisenhower replaced Truman as US President in January 1953. In Australia and New Zealand, policymakers were concerned by new US national security strategies and whether the Eisenhower Administration viewed ANZUS as a serious commitment.

ANZUS Machinery and Membership

After the ANZUS Treaty was finalised and presented to the public, Spender was replaced as Australian External Affairs Minister and reassigned as Australian Ambassador to the United States in April 1951. As he played an instrumental role in concluding the treaty, Spender thought he was best placed to influence decision making in Washington and look after Australian interests. "I believe the next two or three years will be critical years in the history of civilisation", Spender wrote to former US Ambassador in Canberra Myron Cowen on 5 April, "and it is in Washington that the decisions affecting the free world will be made." Spender added that "I believe I can serve my country and the cause of peace in the world better in the USA than I can in any capacity at the moment in Australia."[1] His replacement as External Affairs Minister, Richard Casey, was tasked with ensuring Spender's efforts to secure the ANZUS Treaty were not in vain and worked to serve Australian interests; namely, greater Australian-American strategic cooperation and military information exchange with the Pentagon. He was a more than capable successor to Spender. Serving previously as Australia's first Minister to Washington and a Cabinet Minister during the ANZUS negotiations, Casey's thirty years of experience in international affairs

---

1   Spender to Cowen, 5 April 1951, Spender Papers, Box 1, NLA.

made his appointment as External Affairs Minister a role "for which his whole life seemed to have prepared him."[2]

Figure 11. Australian External Affairs Minister Richard Casey (1951-1960), 1951. Photo by Australian News and Information Bureau (1951), Wikimedia, https://commons.wikimedia.org/wiki/File:Richard_Casey_1951.jpg, Crown Copyright.

Even for Casey, it was not an easy assignment. ANZUS did not require American policymakers to share their strategies with Australia and New Zealand, nor did it specify that Canberra or Wellington must be informed of US intentions before any decisions were made. Annual ANZUS Council meetings between External Affairs and State Department officers, as well as a small representation from the US military, became the basic mechanism for trilateral discussions, yet these meetings were designed mostly for the Americans to outline the plans they had already made, rather than to consult with Australia and New Zealand over

---

2   Christopher Waters, "Cold War Liberals: Richard Casey and the Department of External Affairs, 1951-1960", in *Ministers, Mandarins and Diplomats: Australian Foreign Policy Making, 1941-1969*, Jean Beaumont, Christopher Waters, David Lowe and Gary Woodard eds. (Melbourne: Melbourne University Press, 2003), 89.

their perspectives, objections and interests. US Secretary of State Dean Acheson later recalled:

> Instead of starving the Australians and New Zealanders, we would give them indigestion. For two days we went over the situation in the world, political and military, with the utmost frankness and fullness. At the end they were very happy with political liaison through the Council and military planning through the Commander in Chief Pacific.[3]

United States military officials insisted that discussions should be mostly political and should not offer Australia and New Zealand any concrete information on military planning other than through the US Commander-in-Chief Pacific (CINCPAC).

Members of the New Zealand External Affairs Department generally accepted this structure. As one adviser told Secretary McIntosh less than two weeks before the first ANZUS meeting in Honolulu during early August 1952, New Zealand "did not share the long-standing Australian objective of infiltration into the world's policy-making hierarchy."[4] Instead, Frank Corner suggested that all that New Zealand was seeking from the United States was basic consultation in Far Eastern matters rather than the high-level military and political discussions for which Spender had hoped. "What in fact we are all seeking to establish", Corner told McIntosh, was ANZUS as a kind of "Dominion status with the United States, [and] a right to be consulted in Pacific and Far Eastern Affairs."[5]

George Laking, another New Zealand External Affairs Officer, was not even convinced that ANZUS was in any way useful for New Zealand. "The plain fact is we are getting nothing at all from the Americans, who have a childish faith in their ability to fox one and all", Laking complained to Secretary McIntosh on 25 June 1951. "The chances of our knowing the right answers before the press are five to four against", he added, and "the secret of it all [was] that the Americans don't know the answers themselves until it happens."[6] McIntosh certainly sympathised

---

3 Dean Acheson, *Present at the Creation: My Years in the State Department* (New York: W.W. Norton, 1987), 876-878.

4 Memorandum for McIntosh, 25 July 1952, Archives NZ, EA, 111/3/3/1 Part 8.

5 Corner to McIntosh, 20 February 1953, Archives NZ, EA, 316/4/1.

6 Laking to McIntosh, 25 June 1951, in *Undiplomatic Dialogue*, 76.

with Laking's reservations. Along with Foss Shanahan and Joseph Wilson, two of New Zealand's External Affairs Officers, McIntosh conceded that New Zealand "never wanted the damn Pacific Pact in the first place."[7]

Before the first ANZUS meetings even began in August 1952, Casey recognised the difficulties that ANZUS posed for Australia and New Zealand. "ANZUS represents [two] difficulties: the fact that there is one very strong partner and two others very much less strong, and that any threat to which [Australia] may be exposed must come from the southward expansionist ambitions of Communist China which must come by land", Casey penned in his diary on 1 August. He added that "the fact that the US will not even consider any further land obligations on the Asian mainland makes for an obviously anomalous position." Unfortunately for Casey, he knew that there was little Australia could offer the United States in return for a greater commitment in Southeast Asia. "There are a great many great things that we could ask the Americans for", Casey conceded, but "few things that we could offer them in exchange."[8]

Spender, the architect of ANZUS, was having similar problems in Washington. "We need to put flesh on the bones of the Pacific Pact", Spender argued to Casey, suggesting that the powers needed to agree on a "wide flung strategy" and not ignore the needs of home defence.[9] Much to Spender's frustration, as Australia was not a NATO member, ANZUS was not allowing Australia to get its voice heard in any of NATO discussions. For Spender, this was important for Australia's general strategic planning. "NATO decisions affect everyone and Australia should have the right to be heard, not only with respect to general strategic considerations but especially on matters directly affecting Australia", Spender said in a State Department meeting on 20 May 1952. Spender, in other words, was "not content to be the hair on

---

7   McIntosh to Corner, 3 October 1952, in *Unofficial Channels*, 106.

8   Casey Diary Entry, 1 August 1952, in *Australian Foreign Minister: The Diaries of R. G. Casey, 1951-1960*, T. B. Millar ed. (London: Collins, 1972), 84-85 (hereafter Casey Diaries).

9   Spender to Casey, 25 June 1952, Spender Papers, Box 1, NLA.

the tail of the dog." He felt that Australia should at least be "part of the hide of the dog itself."[10]

Acheson was unprepared to meet Spender's demands. Brushing off these concerns, Acheson proposed that "if the Australians wanted real contact with the American Government and its thinking on world problems, it was highly desirable that they keep in touch with the Department of State and not continue to attempt to establish themselves in liaison with the Pentagon." He added that "with particular regard to Pacific defence and its problems, the real planning was being done by Admiral Arthur Radford (US Chief Commander in the Pacific) and his staff in Hawaii. If the Australians and New Zealanders really wanted contact with US military planning operations, this was the place for it."[11] In short, Acheson advised that the Australians and New Zealanders should stick with their present contacts in the Department to obtain information relating to global strategic plans. The ANZUS Council meetings were Australia and New Zealand's supposed "door of entry" to information on US global planning, but not to NATO.[12]

It was simply not possible for Australia and New Zealand to expect any greater access to the Pentagon through ANZUS. If the ANZUS meetings got through the organisational steps in good order, however, Acheson offered that he would present a total picture that would give them "plenty to think about and work on." It was certainly not the consultation for which Australia had hoped. New Zealand diplomats, on the other hand, believed this method of consultation was appropriate. New Zealand delegates at the first ANZUS Council meeting in Hawaii described the trilateral discussion as "a most successful one."[13]

The US military did have one clear idea how Australia and New Zealand could meaningfully contribute to the relationship. While ANZUS was originally designed to protect against mutual security threats solely in the Pacific theatre, US military planners began to suggest that Australia

---

10 Department of State Memorandum of Conversation, 20 May 1952, Secretary of State File, Acheson Papers, TL.

11 Memorandum of Conversation, 4 August 1952, Secretary of State File, Acheson Papers, TL.

12 Watt to McIntosh, 12 July 1952, Archives NZ, EA, 111/3/3/1 part 8.

13 Memorandum for Holland, 15 August 1952, Archives NZ, EA, 111/3/3/1 part 8; Webb Statement, 12 August 1952, Archives NZ, EA, 111/3/3/15 part 1.

and New Zealand should also be prepared to commit their forces to defending the Middle East. During another joint State Department-Joint Chiefs of Staff (JCS) meeting in late November, JCS Chairman Omar Bradley concluded that it would be "good performance" for Australia and New Zealand to commit infantry divisions to any future hostilities in the Middle East.[14] By JCS estimates, this trans-Tasman contribution would assist in meeting the "ground force deficiencies" under current American contingency plans for war with the Soviet Union in the region. For Bradley, Australian and New Zealand military contributions to the Middle East (as well as contributions from other countries) should still come under the guise of a joint defence Command. There was a "need for the early establishment" of the Middle East Defence Command, Bradly concluded, as this organisation would undertake the joint military planning required to defend the region from Soviet control.

By this stage, however, the Australians had cooled even further towards the idea of the formation of a Command. Australian External Affairs Secretary Alan Watt expressed serious reservations about the Command because it offered Australia absolutely no method of influencing the decision-making process. According to Watt, the proposed Command structure did not give Australia "an adequate political voice in [the] political direction of the Middle East Command."[15] There was also little Australian support for a commitment to the Middle East because policymakers in Canberra believed that the security of the Pacific region was far more important. As New Zealand External Affairs Secretary Alister McIntosh reported from his trip to Canberra on 6 May 1952, "the Australians felt that there was a large element of unreality about the Middle East Command." He suggested that the Australians "preferred a Pacific approach, and the construction of a relationship with the Americans, through a Pacific Defence Council."[16]

For different reasons, New Zealand began to reconsider the usefulness of a Command. McIntosh and Shanahan conceded on 13

---

14 Department of State Minutes of State-Joint Chiefs of Staff Meeting, 28 November 1952, RG 59, NARA, Lot 61, D 417.

15 Middle East Command – Australian Views, 22 May 1952, Archives NZ, EA, 111/39/2 Part 3; Meeting between Watt and McIntosh, 6 May 1952, Archives NZ, EA, 111/39/2 Part 3.

16 Note for File, 6 May 1952, Archives NZ, EA, 111/39/2 Part 3.

June 1952 that "there will probably be some military secrets from which we will be excluded", but did not think this prevented New Zealand from actively supporting the Command. According to McIntosh and Shanahan, there were other more pressing issues about the arrangement that brought its usefulness into question. For one, they both thought that "serious differences in views between the United States and Britain" in the Middle East—such as the make-up of the Command personnel, US policies toward Egypt and the Suez Canal, and British intentions for nearby Sudan—made the proposed Command a potential disaster for Western interests in the region.[17] They also concluded that tense relations with Egypt over British bases near Suez presented a complicated situation to address for the Command powers, especially in the wake of Cairo's refusal to participate.

ANZUS itself was complicated further by the question of British membership. For the first time in Australian and New Zealand history, the two former British colonies signed a major international defence treaty that did not include Britain as a member. London argued that its exclusion was a blow to its international prestige, signalled a clear military weakness in the Commonwealth, and might cause a serious rift in Anglo-American relations. On these grounds, British policymakers ignored Australian and New Zealand representations and strongly objected to ANZUS. After the Foreign Office was initially unable to prevent the treaty's conclusion in early to mid-1951, British policy changed to press upon the ANZUS powers the need for British membership either directly as a signatory to, or indirectly as an observer of, Council meetings. British Foreign Minister Anthony Eden argued on 19 April 1951 that Britain should be included in the alliance because "any threat to either Australia or New Zealand must always be calculated as a threat to [Britain]." He went on to suggest that British interests in Malaya "make it essentially a Pacific Power."[18]

Winston Churchill, who had returned to office in late 1951 for his final stint as prime minister, also staunchly objected to British exclusion from ANZUS. Believing that links between Britain and the Dominions were still strong, Churchill saw the need for his government to play a

---

17   Meeting between McIntosh and Shanahan, 13 June 1952, Archives NZ, EA, 111/39/2 Part 3.
18   Eden Statement, 19 April 1951, UK Parliamentary Debates, Vol. 484, 2007-2008.

larger role in Pacific defence planning to "guide" US strategy against the Communist bloc. In short, without closer Anglo-American strategic cooperation, British interests in the Pacific were likely to become increasingly marginalised by US strategists when they considered issues of concern in this region. Churchill pushed for British inclusion on two fronts: lobbying in Washington on many occasions during 1951-1953, and appealing to Australia and New Zealand to convince the Americans to include Britain in ANZUS.[19] Finding support in Canberra and Wellington would not have appeared too difficult to Churchill, especially since pro-British sentiment in these countries was particularly strong. However, the extent to which the Pacific Dominions would be able to convince the Americans to include Britain in ANZUS was certainly overstated.

The Australians were divided over British membership. Given his well-established predisposition to support Britain and its policies abroad, Menzies was receptive to Churchill's reasoning and agreed that London should be included in ANZUS in some capacity. He told British officials on 5 June that he was "very much in favour" of closer association with the United Kingdom through ANZUS.[20] He then told Casey and Spender that "[Australia] should not place any obstacle in United Kingdom efforts" to join ANZUS Council meetings as an observer [...] provided the Americans are willing to play and provided the United Kingdom request does not involve our acceptance of a string of other countries in the same capacity."[21] These last two points were crucial for Menzies. Firstly, Menzies recognised that American agreement to British observer status was a key condition. This suggests that Menzies had in fact moved away from the idea of British leadership and recognised the need to prioritise the US position. Secondly, if the United States agreed, Menzies was willing to consider British consultation but feared that this might herald the expansion of ANZUS to include other Commonwealth countries. He did not want Australia becoming responsible for defending areas outside of its strategic interests.

---

19   Robb and Gill, "The ANZUS Treaty during the Cold War", 147.
20   Secretary of State for Commonwealth Relations to UK High Commission in New Zealand, 5 June 1952, Archives NZ, EA, 111/3/3/6 part 1.
21   Menzies to Casey and Spender, 5 June 1952, NAA, 5954/1, 1418/3.

Spender was unconvinced. He feared British inclusion might strain Anglo-American relations and Britain's relations with other Commonwealth countries. Most importantly for Australia, British inclusion might dilute the usefulness of ANZUS meetings as a forum to consult with the United States on matters of regional and global strategy. If the United States and Britain were both present at ANZUS meetings and squabbled over their own disagreements, Australia's voice might become increasingly marginalised. Before Britain could be seriously considered as an observer, he told Eden that it was "absolutely essential that the United States and United Kingdom get their lines straightened out and agree upon a common approach" towards pressing disagreements between Washington and London.[22] Spender also told Menzies on 6 June 1952 that "while I appreciate the strength of [your observations] […] before any questions of 'observers' or any extension of the Pact to include other nations should arise, the Council should be first established."[23]

Casey was more sympathetic to British concerns over exclusion from ANZUS. He recognised that the British were "very concerned about their being excluded from any official contact with the ANZUS Council." He was also determined not to pursue closer US consultation at the expense of Australia's relationship with Britain. Casey wrote at the outset of the first ANZUS Council meeting that "Australian relations with the US are close and confident, but I always have in mind the effect of any accord on the British. It would be counter-productive if our good relations with [the] US were at the expense of bad UK-US relations." Along the lines of Menzies's suggestion, he thought he might be able to include "UK people into the ANZUS Council as British Liaison Officers", even though he recognised that Australia must execute "caution in extending 'observer' rights to the United Kingdom or other countries."[24] Even if Britain did not become associated with ANZUS, Casey went as far as suggesting that Australia and New Zealand were already acting as British representatives for Commonwealth interests in the Asia-Pacific region through ANZUS. "ANZUS [was] only a local manifestation of

---

22 Spender to Eden, 15 March 1952, Spender Papers, NLA.
23 Spender to Menzies, 6 June 1952, NAA, A1838/276, 686/6, part 1A.
24 Richard Casey, 3 August 1952, Casey Diaries, 85; Casey to Spender, 11 June 1952, NAA, A1838/289, 250/7/10, part 1.

closer British-American relations", Casey told the Australian Parliament in September 1952."[25] In other words, Australia and New Zealand would retain their roles as British outposts in the Pacific.

While the Australians were divided over the question of British membership, the New Zealanders agreed almost unanimously that Britain must be included in some capacity. New Zealand External Affairs Minister Thomas Clifton Webb thought that while "the Australians saw great difficulty for the United Kingdom to be associated with the Council", New Zealand was "anxious to have the closest consultation with the United Kingdom on operation of [ANZUS]."[26] Wellington had always been reluctant to adjust to American leadership in the Pacific because of its sentimental ties to Britain. Britain's inclusion, even as an observer, was therefore greatly appealing.

Including Britain also countered concerns in New Zealand that Australia and the US would dominate ANZUS discussions. "From New Zealand's point of view", a brief for the New Zealand delegation to the ANZUS Council meeting stated on 25 July 1952,

> British participation would be a most useful counter-weight which would help to guard against [ANZUS] being influenced too much by Australia or the United States or both. United Kingdom would undoubtedly give a stability to the Council which might otherwise be lacking.[27]

In short, while the Australians were primarily concerned that British inclusion might prevent closer consultation with the United States through ANZUS, the New Zealanders wanted British inclusion precisely because it would prevent Australia and the United States from dominating ANZUS discussions.

After the first ANZUS meeting in August, McIntosh and Corner both expressed their concerns about British exclusion. On 3 October, McIntosh told Corner that he had "always wanted to have the United Kingdom in." He even complained that during ANZUS meetings External Affairs Minister Webb "did not put up any fight whatsoever to have the United Kingdom in as observers." In response, Corner replied

---

25   Casey Statement, 24 September 1952, Archives NZ, EA, 111/3/3/6 part 1.
26   Webb to Holland, 8 June 1952, Archives NZ, EA, 111/3/3/6 part 1.
27   Brief for the Council Meeting: Relationship with the United Kingdom, 25 July 1952, Archives NZ, EA, 111/3/3/24.

that US objections to British inclusion were the real problem. "It seems to me", Corner wrote to McIntosh in December 1952, that

> The American unwillingness to include Britain in ANZUS springs from a refusal to share real power in the Pacific with any other country. They will talk to Australia and New Zealand, and will be most forthcoming with us, because we are so unequal and represent no real challenge to their right of decision. But the British are a different proposition and if they were admitted they would bring much greater weight and prestige and would require that America shared its power of decision.[28]

Corner's concerns about US opposition to admitting Britain into ANZUS proved to be correct. Casey told Acheson in the first ANZUS meeting in early August that he was under considerable pressure from the British to have them brought into ANZUS planning. He said that British Foreign Minister Anthony Eden "feels very deeply" on this question and had pressed Casey to push the British case. Acheson, in response, said he felt that this was "completely impossible."[29]

The United States, preferring to "go it alone" in the Pacific rather than including Britain, had no interest whatsoever in including it in ANZUS in any capacity. While Acheson told Menzies that he thought the ANZUS powers should "keep no secrets" from the United Kingdom, he was not prepared to offer them "any special consideration" through ANZUS.[30] After informing Eden of his decision in August 1952, Acheson's stern comments ended any further serious discussion about British membership. Acheson was determined to assert that the United States was indeed the dominant power in the relationship and would not accept changes to the treaty that did not suit US interests. Unable to sway American opinion, British policymakers eventually conceded that "Australia and New Zealand had grown up" and London would not be directly associated with ANZUS in any capacity.[31]

---

28 McIntosh to Corner, 3 October 1952, in *Unofficial Channels*, 106; Corner to McIntosh, 17 December 1952, in *Unofficial Channels*, 112.

29 Memorandum of Conversation, 4 August 1952, Secretary of State File, Acheson Papers, TL.

30 NZ Embassy in Canberra to Webb, 24 July 1952, Archives NZ, EA, 111/3/3/1 part 8; Memorandum for Webb, 14 August 1952, Archives NZ, EA, 111/3/3/1 part 8.

31 Corner to McIntosh, 11 December 1952, in *Unofficial Channels*, 109.

Another interesting element that has recently received greater attention regarding the US response to British inclusion in ANZUS is the issue of race. While Acheson privately stated that there was no capacity for Britain to be involved in ANZUS, US public explanations suggested that including Britain would increase anxieties in the Asia of an "Anglo-Saxon" or "White Man's Club" in the region.[32] This reasoning was hardly convincing, especially since all three ANZUS signatories were already predominantly Anglo-Saxon. It does, however, echo some of the concerns Dulles originally had when conducting treaty discussions in Canberra and explains why he was particularly interested in including the Philippines in the pact. It was certainly not a primary consideration, but perceptions over race did inform Dulles's thinking and influenced broader US concerns about its image in Asia. The US was mindful of domestic race relations with African Americans and certainly wanted to win the propaganda war against the Soviet Union in the developing world. In this case, though, it seems that concerns over an exclusionary defence treaty based on race were something of a convenient excuse for not including Britain in ANZUS.

A Five-Power Staff Agency

After being rejected from ANZUS as an observer, Britain instead pushed for the conclusion of a Five-Power Staff Agency between the United States, Britain, France, Australia and New Zealand for the collective defence of Southeast Asia. In December 1952, British, American and French representatives met in Paris and agreed in principle to a coalition for liaison on intelligence and other defence matters in the region. In a follow-up meeting in London, Churchill stressed that "it was unreasonable for ANZUS staff planners to deal with the Pacific and Southeast Asia without direct assistance from the British."[33] Then, in a separate meeting with Dominion representatives, Churchill told Australian and New Zealand Prime Ministers Robert Menzies and

---

32 Robb and Gill, "The ANZUS Treaty During the Cold War", 145. For a broader examination of the element of race in the Australian-American relationship, see Travis Hardy, *The Consanguinity of Ideas: Race and Anti-Communism in the US-Australian Relationship, 1933-1953*. PhD Thesis, University of Tennessee, 2010.

33 External Affairs Memorandum, 16 January 1953, Archives NZ, EA, 434/8/1 Part 2.

Sidney Holland that the Agency would essentially be a revitalised and widened version of previous ANZAM defence arrangements between their three countries. He handed both Menzies and Holland a newly revised British defence policy document called "The Future of ANZAM", which outlined Britain's plans for the Agency as well as a new focus on defending Malaya from Communist aggression.[34] This plan, in short, aimed to expand previous cooperation between Australia, New Zealand and the British into a defence arrangement for Southeast Asia that also included the United States and France. This arrangement would effectively supersede ANZUS and enable Britain to be as closely involved as possible in the defence planning for the region.

New Zealand Prime Minister Sidney Holland was particularly excited at the prospect of creating a Staff Agency. If the United States agreed to take part, Holland thought it was a fantastic opportunity to incorporate Britain in Pacific defence planning after their attempts to join ANZUS were blocked by the State Department. It would be a "marriage of ANZUS and ANZAM", Holland said, adding that the Agency could become a prelude to a joint machinery in the whole Pacific.[35] In other words, Holland hoped to reignite discussions over including Britain as an ANZUS partner.

Support for the proposal was less forthcoming in Wellington. Frank Corner considered that, given the proposition of French membership coupled with the deteriorating situation in Indochina, the Agency appeared to be intended primarily for multilateral defence discussions about that region. As a result, he questioned whether a focus on Indochina was in New Zealand's best interests. The Agency aimed to deal primarily with the "vital problems in Indochina" and "raise French morale", Corner told McIntosh, and he also thought the Pentagon was only interested in the Agency for "considering practical problems relating to Indochina."[36]

---

34 Meeting between Churchill, Menzies and Holland, 12 December 1952, NAA, A5954/1, 1424/1.

35 Hiroyuki Umetsu, "The Origins of the British Commonwealth Strategic Reserve: The UK Proposal to Revitalise ANZAM and the Increased Defence Commitment to Malaya", *Australian Journal of Politics and History* 50, no. 4 (2004), 517, https://doi.org/10.1111/j.1467-8497.2004.00350.x

36 Corner to McIntosh, 20 February 1953, in *Unofficial Channels*, 125.

In the Australian External Affairs Department, however, Casey and Spender were greatly concerned that the creation of a joint Staff Agency for the defence of Southeast Asia would undermine the importance of ANZUS. Similarly, they were also concerned that an Agency would prevent Canberra from consulting directly with Washington on security issues in the region. As Truman's second term as US President was soon scheduled to end, Casey and Spender thought that Australia should push for an ANZUS Council meeting with the Americans shortly after new President-elect Dwight Eisenhower took office to gauge his Administration's views on the subject. To "offset any danger" that the Agency might undermine ANZUS military planning, Spender urged Casey to call an ANZUS meeting shortly after Eisenhower took office.[37]

Fearing the political effect it would have in London, New Zealand responded unfavourably to an ANZUS meeting. Webb told the Australians shortly after the meeting was proposed that it was untimely "to press for an early ANZUS meeting at least at this juncture" because it might aggravate the British.[38] Secretary in the Australian Commissioner's Office in Wellington J.S. Cumpston then tried to urge New Zealand to reconsider. When meeting with Shanahan and McIntosh in late February, Cumpston attempted to persuade both men of the need for an early ANZUS meeting with the Americans. Their response, however, was again quite negative due to concerns about the effect an early ANZUS meeting would have in London. Wellington dismissed subsequent Australian efforts to urge New Zealand to support an earlier ANZUS meeting in March.

Meanwhile, after initial consultation with London, the United States agreed in principle to the establishment of a Five-Power Staff Agency for the defence of Southeast Asia. While the arrangement did not specifically commit any country to military action, it did provide a basic framework for joint-defence planning in the region. Delegates agreed that each country would appoint a military representative to coordinate defence plans with one another, as well as exchange all available intelligence information useful to the defence of Southeast Asia. As Assistant Secretary for Far Eastern Affairs John Allison advised

---

[37] Spender to Casey, 2 January 1953, NAA, A5954/1, 1424/1.
[38] Webb to Casey, 21 January 1953, NAA, A5461/1, 1/4/2A Part 3.

Secretary of State John Foster Dulles in late January, "I cannot conceive how we can engage in efficient planning for the military defence of the Pacific without engaging in some form of joint planning with our allies."[39]

Allison argued that the Agency must take a different form to ANZUS for two reasons. Firstly, he thought that an enlargement of ANZUS would entail an unwanted US commitment to Hong Kong, Malaya and Indochina. Secondly, he urged Dulles that the Agency would be useful primarily because it would help prevent Chinese aggression in the region. US policymakers such as Allison, in other words, had no intention of expanding ANZUS or merely mollifying British concerns about defence planning for the region. Instead, the Agency "offered the best prospect of causing Communist China to cease an aggression", the State Department concluded on 17 February.[40]

In Australia, policymakers continued to be concerned that the military function of ANZUS would be substantially absorbed by the Staff Agency. Australian Defence Minister Philip McBride told Menzies one week after the Conference that "the accent on planning for South East Asia has been transferred from an ANZUS to a Five Power basis." He added that he was concerned that the Staff Agency might subsume ANZUS and ANZAM in the long-term future.[41] Members of the Australian External Affairs Department were also anxious as to what the Agency would mean for the future of ANZUS military discussions. Assistant External Affairs Secretary Ralph Harry argued that the development of the Agency would lead to "the suspension by ANZUS of its military planning and concentration on political consultation", mainly because the Agency's proposed plan of studies would "seem to render redundant at least some of the current ANZUS military planning."[42]

Given New Zealand's great reluctance to hold an ANZUS Council meeting on the subject, Australia stepped up its own diplomatic efforts to obtain US views. In late May, Minister of the Australian Embassy in Washington Arthur Tange conferred with US Director of the Office

---

39   Allison to Dulles, 29 January 1953, FRUS 1952-1954 Vol. XII Part I, 265.

40   Memorandum for Allison, 17 February 1953, FRUS 1952-1954 Vol. XII Part I, 232.

41   McBride to Menzies, 17 April 1953, NAA, A816/30, 11/301/855.

42   Harry to Hay, 21 April 1953, NAA, A1838/269, TS654/8/3/2 Part 2.

of the British Commonwealth and Northern European Affairs Andrew Foster. Foster made it clear that given the Pentagon's reluctance to underwrite the security of mainland Asia, the US did not think the Staff Agency should be "a formal and elaborate organisation." The Agency should "rest on an ad hoc, on-call-need-to-know basis." He assured the Australians that there was no prospect that the Agency would supplant ANZUS and ANZAM machineries. Regarding the concept of an ANZUS-ANZAM linkage, Foster claimed the US could not establish a firm position until it "learn[s] of any ideas that may come out of conversations" among the Commonwealth states on the reformation of ANZAM."[43] At least for now, Australian concerns about the future of ANZUS had been allayed.

Eisenhower in the Oval Office

As discussions surrounding ANZUS and the Five-Power Staff Agency took place in late 1952 and early 1953, major political changes in the United States complicated the future of defence arrangements in the Asia-Pacific region. President Truman's second term as US President was scheduled to end in January 1953 and an election was planned for November 1952 to decide his replacement. After almost twenty years of Democrat control of the White House, the Republican Party's Presidential candidate, Dwight "Ike" Eisenhower, won the election by campaigning on major changes to US foreign policy. While Ike strongly criticised Truman for plunging the United States into a costly and protracted war, Eisenhower promised he would end the war in Korea and reduce the financial deficit from overspending on the military.

On taking office, Eisenhower's first major foreign policy initiative was appointing John Foster Dulles as his Secretary of State. Given his experience in international affairs, Eisenhower believed that Dulles was an "obvious" choice for the position.[44] In Australia and New Zealand, Dulles's appointment was especially important because both countries had experience in dealing with him during the ANZUS negotiations in early 1951.

---

43 Foster to Matthews, 29 May 1953, NARA, RG 59, 790.5/5-2953.
44 Dwight D. Eisenhower, Mandate for Change: 1953-1956 (New York: Doubleday & Co., 1963), 86.

Figure 12. Eisenhower during the US Election Campaign in Baltimore, MD, September 1952. Credit: Dwight D. Eisenhower Presidential Library, Wikimedia, https://commons.wikimedia.org/wiki/File:I_like_Ike.jpg, Public domain.

Eisenhower's most immediate foreign policy problem was ending a protracted and costly war in Korea. "Of the manifold problems confronting me early in 1953", Eisenhower penned in his memoirs, "none required more urgent attention than the war in Korea."[45] He had famously visited Korea in late 1952, but had no precise idea about how to end the war. Fortunately for Eisenhower, in March US negotiators achieved a breakthrough with their North Korean and Chinese counterparts over an exchange of prisoners of war. After restraining South Korean President Syngman Rhee from continuing the war and accepting a compromise demarcation at the 38th parallel, an armistice was signed on 27 July 1953 that brought the Korean War to an end.

While an end to the fighting in Korea was a welcome development, Eisenhower continued to follow the previous Administration's example and refused to recognise the PRC. In Australia, however, Casey thought that the end of the war made the prospect of recognising Beijing more palatable. Within weeks of the signing of the Armistice, Casey discussed with the Australian Cabinet how to approach China. He felt that it

---

45 Eisenhower, *Mandate for Change*, 171.

Figure 13. US President Dwight Eisenhower (1953-1961), 1952. Photo by Fabian Bachrach (1952), US Library of Congress, https://www.loc.gov/resource/cph.3c17123/, public domain.

was becoming increasingly important to open a dialogue with the Communist regime to prevent Mao from moving "closer into the arms of Moscow."[46]

Across the Tasman, Webb also thought that the end of the Korean War signalled a chance to reconsider the recognition of the PRC and thereby reduce tensions in East Asia. On 6 July, Webb went one step further and made his thoughts on recognising China public. Three days after Webb's address, New Zealand Ambassador in Washington Leslie Munro reported that the speech had gravely concerned policymakers in Washington. The remarks "caused distress" in the United States, Munro told Webb on 9 July, and comments such as Webb's "gravely disturbed the Americans."[47] Munro was especially concerned that the speech might affect New Zealand's relationship with the United States and suggested that, in the future, New Zealand should publicly support the US position on China.

Webb had anticipated that Australia was "inclined to take the American view" on China, and indeed McIntosh told Corner that his comments caused a "dislocation of the eyebrows in American and

---

46 Cabinet Submission, 14 August 1953. NAA, A1838, 3107/33/1, Part 1.
47 Munro to Webb, 9 July 1953, Archives NZ, EA, 264/3/14/1 Part 10; Munro to Webb 31 July 1953, Archives NZ, EA, 264/3/14/1 Part 8.

Australian circles." According to McIntosh, Australia's major concern was that Webb might push New Zealand towards recognising China without prior consultation.[48] This concern suggests that there was little trans-Tasman communication or cooperation regarding the issue of Chinese diplomatic recognition.

Outside of East Asia, another concern for the ANZUS countries was reconsidering policy toward the Middle East. By the time of Eisenhower's inauguration in January 1953, Egyptian General Gamal Abdel Nasser had already overthrown the Egyptian government led by King Farouk and he declared Egypt a republic in June. These dramatic events convinced the Eisenhower Administration that a Command structure was no longer an appropriate means for the defence of the Middle East. "We had decided to put the [Command] concept on the shelf", US Deputy Assistant Secretary of State for Near Eastern Affairs John Jernegan told Counselor of the British Embassy in Washington Harold Beeley on 17 June, citing political instability in the region as the major reason for US reluctance to participate.[49] Beeley replied that the British Foreign Office had a similar view and instead supported the idea of working closely with individual countries that appeared willing to defend Western interests in the region. At Beeley's insistence, this included Australia and New Zealand.

In an NSC meeting, American policymakers confirmed that in their view a formal multilateral defence arrangement was no longer the best way to protect US interests in the Middle East. The Command was "no longer played up as a likely defense arrangement in the future", US National Security Advisor Robert Cutler told the NSC on 9 July, and "Egypt was no longer considered to be the nucleus of an area defence organisation." Secretary of State John Foster Dulles agreed. "The [Command] was too complicated, too much like NATO, and it obviously would not work", Dulles said to Cutler, adding that "something less formal and grandiose was needed as a substitute." The meeting concluded by agreeing that the United States should support Britain "to the greatest extent practical, but reserving the right to act with others or

---

48 Webb to Scotten, 7 July 1953, Archives NZ, EA, 264/3/14/1 Part 8; McIntosh to Corner, 7 August 1953, in *Unofficial Channels*, 147-148.

49 Memorandum by Jernegan, 17 June 1953, NARA, RG 59, 780.3/6-1753.

alone."⁵⁰ In other words, the United States remained committed to the defence of the Middle East, but it wanted greater flexibility in a future response if a crisis developed.

For their part, Australia and New Zealand certainly agreed with abandoning the idea of a Middle East Command. In no uncertain terms, New Zealand Deputy High Commissioner in London Frank Corner argued that "the Middle East is of no direct importance to New Zealand." He concluded that it was completely unsatisfactory "to be committed to fight in an area where we have no representation, no way of making an independent appraisal of conditions in the country where our troops will be placed [and] no way of influencing the governments." Australian military officials reached similar conclusions. In one report, the Australian Defence Committee argued that "the threat to Southeast Asia is greater than that to the Middle East [...] Southeast Asia should be given priority."[51]

Looking more broadly, the Eisenhower Administration also needed new national security strategies. After much deliberation, the National Security Council produced the NSC 162/2 report in late 1953, a formal statement that outlined Eisenhower's "New Look" approach to foreign policy.[52] NSC 162/2 aimed to achieve the same goals as Truman's national defence policies, but would do so through more cost effective means; namely, through a reliance on nuclear weapons, an apparent willingness to use them and the subsequent deterrent effect on the belligerent Soviet bloc. It also relied on forming a number of defence pacts with Allied powers that aimed to ensure the United States would not again have to shoulder the burden of an entire military effort as it did in Korea.

Part of this plan encompassed a continued commitment to the ANZUS treaty. In September, the second round of ANZUS Council meetings were held in Washington. During these meetings JCS Chairman Arthur Radford confirmed this sustained commitment

---

50 National Security Council Meeting Minutes, 9 July 1953, Ann Whitman File, Eisenhower Papers, NSC Series, Box 3, EL.

51 A Strategic Basis of Australian Defence Policy, 8 January 1953, NAA, A5954, 1353/2.

52 NSC Report, 30 October 1953, Ann Whitman File, NSC Series, Box 2, EL. See also Valerie Adams, *Eisenhower's Fine Group of Fellows: Crafting a National Security Strategy to Uphold the Great Equation* (Lanham: Lexington Books, 2006), 63-69.

to the ANZUS partners, emphasising both his "continued interest in ANZUS" and the treaty's overall "importance and value" to US defence planning in the Pacific. Commander of the US Pacific Fleet Admiral Felix Stump expressed similar sentiments. He stated that ANZUS military discussions would be used as "background material to national plans" in the Pacific theatre, particularly in relation to Five-Power Agency defence discussions in Southeast Asia.[53] ANZUS, in other words, would provide one basis for US defence planning in the region. The Australians and New Zealanders welcomed this arrangement, yet similar issues re-emerged to those presented during the first Council meetings one year earlier. Casey again raised the possibility of British membership of ANZUS, asking whether "any link could be created" to satisfy British membership demands. Spender also continued to express his discontent at the "insufficient planning and coordination" between the ANZUS partners in the event of a worldwide war and suggested the smaller ANZUS partners should be privy to US global war plans. Both suggestions, however, were dismissed by US representatives. In short, the United States remained committed to ANZUS under Eisenhower, but it was not prepared to change the membership or consultative arrangements of the alliance.

Outside of these ANZUS discussions, Australian and New Zealand policymakers were seriously concerned by the Eisenhower Administration's new national security policies. On the one hand, an increased US commitment to its formal allies suggests Eisenhower and Dulles were prepared to take ANZUS and the Five-Power Staff Agency seriously and consult more closely with Canberra and Wellington. On the other hand, a reliance on nuclear weapons opened further the serious possibility of another world war in which Australia and New Zealand would undoubtedly have been involved.

New Zealand Ambassador in Washington Leslie Munro suggested that the new Administration would follow a "conservative line", meaning that Eisenhower was looking to cut military spending and reduce direct US military involvement overseas during the 1950s. Such a policy, according to Munro, was not ideal for New Zealand, particularly

---

53 Minutes of the ANZUS Council Meeting, 9-10 September 1953, NARA, RG 59, Lot 60, D 627, CF 163.

for Western defence positions in the Pacific.[54] In terms of broader US strategy, there were similar concerns in New Zealand that Eisenhower's proposed foreign-policy brinkmanship could be disastrous for the West. Many New Zealand diplomats regarded these policies as "misguided", "misconceived" or "extreme."[55]

While still concerned about the potential for global nuclear war, policymakers in Canberra were more optimistic about Eisenhower's new national security strategies. Many officers within the Australian External Affairs Department hoped that increased US reliance on its defence pacts would heighten American involvement in Asia and the Pacific. If used cautiously, they were also optimistic that US nuclear diplomacy could prevent further Communist advances. Casey, for one, was hopeful that the "major re-appraisal of US foreign policy" would benefit Australia because it would create greater US interest in defending a region close to Australian borders. He thought, in turn, that Australia must capitalise on this unprecedented US interest in Southeast Asia and demonstrate that Canberra was a reliable US ally. "It would be bad value", Casey later wrote in his diary, "to give Washington the impression that it was "contemplating retreat from [its] obligations."[56] Testing the ANZUS powers' commitment to defending Southeast Asia soon proved crucial, as Communist forces in Indochina sparked a major international crisis that tested the ANZUS commitment to Southeast Asia.

---

[54] Laking to McIntosh, 25 February 1953, in *Unofficial Channels*, 127-128.
[55] James Waite, "Contesting 'the Right of Decision'", 897-898.
[56] Casey Diary Entry, 16 September 1954, *Casey's Diaries*, 186.

6. Crisis in Southeast Asia

As Australian and New Zealand diplomats contemplated the repercussions of new US national security strategies during the early stages of the Eisenhower Administration, a Communist offensive in North Indochina threatened the French garrison at Dien Bien Phu and raised questions about US involvement in Southeast Asia. Before the outbreak of fighting in March 1954, Communist revolutionaries and the remnants of French colonial forces had been locked in a power struggle over Indochina for almost ten years. To a large extent, Eisenhower's policy options toward this struggle were constrained by the choices of his predecessor. Under Truman, the United States had explicitly stated that France had a right to retake control of Indochina after the Japanese occupation that took place during World War II. From 1950 onwards, the Truman Administration actively aided the French war effort after France's position in the region looked increasingly unstable. After promising an unwavering commitment to stop the spread of Communist aggression during the 1952 election campaign, Eisenhower had little choice other than to continue supporting the French cause in Indochina even if Paris could not continue to hold its position alone.

Similarly, the Menzies and Holland governments had long been concerned about the deteriorating situation in Indochina and outlined a firm commitment to defending Communist aggression. In March 1950, Australian External Affairs Minister Percy Spender thought that Indochina represented the "greatest present danger point" in Southeast Asia.[1] Policymakers in Wellington reached similar conclusions. By 1953, New Zealand High Commissioner in London Frank Corner was

---

1   Spender Statement, 9 March 1950, Commonwealth Parliamentary Debates, House of Representatives, 627.

© 2018 Andrew Kelly, CC BY 4.0   https://doi.org/10.11647/OBP.0141.06

convinced Indochina was the "key" to Southeast Asia. He argued that if the Communists were successful in Indochina, Malaya, Burma and Siam would also fall under Communist control. Corner was also hopeful that New Zealand might be able to work closely with Australia on Southeast Asian issues, even though he complained that "the Australians are often more interested in having a voice than solving practical problems."[2]

Siege at Dien Bien Phu

On 13 March 1954, tensions in Indochina reached a climax after Vietminh forces led an assault against the French fortress at Dien Bien Phu. The siege caused a major strain in Anglo-American relations, prompting Australia and New Zealand to seriously reconsider how closely, if at all, their respective External Affairs departments were prepared to align their policies with Washington. Moreover, even though the security of both countries rested on combating the spread of Communism Southeast Asia, there was no certainty that Australia and New Zealand could reach common ground as to the most appropriate response. On the contrary, two days after the first day of the siege, Frank Corner warned External Affairs Secretary Alister McIntosh that New Zealand should not involve itself in the conflict purely to protect Australian strategic interests. He also doubted whether the future of Southeast Asia was in fact a vital interest for New Zealand. Predicting that Australia would push for joint intervention in Southeast Asia, Corner wrote on 15 March that New Zealand "should resist being dragged by the Australians [...] into premature involvement in Southeast Asia." He concluded that he felt "very dubious about bustling into commitments in Southeast Asia [...] there is no good future for us there."[3]

In Washington, JCS Chairman Arthur Radford warned Eisenhower that the United States must be prepared to intervene militarily in order to prevent the loss of all Indochina. In Radford's own words, the United States "must be prepared [...] to act promptly and in force possibly to a

---

2   Corner to McIntosh, 20 February 1953, in *Unofficial Channels*, 122-127.
3   Corner to McIntosh, 15 March 1954, in *Unofficial Channels*, 158.

Figure 14. Viet Minh soldiers capture French troops and escort them to a prisoner-of-war camp, 1954. Photo by unknown (1954), Wikimedia, https://commons.wikimedia.org/wiki/File:Dien_Bien_Phu_1954_French_prisoners.jpg, public domain.

frantic and belated request by the French for US intervention."[4] Dulles, however, disagreed with Radford's proposal. He feared that the United States might get embroiled in another protracted and costly war. He also thought that even if the Administration wanted to act unilaterally, Congress would be unlikely to authorise such action. Dulles's sharp prediction proved correct; leaders from Republican and Democratic parties told him in early April that they would only sanction the use of US force if the Administration could obtain commitments from other allies, particularly Britain.

At the time, political discussion about combatting Communism and US defence was very heated. The Eisenhower Administration was under constant attack from hardline senators such as Joseph McCarthy who argued strongly that the United States was not doing anywhere near enough to combat Communism at home and abroad. Much to Eisenhower's annoyance, these attacks separated the House of Representatives and Senate on almost every issue and often froze Congress so that it became an impractical and unmanageable sector

---

4   Radford to Eisenhower, 24 March 1954, NARA, RG 59, 751.00/3-2454.

of government. In short, Congressional backing for any short-term policy in Indochina was close to impossible. "It is close to disgusting", Eisenhower wrote angrily, "it saddens me that I must feel ashamed for the United States Senate." Already in his own fight with Congress, the President wrote in frustration several days later on 18 March that the Indochina Crisis was "just another of the problems dumped on [his] lap."[5]

In an effort to alleviate any domestic criticisms of US inaction, Eisenhower declared publicly that his government was committed to preventing the spread of Communism. He warned that the loss of French Indochina would have a domino effect that would leave the rest of Southeast Asia vulnerable to Communist control. In order to respond to this threat as well as curb domestic concerns of unilateral action, Dulles then proposed that the United States should act jointly with its allies in preventing the loss of Indochina to Communist forces. Advising the NSC that "there was no need" for immediate unilateral action, Dulles suggested making US intervention provisional on whether US allies would be willing to support such action. After Eisenhower agreed to this approach, Dulles followed up the "domino theory" speech with his own public call for a multilateral response to Indochina. Privately, plans were also made between Eisenhower and Dulles to use ANZUS meetings to consult with Australia and New Zealand. Knowing Canberra's earnest desire for closer consultation with the United States, Eisenhower commented that this plan would make the Australians "terribly excited."[6]

In order to convince Canberra and Wellington that their participation in Indochina was important, Dulles made a decided effort to urge the respective Australians and New Zealand Ambassadors in Washington, Percy Spender and Leslie Munro, that the loss of Indochina would directly threaten the security of both of their countries. "If Indochina goes", Dulles told Spender and Munro, "Australia and New Zealand will be directly threatened." Dulles had already built a strong reputation as an astute diplomat with the Tasman countries following ANZUS

---

5   Eisenhower to Hazlett, 18 March 1954, Ann Whitman File, DDE Diary Series, Box 6, EL.

6   Eisenhower-Dulles Conversation Memorandum, 3 April 1954 Dulles Papers, Telephone Conversation Series, Box 6, EL.

negotiations several years earlier, which he surely hoped would work in his favour when speaking directly about the importance of multilateral participation with Australian and New Zealand representatives in Washington.

Still concerned that London would not be willing to participate in multilateral intervention, Dulles also requested that US Ambassador to Australia Amos Peaslee make similar efforts to persuade policymakers in Canberra to support the American plan rather than aligning with British policy. "I hope you will take appropriate occasion to spell out our views in discussions with top officials", Dulles told the US Embassy in Canberra, as he was concerned that the Australians would take a "similar line to [the] British." It is indeed telling that Dulles made a point to stress directly that Peaslee should clearly outline US views on this topic, since it would already fall well within the scope of expected ambassadorial duties to share such views with top Australian officials. It suggests how important he thought it was to secure their support. Dulles, to be sure, remained hopeful that Australia and New Zealand could convince policymakers in London to participate. Whilst predicting there would be "great difficulties" in securing British support, Dulles thought that Australia and New Zealand would be "willing to urge the British in the right direction."[7]

Dulles, who shrewdly assessed that the Britons were highly unlikely to agree to his plan, highlighted the increasingly untenable position the Americans found themselves in regarding Indochina. Indeed, while the British were certainly keen for the French to retain control of Indochina, they were not prepared to use force due to fears that this could escalate into a larger war in the region. Even US Chairman of the Joint Chiefs of Staff Arthur Radford, who visited London in April to convince the British to support military action, could not sway Churchill or Eden to back the American proposal. Instead of a military approach British Foreign Secretary Anthony Eden reasoned that a better course of action was to pursue a negotiated settlement, particularly because there was a conference in Geneva scheduled in a few weeks that would involve deep discussions about the situation in Indochina. If there was any possibility to steer British views toward a military solution before Geneva, Dulles

---

7   Dulles to Peaslee, 1 April 1954, FRUS 1954 Vol. XIII Part I, 1204.

saw Australia and New Zealand, two countries that still held strong ties to the British Commonwealth, as key negotiators that might be able to stress the value of a united military response in London.

On its surface, it was somewhat naïve of Dulles to think the two small Tasman countries may succeed where the United States could not in assuaging British concerns regarding Indochina. His initial discussions with Australian and New Zealand diplomats did, however, illustrate the increasingly important role that Canberra and Wellington could play in mitigating tensions in the Anglo-American relationship. It is also important to note that Dulles fully recognised the potentially disastrous consequences of a unilateral military response and that the American public had no appetite for another protracted war like the one fought on the Korean peninsula. Conceding that British acquiescence to the proposals of the United States would be extremely difficult to obtain, it is fair to assess that Dulles had few other options at his disposal to gather support for multilateral intervention. The stakes were extremely high, especially since US military planners had been seriously contemplating the use of nuclear weapons in Indochina while simultaneously questioning the usefulness of their alliance with Great Britain.[8]

In this light Dulles formally proposed "United Action" to Spender and Munro in early April, a term that referred to the US plan for a multilateral response in Indochina. Echoing Eisenhower's earlier words, Dulles said that if Australia and New Zealand were not prepared to be "excited" by the coalition then the United States would not take action.[9] Again, Dulles stressed that British participation in this plan was crucial. He told both Spender and Dulles that a new military force was needed in Indochina and it "had to include Britain." That being the case, Dulles asked both men to meet with diplomats in the British Embassy in Washington and urge them that the United States, Britain, Australia and New Zealand must all unite for the defence of Indochina to repel the Communist advance in Southeast Asia.

---

[8] Matthew Jones, "Great Britain, The United States, and Consultation over Use of the Atomic Bomb", *The Historical Journal* 54, no. 3 (2011), 797-828, https://doi.org/10.1017/S0018246X11000240

[9] Memorandum of Meeting with Dulles, Spender and Munro, 4 April 1954, NARA, RG 59, 751.00/4-454.

As far as the Australian position was concerned, Spender told Dulles that he could not commit his government while it faced a general election for the House of Representatives which was set for 29 May. On the surface, Australian reservations about a multilateral response appeared less about British inaction and more about domestic policy. Another domestic concern was the recent development of the Petrov Affair in early April, an event that saw Third Secretary of the Soviet Embassy in Canberra Vladmir Petrov offer details of Soviet espionage in Australia in exchange for political asylum. The Petrov Affair sparked considerable public outcry in Australia that the Menzies Government must do more to combat Communist threats domestically instead of focusing solely on overseas developments in Indochina. As one American report concluded, Petrov's defection was the "biggest story of its kind that has ever happened in Australia." As a result, Indochina had been "all but shoved of [the] front pages of newspapers by [the] Petrov Affair."[10]

Once Spender described his conversation with Dulles to Casey, however, he urged that Australia should accept this proposal as a means to increase US interest in defending Southeast Asia. As he told Casey,

> One of the primary aims of our policy over recent years has been, as I understand it, to achieve the acceptance by the USA of responsibility for [South East] Asia. It is for consideration whether, if we fail to respond at all to the opportunity now presented, what US reactions are likely to be if and when areas closer to Australia are in jeopardy.[11]

Casey agreed it was crucial for Australia to support the US position in Indochina. As he penned in his diary one day after receiving Spender's message, the United States "won't go in alone" in Indochina and if "Australia and others don't respond they may change their South-East Asia attitude."[12] As the defence of Southeast Asia was crucial to Australian security, any decline in US interest in the region was a very

---

10 Report from the United States Naval Attaché in Melbourne to the Department of Army, 2 April 1954, NARA, RG 59, 743.00W/4-254. For more on the Petrov Affair, see David Horner, *The Spy Catchers: The Official History of ASIO, 1949-1963* (Sydney: Allen & Unwin, 2014); Robert Manne, *The Petrov Affair* (Sydney: Text Publishing, 2004).

11 Spender to Casey, 6 April 1954, NAA, A5462/1, 2/4/1 Part 2.

12 Casey Diary Entry, 7 April 1954, NAA, M1153, 34.

serious concern. Casey tried to urge the seriousness of the Indochina situation to the Australian public in the event that Australia might have to follow the United States into a war there. Gathering public support was crucial, as a large segment of the Australian public were still confused about what United Action entailed and what Australia's role would be in such a plan. "If Indochina were to fall to the Communists the whole of Southeast Asia would be threatened", Casey proclaimed in the House of Representatives on 7 April.[13] This statement mirrored Eisenhower's sentiments about the loss of Indochina having a potential domino-like effect on the rest of Southeast Asia.

Yet despite how seriously Casey feared the deteriorating situation in Indochina and any decline in US interest in Southeast Asia, he was unsure whether the United Action proposal was the best course. After speaking with British Foreign Minister Anthony Eden on 15 April, it was clear to Casey that Britain would not participate in the plan regardless of Australian efforts to encourage a military response. In any case, Casey thought personally that were substantial risks involved if Australia participated in joint military intervention without Britain. Describing the American plan for mass intervention as "wrong", Casey stressed that United Action would not stop the fall of Dien Bien Phu and risked putting Australia "in the wrong with world opinion particularly in Asia." He also thought such action could potentially risk war with China.[14]

For these reasons, Casey thought that United Action should not be pursued and probably did not push the importance of this plan to the Britons as strongly as the Americans had hoped. This action—or lack thereof—did little to foster closer Anglo-American relations, but Casey's mindfulness about the direct political and strategic consequences for Australia was commendable. His recognition of the implications should Asian countries develop a poor opinion of Australia also dovetailed with his broader efforts for a strategic refocus toward Southeast Asia. Casey aptly recognised that Australia's future would depend on peace and stability in this part of the world and took a keen interest in cultivating closer relationships with Southeast Asian countries.

---

13 Casey Statement, 7 April 1954, Commonwealth House of Representatives Debates, Vol. 3, 122-126.

14 Casey Diary Entry, 15 April 1954, NAA, M1153, 34.

He travelled regularly throughout the region and even published a somewhat insipid yet purposeful book appropriately titled Friends and Neighbours, in which he made a case for wanting Australia to live peacefully with Asian countries amidst increasing nationalistic and Communist-driven insurgencies.[15] These efforts did little to convince other Australian cabinet members of the importance of fostering friendlier relationships with Asian countries, but at the very least helped encourage more positive perceptions of Australia at a time when Australian views about Asian people were often noticeably racist. Casey even had to condemn Australian newspapers for using the term "White Australia"—an immigration policy implemented in the early twentieth century that aimed to exclude people from non-Anglo backgrounds—due to concerns that it would be "most offensive to all Asian peoples" even though a more relaxed form of the original immigration policy was still in effect during the 1950s.[16]

Nevertheless, Casey's arguments regarding Indochina were successful and the Australian government agreed that it could not commit to the United Action proposal in the current political climate. While the Cabinet concluded that Australia should encourage the French to continue fighting and support US military involvement in the region, it could not commit to Dulles's plan for multilateral intervention because of the political pressures leading up to a general election in May. The Cabinet also concluded that because Australia had defence arrangements with Britain in the region it would be unfavourable to join in a US military response if Britain did not participate. Overall, the Cabinet decided Australia could not commit to the plan but still

---

15 R.G. Casey, *Friends and Neighbours: Australia and the World* (Melbourne: F.W. Cheshire, 1954). For a more detailed analysis of Casey's international outlook and views on Australian engagement with Asia, see J Cotton, "R.G. Casey and Australian International Thought"; James Cotton, "R. G. Casey's Writings on Australia's Place in the World", in Melissa Conley Tyler, John Robbins, and Adrian March eds. *R.G. Casey: Minister for External Affairs, 1951-1960* (Sydney: Australian Institute of International Affairs, 2012), http://www.internationalaffairs.org.au/wp-content/uploads/2014/01/casey-book-final-revised.pdf

16 "Offends Asia", *The Courier Mail*, 7 June 1952. The White Australia Policy and its implications for Australia's relationship with the world have been dealt with extensively elsewhere. See, for example, James Jupp, *From White Australia to Woomera: The Story of Australian Immigration* (Cambridge: Cambridge University Press, 2002).

must somehow show the United States that it was "not lukewarm in supporting proposals designed to ensure that Communism in Southeast Asia is checked."[17] With regards to Indochina and US interest in Southeast Asia, Australia simply wanted to have its cake and eat it too.

Meanwhile, policymakers in New Zealand wanted to know the British response before they made any decision. Writing to the New Zealand High Commission in London, McIntosh told Corner that his personal preference was that New Zealand should "tell the Americans we will join them on the understanding that the British […] come in also."[18] In Washington, New Zealand Ambassador Leslie Munro suggested that Dulles's plea for United Action signalled a new course of American policy in Indochina, indicating that the United States could not accept under any circumstances that Indochina fall completely to the Communists. As a result, Munro concluded that New Zealand "had little alternative but to join the coalition" because New Zealand valued its close relations with the United States especially due to Indochina's proximity to Australia and New Zealand. Munro, however, thought along similar lines to McIntosh and attached one very important condition to New Zealand participation: the United Kingdom "must also participate."[19] McIntosh also thought that New Zealand should encourage the French to commit to the US plan for multilateral intervention. He reasoned that this response would prevent New Zealand from falling out with the Americans (who desperately wanted the French to continue fighting in Indochina) while simultaneously meaning that New Zealand would not commit without British support.

On 7 April, Australia and New Zealand exchanged some of their defence policy conclusions with respect to Indochina. The Australian position, which was developed by the Joint Intelligence Committee and primarily focused on broader strategic and military considerations, determined that every effort must be made to strengthen the will of the French. It also determined that "Australia should also encourage Indochina governments to reach agreements with the French in establishing their independence and continue the Communist resistance." In order to

---

17 Minutes of Cabinet Meeting, 6 April 1954, NAA, A1838/276, TS383/4/1 Part 1.
18 McIntosh to Corner, 12 April 1954, in *Unofficial Channels*, 164.
19 Munro to Corner, 6 April 1954, Archives NZ, EA, 316/4/1 Part 6; Munro to Webb, 6 April 1954, Archives NZ, EA, 316/4/1 Part 6.

achieve this objective, the document even concluded that "Australia should participate in United Action because doing otherwise might compromise the present helpful trend of American policy towards the security of the Pacific."[20] This was in glaring contrast to Casey's views on the untenability of United Action, highlighting that the Departments of Defence and External Affairs held noticeably different views on the strategic benefits of a military response. In short, military planners instead proposed a two-fold objective in the Indochina Crisis: encourage the French to continue fighting, and assure the Americans that Australia was committed to the defence of Southeast Asia even though upcoming elections delayed an immediate public response. British participation was desirable for the Australians, but not essential.

In contrast, the equivalent New Zealand policy document on Indochina revolved around British participation, UN involvement and avoiding a confrontation with China. It determined that New Zealand would only participate in United Action "under the condition that Britain [was] also a participant" and such a coalition fell under the "aegis of the United Nations." Moreover, due to concerns that intervention might escalate into a wider war, the document claimed that a Western multilateral response must make "every effort to avoid confrontation with China."[21] Much like British views, New Zealand prioritised a diplomatic solution over a military response.

Australia and New Zealand greatly differed in their assessments about the possibility of Chinese intervention. The Australians were aware of New Zealand's policy position that "armed intervention in Indochina may lead to involvement with China and possibly even with the Soviet Union itself", as an Australian Joint Intelligence Committee report concluded, adding that Wellington was "more doubtful whether it could be possible to avoid conflict with China." Australia predicted instead that it "was not likely that the Chinese would abandon their profitable policy for one of open intervention which carries the risk of retaliation."[22]

---

20   Australian Policy on Indochina, 7 April 1954, Archives NZ, EA, 316/4/1 Part 2. See also Joint Intelligence Committee Report, 14 April 1954, NAA, A5954, 2298/2.

21   Collective Action in Indochina Policy Document, 6 April 1954, Archives NZ, EA, 316/4/1 Part 6.

22   Joint Intelligence Committee Report, 14 April 1954, NAA, A5954, 2298/2.

Irrespective of whether China would act in Indochina after possible Western intervention, the British strongly opposed the United Action proposal. As part of his initial pursuit of United Action, Dulles met with British Ambassador Roger Makins on 2 April. During the meeting, Anglo-American differences over supporting French action in Indochina were sharply exposed. While Dulles warned against the "dangers of a French collapse" and that the "French accepting a settlement would be disastrous for the free world", Makins responded that his government regarded "the deteriorating situation in Indochina in more pessimistic terms" and was inclined to accept a settlement in Indochina.[23]

Shortly thereafter, Eisenhower wrote to British Prime Minister Winston Churchill and declared that his Administration had no intention of searching for a peaceful solution. Churchill, however, was reluctant to commit to any action. Churchill told Eisenhower directly that he feared multilateral intervention would lead to a wider war and threaten British interests in Hong Kong, Malaya and Singapore. In short, Churchill said that the US plan for multilateral action simply "raised too many problems" for Britain. Privately, Churchill confessed that he had no interest in putting British troops "in the jungle" and thought that Malaya could still be held even if Indochina fell.[24]

As the weeks passed and the US mustered little support for United Action, the situation in Indochina worsened. Eisenhower again wrote to Churchill, hoping that the British might reconsider their position on Indochina as the Geneva Conference approached. "I am deeply concerned by the seemingly wide differences in the conclusions developed in our respective governments", Eisenhower wrote to Churchill on 26 April, "especially as these conclusions relate to such events as the war in Indochina."[25] Even though France was quickly losing control over Indochina, Eisenhower had problems convincing the French to consider multilateral support for their position. "For more

---

23 Conversation between Dulles and Makins, 2 April 1954, FRUS 1954 Vol. XIII Part I, 1216.

24 Churchill to Eisenhower, 7 April 1954, Ann Whitman File, DDE Diary Series, Box 6, EL; James, *Churchill and Empire*, 379. See also Daniel Williamson, *Separate Agendas: Churchill, Eisenhower and Anglo-American Relations, 1953-1955* (Lanham: Lexington Books, 2006).

25 Eisenhower to Churchill, 26 April 1954, Ann Whitman File, DDE Diary Series, Box 6, EL.

than three years I have been urging upon successive French governments the advisability of finding some way of 'internationalising' the war", Eisenhower confessed, but:

> The reply has always been vague, containing references to national prestige, Constitutional limitations, inevitable effects upon the Moroccan and Tunisian peoples, and dissertations on plain political difficulties and battles within the French Parliament. The result has been that the French have failed entirely to produce any enthusiasm on the part of the Vietnamese for participation in the war.[26]

Eisenhower concluded that the situation in Indochina had gotten to a point where "the French have used weasel words in promising independence and through this one reason as much as anything else, have suffered reverses that have really been inexcusable."

Figure 15. French Foreign Minister Georges Bidault (left), British Foreign Secretary Anthony Eden (centre), US Secretary of State John Foster Dulles (right). Photo by unknown (n. d.), Wikimedia, https://commons.wikimedia.org/wiki/File:Georges_Bidault,_Anthony_Eden_and_John_Foster_Dulles.jpg, CC BY 3.0.

As American frustrations with British and French policies toward Indochina increased, the possibility of unilateral action resurfaced

---

26 Eisenhower to Hazlett, 27 April 1954, Ann Whitman File, DDE Diary Series, Box 6, EL.

in Washington. During an NSC meeting on 29 April, Vice President Richard Nixon and Director of the Mutual Security Agency Harold Stassen argued that the United States "should not let the British have a veto over our freedom of action." Eisenhower disagreed, believing that the United States was not able to be the non-Communist world's sole policeman and would be looked upon unfavourably by the rest of the world if it took unilateral action. "To go in unilaterally in Indochina", Eisenhower said, "amounted to an attempt to police the entire world." He added that if the United States attempted such a course of action, "we should everywhere be accused of imperialistic ambitions."[27]

Meanwhile, the Geneva Conference began on 26 April 1954. Two weeks into the Conference, after the US refused to act unilaterally and did not gather support for United Action, Dien Bien Phu fell to the Communists on 7 May 1954. Although American delegates continued to press the British for joint military action and urged the French to continue fighting, by June the Eisenhower Administration abandoned its plans for multilateral intervention and instead looked towards finding a diplomatic solution in Indochina. As with the post-war division of Korea, delegates at Geneva agreed that Indochina would be divided into two regions, with the Vietminh occupying the North and the French occupying the South. The decision awarded the Soviet bloc a major diplomatic victory in the face of French defeat. Likewise, the decision was a significant blow to Western prestige. After having failed to defend Dien Bien Phu, the Eisenhower Administration then turned its attention to the possibility of a collective defence arrangement in Southeast Asia.

Formation of SEATO

Having to resort to reaching a diplomatic solution in Indochina was disappointing for US policymakers. After sending the French $2.6 billion in military assistance between 1950 and 1954, Washington's failure to prevent a Vietminh victory in Indochina damaged Eisenhower's credibility in fulfilling his promise to limit Communist expansion. Nevertheless, the end of the fighting and the formalisation of a North

---

27 NSC Meeting, 29 April 1954, Ann Whitman File, NSC Series, Box 4, EL.

Vietnamese Communist state enabled the Eisenhower Administration to pursue a broader collective security pact for Southeast Asia, especially because the Five-Power Staff Agency talks had produced few tangible results since its inception a year earlier. Rather than dwell on the loss of Indochina, the United States needed to seize the opportunity to deter the expansion of Communism in Asia through a regional defence arrangement.

Discussions for such an arrangement in Southeast Asia began in the National Security Council. From a military point of view, questions were raised about the desirability of a pact when few states in the region were capable of defending themselves. At an NSC meeting on 23 July, Chairman of the Joint Chiefs of Staff Arthur Radford said that "we [the United States] are now talking about an area where there are no developed military forces." He added that the US could build military power in the region, but "only at considerable cost." Overall, he argued that the United States "should take a good look at the idea of a defence alliance for this area to be sure we are not making a mistake [...] from a military point of view a Southeast Asia defence pact seems undesirable and unwise."[28]

The State Department, however, saw clear advantages in concluding a defence pact. Such a pact would signal an evident US willingness to prevent the spread of Communism and ensure that countries at risk of Communist subversion would be provided with American assistance. At a follow-up meeting about American policy toward Southeast Asia on 24 July, Dulles argued that a defence pact would have two significant advantages: it would give Eisenhower discretionary authority (which he did not already have) to use in the event of overt Chinese aggression in the area, and it would ensure that Washington had the support of other nations in any action it might be forced to take. Moreover, as a means to offset Radford's concerns about an undesirable military commitment, Dulles suggested that the treaty would not be drafted in such a way "so as to lead other signatories to expect large amounts of US military

---

28 Memorandum of a Department of State-Joint Chiefs of Staff Meeting, 23 July 1954, NARA, RG 59, Lot 61, D 417.

assistance."[29] In order for such a pact to be effective, it would require support from other countries willing to enter into the agreement.

Most importantly for the prospects of concluding a regional defence treaty, Britain quickly signalled its willingness to enter into a defence pact despite sharp differences with the Americans over Indochina in Geneva. Fearing that British bases in Malaya and Hong Kong were at risk, Churchill wrote to Eisenhower on 21 June stating that Britain and the United States should "establish a firm front against Communism in the Pacific sphere." More specifically, Churchill suggested that there should be a Southeast Asian Treaty Organisation (SEATO) similar in structure and purpose to the North Atlantic Treaty Organisation for Europe.[30] Concerned that the Communist diplomatic victory in Geneva might spur further aggression in the region, there was a clear sense of urgency about Churchill's efforts to secure the treaty. New Zealand Ambassador in Washington Leslie Munro reported to Wellington that at a luncheon meeting in Washington a week later, Churchill said that plans for the defence of Southeast Asia would be "pressed forward now, immediately."[31]

Meanwhile, an ANZUS meeting took place in Washington on 30 June. Dulles told Casey and Munro that as agreements for Indochina took place in Geneva, the United States was "very deeply concerned" about developments in the area. Moreover, he stressed that the United States could not "fight their own way into the area, alone, and under conditions by no means clear." Dulles then suggested that it would be especially useful for the United States to be briefed on Australian and New Zealand views on Indochina, because France was "fading away" and Britain was "badly overextended."

In response, Casey suggested that reaching a SEATO-type arrangement would be useful for Australia. However, he thought that a temporary "ad-hoc SEATO" would be practical until a formal multilateral agreement could be agreed upon by Washington and London. He proposed a public non-aggression pact with as many Asian countries as possible. "Such a document would have no teeth

---

29 Minutes of a Meeting on Southeast Asia, 24 July 1954, NARA RG 59, Lot 60, D 627, CF 348.

30 Churchill to Eisenhower, 21 June 1954, FRUS 1954 Vol. XIII Part II, 1728.

31 Munro to Holland, 30 June 1954, Archives NZ, EA, 434/8/1 Part 4.

and involve no obligations for its parties", Casey conceded, but once a more binding agreement could be reached, he thought that "the teeth of an alliance would be in SEATO."[32] Casey, in short, was in favour of an immediate defence structure for Southeast Asia that included countries in that region and hoped both Britain and the United States would be involved. "We could not be belligerent while the United Kingdom was not", Casey wrote in his diary after the meeting. He added, almost excitedly, that since Australia was "poised rather delicately" between the United States and Britain in international affairs, Canberra was "in a position to exercise some influence on each."[33]

Speaking on New Zealand's behalf, Munro mirrored Casey's sentiments and suggested Wellington was in favour of an immediate defence arrangement in Southeast Asia. He noted New Zealand's concerns about Communist aggression in the area and argued that his country would "firmly resist" any further advances. However, he made two unique points. Firstly, he thought that any immediate aggression before SEATO could be established should be referred to the United Nations rather than dealt with through Casey's proposed temporary non-aggression pact. Secondly, he reiterated that New Zealand would only participate in SEATO if Britain was also a member. "It was a principle of our policy and negotiation that [Britain] should be a party to the SEATO arrangement." Munro told Dulles on 30 June 1954.[34]

Dulles, however, made it clear that the United States would only commit to an arrangement that specifically aimed to stop Communist aggression. "The United States would be prepared to take positive action if there were any substantial extension of Communist power", Dulles said to Casey and Munro, but he stressed "there would be nothing in the nature of a blanket commitment."[35] He repeated these views later on 28 July to US Ambassador to the United Kingdom Roger Aldrich, requesting he make it clear to London that the United States "did not envisage the Southeast Asia pact developing into a NATO-type organisation with [a] large permanent machinery [and]

---

32 Notes of the ANZUS Meeting, 30 June 1954, Archives NZ, EA, 434/8/1 Part 4.
33 Casey Diary Entry, 30 June 1954, NAA, M1153, 34.
34 Notes of the ANZUS Meeting, 30 June 1954, Archives NZ, EA, 434/8/1 Part 4.
35 Ibid.

substantial US financial support."[36] The US military supported this limited commitment. The SEATO machinery "should be similar to the ANZUS arrangements", US Acting Secretary of Defense Robert Anderson told the State Department, insofar as it should function more as a "consultative arrangement" rather than representing definitive American military commitments in Southeast Asia. Anderson went on to suggest that these views reflected "the thinking of this Department at this time."[37]

While Australia and New Zealand reasoned that their influence on US policy was perhaps greater than it had ever been, neither government could convince Washington to sign anything other than a very limited defence treaty. The United States, in short, would only commit to respond to Communist aggression. The Southeast Asia Treaty Organisation was subsequently signed into effect on the 8 September 1954 at the Manila Conference between the ANZUS powers as well as Britain, France, the Philippines, Thailand and Pakistan. The three Associated States, South Vietnam, Laos and Cambodia, were also awarded observer status and included under the area protected. Its scope was very similar to ANZUS, stating that all signatories would respond to meet a common danger in accordance with its constitutional processes.

Overall, SEATO's conclusion was ultimately born out of Western failure in Indochina and concerns about further Communist aggression in the area. It had a number of weaknesses: its scope was limited, and there was no clear machinery for intelligence cooperation or military consultation between the signatories. Ultimately, even though the siege at Dien Bien Phu and the conclusion of SEATO offered Australia and New Zealand an opportunity to play more important roles in US strategy, there were few positives that could be drawn from the ANZUS response to the crisis.

---

36 Dulles to Aldrich, 28 July 1954, FRUS 1952-1954 Vol. XII Part I, 680.

37 Anderson to Murphy, 19 August 1954, FRUS 1952-1954 Vol. XII Part I, 767-768.

7. A Horrible Dilemma in the Taiwan Straits

While Australian, New Zealand and American delegates met in Manila to finalise SEATO in September 1954, another crisis broke out in the Taiwan Straits after the People's Republic of China (PRC) began shelling the Nationalist-held offshore islands of Quemoy and Matsu. Even though by sheer geographical size and position alone it would be unthinkable that a global war might erupt over such small islands, there was a very real possibility that any miscalculation by the United States could spark a war with China, and by extension, the Soviet Union. America had long established its determination to prevent Taiwan and the Pescadores falling into Communist hands, but to achieve this, Eisenhower's Joint Chiefs of Staff (JCS) thought it was important that these lesser offshore islands also remain in Nationalist hands. Others, such as Australia, New Zealand, Britain and most of the American public, were not convinced. US Secretary of State John Foster Dulles, for one, described them as "a bunch of rocks."[1]

Less than nine months before the PRC shelled Quemoy, Secretary of Defence Charles Wilson approved a JCS recommendation to loan US naval vessels to the Nationalists to assist in the defence of the offshore islands. These loans included two destroyers, ten patrol crafts, two landing repair ships, and less than one hundred small landing crafts. Approving these loans meant that, at the very least, Eisenhower and his military staff hoped that the Nationalists could hold these islands if hostilities broke out in the immediate future.[2] Yet once the crisis began, Eisenhower was certain that

---

1 Department of State Conversation, 19 January 1955, FRUS 1955-1957 Vol. II, 47.
2 Wilson to Dulles, 7 December 1953, FRUS 1952-1954 Vol. XIV Part I, 339.

the offshore islands could not possibly be defended by the United States. After Dulles presented the NSC with the "horrible dilemma" that confronted the United States on 12 September, Eisenhower stressed that "Quemoy is not our ship." According to the former General, defending Quemoy by force would lead to war with China. Public opinion seemed to support this position. Eisenhower went on to tell the NSC that he had constantly been receiving letters from the American public saying "please do not send our boys to war" and "do we really care what happens to those yellow people out there?"[3]

Political opinion aside, most US military planners argued that the offshore islands were important to the defence of Taiwan. A JCS report, submitted to the President on the afternoon of 3 September, recommended that current American policy towards the Taiwan Strait area be changed to assist in the defence of Quemoy as well as nine other offshore islands. The JCS Chairman Arthur Radford, a strong-minded former admiral with a wealth of experience in Pacific naval planning, argued particularly strongly for the defence of the islands. He recommended to the State Department that the United States commit to defending Quemoy and Matsu even with the use of tactical nuclear weapons. Not all of the Chiefs of Staff agreed with Radford's radical approach, but along with the Chief of the Air Force Nathan Twinning and Chief of Naval Operations Robert Carney, the JCS majority opinion concluded that defending the offshore islands was important and any withdrawal would have a considerable psychological effect on Nationalist morale.[4] In opposition, Army Chief of Staff Matthew Ridgeway and Secretary of Defence Charles Wilson thought that any psychological effect did not outweigh the alarming consequences that could ensue if the United States committed to defending these islands. Ridgeway argued that defending Quemoy was "not substantially related to the defence of Taiwan", whereas Wilson simply saw no worthwhile reason for the US to defend those "doggoned little islands."[5]

---

3   NSC Meeting, 12 September 1954, Ann Whitman File, Eisenhower Papers, NSC Series, Box 6, EL.

4   Anderson to Eisenhower, 3 September 1954, Ann Whitman File, Eisenhower Papers, Dulles-Herter Series, Box 3, EL.

5   NSC Meeting Notes, 10 September 1954, Ann Whitman File, Eisenhower Papers, NSC Series, Box 6, EL.

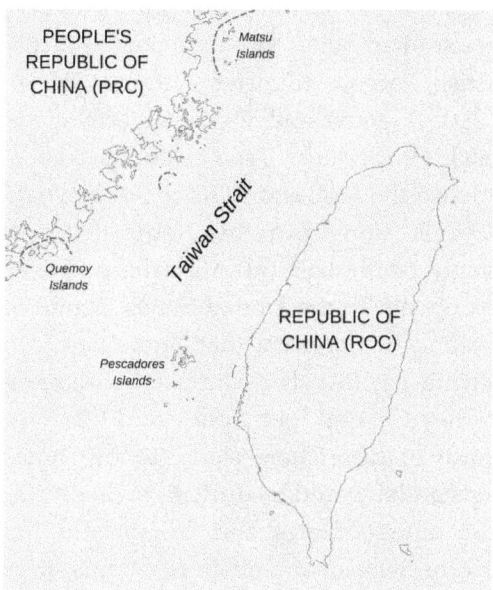

Figure 16. Map of the Taiwan Strait. Created by Andrew Kelly, adapted from map by NordNordWest (2008), Wikimedia, https://commons.wikimedia.org/wiki/File:Taiwan_location_map.svg, CC BY 3.0.

In Canberra, opinion was unanimous that defending the offshore islands was out of the question. Even before the outbreak of hostilities, Casey drew a line between the defence of Taiwan and the offshore islands. On 25 August he told Spender that there was a "distinction" between the two and "hoped that the US could see that."[6] Thomas Critchley, Head of Australia's East Asia Section in the Department of External Affairs, echoed Casey's concerns over American policy. According to Critchley, "[the offshore islands] problem was critical [...] because of the dangers of US involvement." He was particularly concerned that ANZUS obliged Australia to respond if the United States was attacked in the Taiwan Strait. In this event, any Australian failure to respond would be catastrophic for its relationship with the United States, even if Canberra was "left free" of any strict military obligation to defend the offshore islands.[7]

---

6   Casey to Spender, 25 August 1954, NAA, A1838, 519/3/1 Part 1.
7   Critchley Memorandum, 25 August 1954, NAA, A1838, 519/3/1 Part 1; Critchley Memorandum, 19 October 1954, NAA, A1838, 519/3/1 Part 1.

Casey and Critchley's position did not change once the attacks began. In fact, Australian policy closely matched British policy toward the islands. British Foreign Minister Anthony Eden told Dulles on 17 September that Quemoy and the other offshore islands had "no conceivable strategic importance", and he hoped to keep "as much water as possible" between the PRC and ROC.[8] To achieve this, Eden argued that Chiang Kai-shek should evacuate Nationalist troops stationed on the offshore islands. Although the Australians did not express their disagreement as openly to the United States in mid-September, there was a strong feeling in Canberra that Australian interests were best served by following the British example. "We agree with the United Kingdom", Attorney General John Spicer told Casey on 16 September, "with the proximity of the offshore islands to the Chinese mainland [...] fighting [for the islands] would be difficult to justify."[9]

Although the United States and Britain did not agree on the defensibility or otherwise of the offshore islands, they did agree that war must be avoided at all costs. With this thought in mind, Eden and Dulles met in London during September to plan for a potential UN resolution that would call for a ceasefire in the strait. Eden felt that it would be best if the United States did not itself initiate action in the United Nations, fearing that the PRC might respond aggressively. Instead, Eden suggested that New Zealand might propose the resolution because at the time it was a temporary member of the Security Council. Moreover, as New Zealand was a much smaller power than the United States or Britain, a call for a ceasefire from Wellington was far less likely to provoke a strong international backlash from China or the Soviet Union. Dulles agreed with Eden's recommendation, believing that a UN resolution had substantial political benefits.[10] He had told the NSC before he left for London that if a joint US-UK resolution could be reached in the Taiwan Straits, it may lead to a "coming together" of Anglo-American policy in the Far East. In Dulles's view, it had an additional benefit. If the Soviet Union vetoed the resolution, it would

---

8   Australian High Commissioner's Office to Canberra, 17 September 1954, NAA, A5954, 1415/3.
9   Spicer to Casey, 16 September 1954, NAA, A5954, 1415/3.
10 Dulles to Eisenhower, 18 September 1954, John Foster Dulles Papers, JFD Chronological Series, Box 9, EL.

demonstrate the aggressive and dangerous threat that Communism posed and spur allied support. If Moscow supported the resolution, it would mean the PRC was acting "against the will of the majority in the UN."[11]

Dulles and Eden proposed a UN resolution codenamed "Oracle" to New Zealand's Acting High Commissioner in London Richard Campbell on 29 September. Interestingly, they both stressed the "extreme secrecy" of the proposal. In other words, even with an ANZUS Council meeting scheduled in less than a month, the Australians were not to be told.[12] Upon hearing about the proposal, New Zealand policymakers were excited by the opportunity to assist in an international crisis. They were also hopeful that a resolution might encourage US-UK rapprochement vis-à-vis China. New Zealand Prime Minister Sidney Holland believed that his government should accept responsibility and move ahead with the UN resolution as it presented New Zealand with an "opportunity of playing a constructive role" in joint US-UK policy regarding Far Eastern matters.[13] New Zealand External Affairs Minister Thomas Macdonald agreed, but emphasised that New Zealand should not commit beyond the introduction of the resolution to the United Nations unless the United States and Britain were certain they could cooperate. As Macdonald explained, New Zealand might be placed in an immensely difficult position if the United States and British differences on China were exposed publicly once the resolution was presented to the Security Council. "We may find ourselves able to play a useful part", Macdonald told Munro on 1 October, "but my inclination is not to commit ourselves to any particular course in the UN beyond initiation of the debate."[14]

Nevertheless, these concerns were put aside and the next day New Zealand notified the United States and Britain that it was prepared to assist in the project and propose Oracle to the United Nations. All states agreed to submit it under Article VI of the UN Charter, declaring that the crisis threatened international peace and security. As for when the resolution should be submitted, Under Secretary of State W. Bedell

---

11   NSC Meeting, 12 September 1954, Ann Whitman File, Eisenhower Papers, NSC Series, Box 6, EL.
12   Campbell to Macdonald, 30 September 1954, Archives NZ, EA, 264/2/2 Part 1.
13   Holland to Munro, 30 September 1954, Archives NZ, EA, 264/2/2 Part 1.
14   Macdonald to Munro, 1 October 1954, Archives NZ, EA, 264/2/2 Part 1.

Smith told New Zealand Ambassador in Washington Leslie Munro that the submission must wait until after the US mid-term elections in November. Macdonald also asked Munro to find out whether the United States would object to briefing the Australians on the resolution. Macdonald suggested that it would be "highly embarrassing" if Casey found out at the upcoming ANZUS Council meeting in October that discussions had been taking place between America and New Zealand without Australia even knowing about them. Macdonald, in short, thought that it might be best to include Australia in these plans before proceeding to the Security Council.[15] When asked about informing the Australians, Dulles told Munro that he preferred that Australia not yet be told but would not object if New Zealand thought it essential. On further reflection, Munro seemed to agree with Dulles that Australia should not be told until the last possible moment. "There is always the risk of Australian intervention at an inappropriate stage and pursued by Spender in his own peculiar style", Munro told Macdonald, "I do not like the risks that involves."[16]

Despite reservations from Munro and Dulles, Casey was told about the Oracle project in mid-October as part of preparations for the ANZUS Council meeting in Washington. Upon being briefed by New Zealand, Casey had immediate objections. He did not understand why his American and New Zealand counterparts could not see that potentially serious issues could occur if a UN resolution was pursued. For one, Casey thought the prospects of a successful UN submission would be "so remote as to throw in doubt [the] value of [the] exercise." Even in the unlikely event that a resolution was passed, it was clear neither how the full cooperation of the Nationalists in neutralising the islands could be obtained nor how this would be implemented. So far as Casey was concerned, there was also a disconcerting possibility that a Soviet veto could "stimulate pressure" in the United States to defend the offshore islands.[17] In short, although Casey wanted a ceasefire in the Taiwan Straits as soon as possible, he did not agree that the New

---

15 Macdonald to Munro, 7 October 1954, Archives NZ, EA, 264/2/2 Part 1.

16 Munro to Macdonald, 9 October 1954, Archives NZ, EA, 264/2/2 Part 1.

17 Caseyto Spender, 5 November 1954, NAA, A5954, 1415/3.

Zealand-American-British UN resolution was the most appropriate action to achieve that objective.

A Mutual Defence Treaty

By late 1954, the United States was also moving ahead with the conclusion of a binding commitment to defend Taiwan and the nearby Pescadores. Due to the close cooperation between the US and New Zealand in the service of the Oracle project, the Americans told the New Zealanders about this plan before the Australians and left it to New Zealand to "keep Australia adequately informed if and when a decision seemed likely." Once the Australians were briefed about this plan, Spender immediately called a meeting with Dulles on 31 October to express his dissatisfaction with the proposed treaty and the lack of consultation with Australia. During the meeting Spender "expressed some annoyance that the Australians had not been brought into these talks" for the mutual defence pact with Taiwan. He also suggested that a pact would be "unwise" because it would "compel a clarification of the situation with reference to the offshore islands and that a somewhat indeterminate status was preferable."[18] In other words, Spender thought that the United States should avoid a clear-cut commitment and instead keep the PRC guessing as to American intentions in the Taiwan Straits.

Nonetheless, a mutual security treaty between the United States and the Nationalist Government was eventually signed on 2 December 1954. This treaty guaranteed that the United States would defend Taiwan, potentially even with the use of nuclear weapons. It also required Chiang to consult with the United States before launching any attack on the Chinese mainland. This provision ensured that the Nationalists could not drag the United States into an unwanted war over mainland China. As Dulles had hoped, the wording over the commitment to defend the offshore islands was left unclear. Eisenhower stressed later that the decision to defend Taiwan's "closely related territories" would be made by the President.[19]

---

18 Memorandum of Conversation between Spender and Dulles, 31 October 1954, NARA, RG 59, 611.43/10-3154.
19 NSC Memorandum, 2 November 1954, Ann Whitman File, Eisenhower Papers, NSC Series, Box 6, EL.

Once the treaty was put into force, Dulles hoped to clear up this fuzziness with American allies. He spoke with New Zealand Ambassador Leslie Munro and British Ambassador Roger Makins about US willingness to commit privately to defending Quemoy and Matsu even with the use of nuclear weapons. To be sure, neither Munro nor Makins were pleased with this new American policy. Determined to sway allied opinion, Eisenhower went one step further and wrote to Churchill directly to stress the strategic usefulness of using these types of catastrophic weapons. Believing that the British were not properly seeing how effective a nuclear response could be, Eisenhower argued that even the tactical deployment of a dozen atomic bombs on critical defence infrastructure could effectively paralyse the PRC and award the Western powers a decisive upper hand in the Northeast Asian region.[20] It was quite a startling suggestion from the former US Chief of the Army, particularly because the use of nuclear weapons could provoke a Soviet retaliation and escalate a regional crisis into a much larger international war.

Despite his vast military experience, Eisenhower failed to convince the Britons of the feasibility of a nuclear approach. Churchill, Eden and the British Foreign Office were not just concerned by the escalation of war in the Taiwan Straits; a nuclear attack might have provoked the Soviets to launch their own nuclear warheads in Europe, much closer to Britain and its critical strategic interests. Upon hearing about the policy, Eden asserted that Oracle should not be pursued until the United States gave up its proposal to defend Quemoy. He simply refused to entertain the idea of using nuclear weapons, going so far as to insist that the search for diplomatic solutions through the UN could not continue until the US abandoned these reckless ideas. Eden was also particularly critical of any of his own policymakers who even hinted that Britain would support US policy in the Taiwan Straits. After British Ambassador to the United Nations Anthony Nutting made several comments about Britain supporting the United States over Quemoy and Matsu, Eden wrote scornfully to Nutting that:

---

20 David Watry, *Diplomacy at the Brink: Eisenhower, Churchill and Eden in the Cold War* (Baton Rouge: Louisiana State University Press, 2014), 79.

Criticism of your interview is principally directed against implications that United Kingdom will necessarily be involved in hostilities if China attacks Formosa. It is by no means certain that an attack on Formosa 'would no doubt call for collective action of the United Nations' [...] they seem cumulatively to create the impression that it was your intention to declare that the United Kingdom would answer the war on the side of the United States if the Chinese launched an attack. "Times" Washington correspondent in his full account of your interview today states that you have in fact created the impression in America, and imply that we have undertaken something new [...] I rely on you to say as little as possible on this thorny subject and to limit your pubic interviews to the utmost.[21]

In Australia, once Eisenhower announced publicly his intention to defend Taiwan—and, if he thought it necessary for Taiwan's defence, its "closely related territories"—Casey grew similarly concerned that a war over the offshore islands may eventuate. For the mindful External Affairs Minister, it was just as dangerous as a possible UN resolution. "We are considerably concerned", Casey told Spender, "it seems equally foolish and dangerous to contemplate [war] in the defence of islands whose security value is, to say the least, doubtful." In summation, he "[did] not regard these islands as worth the risk of war."[22] Casey, a long-time advocate of a more realistic approach to China, explored the alternative possibility of recognising the PRC in an effort to reduce tensions. He wrote to Menzies on 10 December suggesting that on balance, the "majority of the Australian press seemed to be in favour *for* recognition" of the PRC. He also stressed that even though free world nations should not condone Communist aggression, current relations with Beijing were not on a satisfactory basis.[23]

Casey continued to make a connection between recognizing the PRC and reducing the tensions in the Taiwan Strait. When drafting an announcement about the current situation in East Asia, Casey reasoned that "the conduct of international affairs is made more difficult so long as the PRC is not recognised and so it would be logical to change this situation."[24] Although Casey concluded that the offshore island crisis

---

21 Eden to Nutting, 14 December 1954, as cited in Watry, *Diplomacy at the Brink*, 78.
22 Casey to Spender, 21 January 1955, NAA. A5954, 1415/3.
23 Letter from Casey to Menzies, 10 December 1954, DAFP: China, 87.
24 Letter from Brown to Menzies, 28 December 1954, DAFP: China, 91.

should be settled first before considering "recognition later", he clearly thought that recognising the PRC might in some way reduce tensions or prevent future Chinese aggression. This part of his statement was never publicised, as Menzies opposed any suggestion that Australia was at the time considering changing its public opposition to recognition of the PRC. Nevertheless, policymakers such as Casey appeared willing to consider the possibility of recognition far more openly than policymakers in the United States.

There was strong support in Australia for Casey's suggestion. Casey was encouraged by both the public and the federal opposition to pursue recognition in exchange for a ceasefire in the straits. For example, an article written by journalist John Bennetts published in the Sunday Times in early 1955 suggested that Australia, the United States and Nationalist China should abandon any interest in the offshore islands as a quid pro quo for recognition of the PRC. For "assurances and demonstrations of goodwill and peaceful intentions" in the Taiwan Straits, Bennetts wrote that Communist China should be "offered eventual membership of the United Nations and general recognition as the lawful Government of mainland China in return."[25] Reports emerged later that Labor backbencher Allan Fraser accused Casey of not "seeking to exploit every opportunity for negotiation with Red China" while the offshore island crisis remained unresolved. Casey should be "prompting the recognition of the Chinese mainland Government", Fraser told the press, "as a means to pave the way for a long-term settlement."[26]

On mainland China, Mao's response to the recent US-ROC defence treaty was particularly aggressive. On 10 January 1955, he ordered an attack on the Tachen Islands. Eight days later, PRC forces also attacked and captured nearby Ichiang Island. The Tachens themselves were approximately 320 kilometres north of Taiwan, far outside the original area the US considered strategically important for defending the island. Nonetheless, Eisenhower and Radford thought these attacks indicated the PRC's "clear intent" to capture all offshore islands, with the ultimate

---

25 John Bennetts, "Australia Moves Fast to End Red China Crisis", *Sunday Times*, 30 January 1955.

26 "Casey Accused of Playing-up Hostility and Hatred", *The Canberra Times*, 31 March 1955.

purpose of taking Taiwan and the Pescadores.²⁷ To combat this, the US convinced a reluctant Chiang Kai-shek to evacuate the Tachens in exchange for a private commitment to defend Quemoy and Matsu in the event of a full scale attack. This drastic change in American policy confirmed that Dulles's original plans had "backfired." As Wilson told the NSC on 20 January, US "diplomatic efforts [...] had failed."²⁸

Given this failure, military options were revisited. Earlier on 20 January, a meeting was held between the State Department, Joint Chiefs of Staff and several Congressmen to brief Capitol Hill on new developments in the Taiwan Straits. Dulles said that the situation in the Taiwan area was developing "in an acute way which seems to call for a sounder defensive concept. There is no doubt in [my] mind that the ultimate purpose of the Communist Chinese is to try and take Taiwan and the Pescadores", Dulles stressed, "the problem had reached such magnitude that it had to be dealt with in a comprehensive way." On the advice of Admiral Radford, Dulles said that there would be a regrouping of Nationalists forces and with help from the United States they would hold the remaining islands (Quemoy and Matsu). Hoping to secure Congressional support for such action, Dulles argued that "it would be criminal folly on our part to sit and watch these islands be taken which could be held with minor help on our part." Most of the Congressmen agreed with this approach, but they wanted Eisenhower to make it extremely clear that US military action was limited only to reorganising Nationalist forces on Quemoy and Matsu and defending these islands in the possibility that they were attacked. As Senator Earle Clements told Dulles, the President must make clear "what we are willing to defend, where we will draw the line, and where we will retreat no further."²⁹

In Canberra, the Tachen attacks presented an increasingly dangerous and uncertain period for Australian policymakers. Yet instead of making any immediate public statement, the Australian Department of External Affairs kept their policies behind closed doors in the belief that the State

---

27 State Department Meeting, 19 January 1955, FRUS 1955-1957 Vol. II, 50.
28 NSC Meeting, 20 January 1955, Ann Whitman File, Eisenhower Papers, NSC Series, Box 7, EL.
29 Meeting of Secretary with mional Leaders, 20 January 1955, John Foster Dulles Papers, White House Memoranda Series, Box 2, EL.

Department was best placed to handle the crisis. The ever-tactful Casey reasoned that his Government's interests were best served by simply staying quiet, because announcing that Australia saw a clear distinction between Taiwan and the offshore islands could only complicate the situation for the United States. "The attitude I have been taking", Casey penned in his diary on 28 January, "is not to talk unless it would do more good than harm." He also recommended against an ANZUS meeting on the crisis, thinking that at that time Australia had "nothing positive to suggest that had not already been considered by the US."[30]

Escalating tensions, however, forced him to outline Australian policy publicly. In an address given almost a month after the Tachens were first shelled, Casey stated the Australian Government's desire for "disengagement" from the offshore islands as these were clearly part of Chinese territory. This position sat uneasily with his US counterparts, who had determined so recently to hold Quemoy and Matsu. It was also no coincidence that Casey's statement came after Eisenhower's address to Congress on 24 January that outlined only the President had the power to decide whether the US would defend Taiwan's "closely related territories." Though Casey recognized in his statement that the situation was "in the hands of President Eisenhower more than anyone else", his timing affirmed Australian discontent over defending the islands.[31]

Although New Zealand shared Australian concerns over the Tachen attacks and recent changes to American policy in the Taiwan Straits, the New Zealand External Affairs Department still believed that Oracle should be pursued rather than defending the offshore islands or pursuing recognition as a quid pro quo for the cessation of PRC aggression. "The Government has no intention of entering into any sort of commitment involving New Zealand in developments around Taiwan", New Zealand External Affairs Minister Thomas Macdonald announced on 27 January. Instead, Macdonald suggested that New Zealand was "anxious that the threat to peace which appears to be developing in that area should be dealt with by the normal machinery of the United Nations."[32]

---

30 Casey Diary Entry, 28 January 1955, Casey's Diaries, 200.
31 Press Statement, 7 February 1955, CNIA Vol. 26, no. 2, 128.
32 Macdonald Statement, 27 January 1955, NZFP: SD, 377-378.

In Washington, Munro agreed wholeheartedly with Macdonald's announcement. He certainly did not agree with the US decision to secure a formal defence treaty for Taiwan and its efforts to create uncertainty over the potential American reaction to attacks on the offshore islands, describing both responses as the "two worst courses of action." "I must say I am seriously disturbed by the American course of conduct", he told Macdonald on 21 January 1955.[33] Munro still believed Oracle could serve a useful purpose, but it could only proceed if the US and UK could agree to support the resolution. This seemed increasingly unlikely once Britain signalled its complete opposition to America's commitment to defend Taiwan and possibly the offshore islands. After Dulles informed British Ambassador in Washington Roger Makins on 19 January that the United States would assist in the defence of Quemoy, Makins responded a day later with British views on the subject. Its message was clear: "the British government is disturbed by developments", Makins told Dulles on 20 January, and "the Cabinet did not like the idea of a 'provisional guarantee' of Quemoy.[34]

Upon receiving word that Britain was unlikely to support a UN resolution while the United States committed privately to the defence of Quemoy and Matsu, Dulles backed down and agreed to reconsider presenting Oracle to the UN instead of committing to defend Quemoy and Matsu. American, British and New Zealand delegates met on 23 January to decide how the resolution might be proposed. It was decided that Britain should inform Beijing and Moscow of Oracle, then New Zealand would invite the PRC to attend UN discussions after the presentation of the resolution. On 31 January the United Nations invited China to attend the debate on the offshore islands, but Chinese Premier Zhou Enlai rejected the invitation. He stated that Oracle opened the door to the possibility of "two China's" and was an illegal intervention into Chinese internal affairs.[35]

---

33   Munro to Macdonald, 21 January 1955, Archives NZ, EA, 264/2/2 Part 2.
34   Memorandum of Conversation, 20 January 1955, NARA, RG 59, 793.5/3-2958.
35   Victor Kaufman, "Operation Oracle: The United States, Great Britain, New Zealand and the Offshore Island Crisis of 1954-55", *Journal of Imperial and Commonwealth History* 32, no. 3 (2004), 106-124, https://doi.org/10.1080/0308653042000279687. See also Williamson, *Separate Agendas*, 121.

Commonwealth Discussions for a Ceasefire

Once the PRC declared that it was unwilling to discuss the offshore island problem in the United Nations, Commonwealth countries grew further concerned that the United States would defend the islands if an invasion took place. These issues were discussed at length during the Prime Ministers' Conference in London from 31 January to 8 February 1955. Aside from discussions over the insurgence of Communist forces in Malaya, delegates discussed reaching an agreement on the Quemoy-Matsu Crisis. Menzies was especially determined to influence British opinion when relaying at the conference that his Cabinet agreed unanimously that the Nationalists should disengage from the offshore islands. Eden agreed firmly with this policy, in line with what he had said to Dulles previously about the offshore islands holding "no conceivable strategic importance." Feeling that this summarised neatly the "consensus of opinion" from the conference, Eden asked Menzies to write to Dulles and outline the position of the Commonwealth nations. The letter stressed that delegates at the Prime Ministers' Conference were convinced that "further resolutions and debate in the Security Council at present would do harm" and that "Australia and Britain were very much opposed to the risk of war over the offshore islands."[36]

Menzies's letter provided the State Department with a clear warning that Britain and Australia were moving away from supporting a UN solution to the crisis. Even New Zealand Prime Minister Holland, who had been a strong supporter of Oracle and was concerned by American action in the Taiwan Straits, pledged his support to Australian and British efforts to at least delay Oracle.[37] In response, Eisenhower wrote to Churchill and noted that while he appreciated British efforts to avoid a rift in Anglo-American relations, in his view the British did not understand fully the Communist's "constant pressing on the Asian frontier."[38] Churchill, however, remained steadfast on his government's position on China and later informed Washington that Whitehall

---

36   Aldrich to Department of State, 4 February 1955, NARA, RG 59, 793.5/2-455.

37   US Embassy in London to State Department, 1 February 1955, NARA, RG 59, 741.13/2-155.

38   Eisenhower to Churchill, 10 February 1955, Ann Whitman File, DDE Diary Series, Box 9, EL.

no longer supported Oracle. As a result, the United States could not realistically hope to find a long-term solution or even a temporary ceasefire through the UN.

During the Prime Ministers' Conference, Spender cabled Menzies on 6 February to offer a more detailed assessment of the situation as it stood in the Taiwan Strait. Even though he was unaware of the importance the American JCS attached to holding the offshore islands, he told Menzies the problem was because of a continued Nationalist military presence on the islands rather than American insistence that protecting the islands was essential. Believing that Chiang would be a difficult man to convince, he proposed that in return for Nationalist withdrawal from the islands, Australia and other Commonwealth countries should declare their intention to defend Taiwan if attacked. Although Menzies did not take up Spender's suggestion immediately — like many Australians, Menzies was reluctant to commit to Chiang's defence and only considered doing so in the hope that it might prevent a wider war with the PRC — it did form the basis for a proposal that Menzies submitted to the United States after the crisis came to an end.[39]

In any event, Spender had more pressing matters on his agenda. Following the Prime Ministers' Conference, Dulles held an important meeting with Spender on 11 February to discuss the Australian and Commonwealth position on Taiwan and the offshore islands. Spender opened the meeting by first relaying the consensus of opinion reached in London. In outlining the Australian position, he stressed that:

> It is causing us deep concern [...] we cannot see that [the offshore islands] are either vital, or even important, to Taiwan-Pescadores defence. It is, therefore, hard for us to see why they are made a policy issue. Our view is that the correct aim is disengagement from the islands [...] these views are not dissimilar to those already expressed by Canada, the United Kingdom and New Zealand.[40]

Dulles appreciated Spender's open yet firm expression of Australian and Commonwealth policy. He told Spender that "none of his colleagues

---

39   Menzies, Cablegram to Canberra, 17 March 1955, DAFP: China, 99; David Lee, "Australia and Anglo-American Disagreement over the Quemoy-Matsu Crisis, 1954-55", *The Journal of Imperial and Commonwealth History* 23, no. 1 (January 1995), 112, https://doi.org/10.1080/03086539508582946

40   Spender to Canberra, 12 February 1955, NAA, A1838, TS519/3/1 Part 3.

had so clearly or so categorically" been as helpful on the offshore island issue. Australia was "more engaged in the area than others", Dulles added, "Australia is not a country on the sidelines."

Dulles was not surprised by the Australian position. It was, as he pointed out, not too dissimilar from the views reached in the NSC meeting in mid-September 1954. Nevertheless, he told Spender that the US now considered that withdrawing from the offshore islands would have a substantial psychological effect on Taiwan and nearby areas. Dulles also shared with Spender that the JCS thought the islands held strategic importance because (1) they blocked two natural harbours and (2) their proximity to the Chinese mainland made them a useful staging area for potential counterattacks. In short, Dulles stressed that the United States had been "reluctantly compelled" to move from its original position (which generally coincided with current Australian policy) to its present position.

Neither Spender nor Dulles wanted war in the strait. They both agreed on the strategic necessity of keeping Taiwan and the Pescadores out of Communist hands, but disagreed on the way that it should be done. For Dulles, it was important to highlight that although the US had determined Quemoy and Matsu be defended, there was considerable flexibility in any decision to do so. In his view, the decision "was entirely ours." Spender—and, for that matter, almost all other Commonwealth nations—seemed unconvinced by this reasoning. Though Spender well understood Dulles's arguments for the defence of the offshore islands and sympathised with his awkward position, Menzies's recent letter to Washington best captured the majority of Australian opinion over American involvement in the strait. American Ambassador to the United Kingdom Winthrop Aldrich also informed Washington that Australia and Britain were deeply concerned that they might be dragged into an unwanted and unnecessary war. He told the State Department that a recent Walter Lippman article called "Towards a Ceasefire"—based on the agreements reached at the Prime Ministers' Conference—argued that "sound American policy would be to do what is being done in the Tachens to Quemoy and Matsu." In other words, Australia and Britain believed the ROC and US should evacuate all offshore islands. This, according to Aldrich, summarised the Commonwealth position to an "extraordinarily exact degree."[41]

Consistent with the summary Aldrich gave to the State Department, Eden rejected flatly Dulles's view that evacuating the offshore islands would seriously affect Nationalist morale. Even if it did, he told Dulles on 26 February that "further deterioration in morale is preferable to breaking up the [Anglo-American] alliance." This presumably meant that if push came to shove, London would not support Washington on the offshore island issue.[42] Fearing further rifts between Washington and its allies, Dulles took the opportunity to remind Casey and New Zealand External Affairs Minister Macdonald that "if fighting broke out in the future over Taiwan [...] Australia and New Zealand would be concerned as partners of ANZUS."[43] It was a disconcerting situation for Australia to be in. If Canberra supported Washington, it risked isolating itself from Britain and the Commonwealth. It also risked placing itself on the frontlines of a nuclear war over islands that Australians policymakers had consistently determined to be strategically insignificant. However, if Canberra supported London, it would both marginalise its relationship with Washington and call into question the usefulness of ANZUS.

Prompted by these Australian-American-British divisions, Menzies visited Washington to discuss possibilities for bringing the crisis to an end. In a meeting with Dulles on 14 March, his first agenda item was to gather US financial and military support for the defence of Malaya, one of Australia's most important strategic interests. As part of Australia's forward defence policy in Southeast Asia, Australian and British defence talks had been moving recently towards creating a Far East Strategic Reserve (which came into effect later in April) that would entail a joint military force stationed in the region to protect Malaya and other Commonwealth interests. Unfortunately for Menzies, he convinced neither Dulles nor the American JCS to commit to Malaya's defence or a broader defence scheme outside of SEATO.

Next, talks moved to the escalating situation in the Taiwan Straits. He first asked Dulles to explain the difference between his position and

---

41 Aldrich to the Department of State, 11 February 1955, NARA, RG 59, 793.00/2-1155.
42 Glen St. John Barclay, *Friends in High Places: Australian-American Diplomatic Relations Since 1945* (Melbourne: Oxford University Press, 1985), 77.
43 Casey Diary Entry, 26 February 1955, Casey's Diaries, 206-207.

that of Casey and Eden's. According to Dulles, there were two elements informing these differences: a misunderstanding of the US approach and questions of judgment as to the best way to achieve the same objective. Dulles stressed that the British House of Commons did not understand that psychological and political factors were just as important as military considerations and that these factors were shaping the US position. He also suggested that there could be no categorical assertion whether the US would or would not defend the islands.[44] Menzies sympathised with Dulles's difficult position. However, American ambiguity ultimately sat uneasily with Australian policy. Menzies, who believed that the "unconditional surrender of offshore islands would intensify Communist truculence", asked Dulles about the possibility of a ROC withdrawal from the islands in exchange for a group of nations guaranteeing the defence of Taiwan (Australia, Britain, New Zealand, and any other Commonwealth nation willing to commit to this scheme). Dulles quite liked this idea. He thought the suggestion had "merit" and would "give further thought" to the proposition. He even told Menzies that he had proposed a similar idea to Eden previously, but had received no response.[45] The unfortunate reality was that Chiang was unlikely to agree. The Generalissimo had already secured a guarantee from the United States, and any offshore island evacuation would work against his plans to recover the Chinese mainland.

Even if a Commonwealth guarantee could not be reached, Menzies wanted to make sure that Dulles understood how the Australian public viewed the situation. While the Australian public might support holding Taiwan if a broader war broke out, he told Dulles that there would be no support whatsoever for a war fought over the offshore islands. In Menzies's view, there was only support for larger efforts to prevent aggressive Communist behaviour. "The Australian public would support a war in the defence of freedom", Menzies stated, "but not of Governments per se (such as Chiang's regime) or offshore islands."[46] Dulles could at least be certain of Australia's commitment

---

44 State Department Meeting, 14 March 1955, FRUS 1955-1957 Vol. II, 368-372.
45 Memorandum for the President, 27 June 1955, White House Central Files, Confidential File, Box 28, EL; State Department Meeting, 14 March 1955, FRUS 1955-1957 Vol. II, 368-372.
46 Ibid., 368.

if war eventuated, but did not find the agreement on offshore island policy he was looking for.

While Spender and Menzies met with Dulles in an attempt to find a resolution to the crisis, New Zealand policymakers continued to debate whether pursuing Oracle might still serve a useful purpose despite Zhou's rejection in late January. In March, Ambassador Munro wrote to Macdonald and explained his thoughts on the project. In his mind, New Zealand could either introduce the Oracle resolution on its own or jettison the idea entirely. Munro appeared to favour the first option, fearing that if New Zealand postponed Oracle and then the United States went ahead with the resolution it would make New Zealand's "position in the operation [...] very invidious."[47] Concerned by this prospect, Munro suggested to Dulles that while New Zealand was not prepared to abandon the Oracle project, it made sense to delay a decision to see whether tensions could be relieved on their own accord.

In response, Dulles suggested to Munro on 23 March that New Zealand's role in the Oracle project was still important and that its presentation to the United Nations should not be delayed. He argued that while tensions had calmed in recent weeks there was no telling when the PRC might mount another attack. Moreover, in April the Soviet Union would assume the Security Council presidency, making it even more difficult to proceed with Oracle. However, this pressure from Dulles to introduce the resolution concerned Munro. He believed that it forced New Zealand to "choose between the British and American points of view in an area where action by the United States, our chief bulwark in the Pacific, might not be supported by the United Kingdom."[48]

Fortunately for the Oracle sponsors, tensions eased on 23 April 1955 when PRC Premier Zhou Enlai announced that China did not want war with the United States and was willing to enter into negotiations. Zhou's announcement meant that Oracle would not have to be introduced in the United Nations in order to resolve the crisis. Though sceptical of Chinese intentions, the Americans agreed and entered into ambassadorial talks in Geneva from August 1955. Realising the weight of domestic and international opinion against any American action in

---

47 Munro to Macdonald, 9 March 1955, Archives NZ, EA, 264/3/2 Part 3; Munro to Macdonald, 15 March 1955, Archives NZ, EA, 264/3/2 Part 3.

48 Munro to Macdonald, 26 March 1955, Archives NZ, EA, 264/3/2 Part 3.

the defence of the offshore islands, President Eisenhower was surely relieved that he never had to decide between whether to intervene militarily or concede defeat to a Communist government. At least for now, the United States had avoided the "inevitable moment of decision between two unacceptable choices" in the Taiwan Straits.[49]

Alongside American trepidations, Menzies could not be certain whether Zhou's offer to negotiate was genuine or not. Either way, he thought that future hostilities with the PRC were still likely. Menzies thought future tensions in the Taiwan Strait could be settled if the PRC was part of an international discussion to achieve its recognition, just as Casey had believed that this approach might reduce the bellicosity of the PRC. Menzies took this idea one step further, proposing to the State Department that the PRC attend a Four-Power Conference to address current Sino-American differences. Menzies's proposal outlined that there was a clear "danger of fighting over the offshore islands [because it] could develop into a major war." Recognition of the PRC should be reconsidered due to "the difficulty of doing anything about the offshore islands while an atmosphere existed of Communist threats to attack the offshore islands and Taiwan."[50] Washington, however, was not convinced that Menzies's proposal addressed its own interests. Dulles first told Spender on 3 May that the idea was "unfavourable" and the American public would be very much opposed.[51] US Ambassador to Australia Amos Peaslee was even more vocal about his dislike for the plan, stating that he was "astonished" and "disturbed." According to Peaslee, the Australian Government was "180° off course" with this idea.[52]

After Menzies's failed proposal, the Australian Joint Planning Committee (JPC) formally reconsidered Taiwan's strategic importance for future defence planning. Offshore island policy was not in question: as late as May, the Australian Government continued to draw a distinction

---

49 Eisenhower to Dulles, 5 April 1955, Ann Whitman File, Dulles-Herter Series, Box 5, EL.

50 Record of Conversation between Tange, Critchley and Peterson, 5 May 1955, NAA, A1209, 1957/5035.

51 Cablegram to Canberra, 3 May 1955, DAFP: China, p.103.

52 Record of Conversation between Tange, Critchley and Peterson, 5 May 1955, NAA, A1209, 1957/5035.

between Taiwan and the offshore islands, claiming that the latter were "not regarded as important."[53] Yet as far as Taiwan was concerned, the JPC report concluded it was now more strategically important because of its proximity to China and the control it afforded over the Taiwan Straits. More importantly for Australian strategy, the report reasoned that the PRC could only "concentrate their military effort at one point at a time." In other words, as long as the PRC's attention was drawn to Taiwan, it acted as a "constant deterrent to further Chinese Communist adventure in Southeast Asia."[54] These JPC findings laid out several reasons why Taiwan was, in fact, an important regional base that had to be kept out of Communist hands, but its strategic importance was considered only in light of Australian interests in Southeast Asia rather than with the intention of coordinating defence policy with the United States.

Moreover, the Department of External Affairs agreed neither with American policy nor that continuing to defend Taiwan was in Australia's best interests. Casey, for one, told Plimsoll on 13 April that "we're not as convinced as the Americans are of Chiang and his forces." He suggested further that American policy was based on a "lie" and that they were "prisoners of their past attitudes." "For Chiang and his Taiwan forces", Casey stated bluntly, "common-sense prompts one to believe that they must be a factor of declining importance in the scheme of things [...] as time goes on, Taiwan will decline."[55] Convinced that the External Affairs Department should reconsider its China policy, Casey commissioned a major study for the Cabinet in June 1955 titled "The Situation in East Asia: Taiwan and Recognition of China." Although the report concluded that Australia was not yet in a position to recognise the PRC due to the US position, it stated that the prospects of finding long term peace in the Far East through potential recognition were now greater than they had ever been. This was due at least in part to Beijing's recent softer diplomacy, which suggested a "genuine [Chinese] desire for a policy of live and let live." In other words, Casey thought that despite the PRC's initiation of the Quemoy-Matsu Crisis, Mao's Government was

---

53 Department Memorandum, 13 May 1955, NAA, A1209, 1957/4844.

54 Joint Planning Committee Report, 27 April 1955 NAA, A5799, 5799/15.

55 Casey to Plimsoll, 13 April 1955, NAA, A1838, TS519/3/1/ Part 4; Casey to Plimsoll, 12 April 1955, NAA, A1838, TS519/3/1/ Part 4.

beginning to act more responsibly and Western powers should award recognition accordingly in the short-term future. "So far as recognition and representation in the United Nations is concerned", Casey's report concluded, the issue was "perhaps now one of timing rather than of principle."[56]

In the immediate aftermath of the 1954-55 Quemoy-Matsu Crisis, Australian, New Zealand and American policymakers were certainly relieved that the crisis did not escalate into a wider war. Nevertheless, there were heightened concerns in these countries that their respective relationships with Beijing were not working and that opposing recognition might in fact be encouraging further aggression in East Asia. This was especially true in Canberra and Wellington, where recognition was discussed before, during and after the Quemoy-Matsu Crisis despite much stronger opposition to recognising the PRC in the United States. Even then, trans-Tasman views vis-à-vis China were by no means identical. Policy differences between the ANZUS powers, however, soon manifested elsewhere. In the Middle East, the trilateral relationship was seriously strained amidst major British strategic miscalculations in the region.

---

56 The Situation in East Asia: Formosa and Recognition of China, 29 June 1955, NAA, A4906, 404.

8. Suez

Shortly after an uneasy peace settlement was reached in the Taiwan Straits, longstanding tensions in the Middle East erupted into open conflict during the 1956 Suez Crisis. Egyptian leader Gamal Abdel Nasser—who had already overthrown the Farouk government in 1952, declared Egypt a republic and publicly advocated a Pan-Arab movement against the West—nationalised the Suez Canal after Britain and the United States removed its support for the construction of the Aswan Dam. The canal had previously been under British control since the late nineteenth century and was an important shipping route to countries in Southern Africa and the South Pacific.

Before the crisis reached a climax in late 1956, the Britons and Americans discussed different options for subduing Nasser. Eisenhower hoped to encourage local and international political resistance against him through a secret operation called Operation Omega, which aimed to use both diplomacy and covert action to thwart his ambitions in the Arab world. Anthony Eden—who had succeeded Churchill as British Prime Minister in 1955—instead wanted to take a much more direct approach. In conjunction with the British Secret Intelligence Service (SIS), Eden worked on plans to assassinate Nasser either covertly or through a large-scale invasion. In his eyes, Nasser was comparable to Hitler and needed to be eliminated as soon as possible. In letters to Eisenhower and in discussions with the SIS, he made frequent comparisons between Nasser, Hitler and Mussolini.[1] "I feel myself that we can no longer safely wait on Nasser", Eden wrote to Eisenhower in

---

1   Eden to Eisenhower, 5 March 1956, in *The Eden-Eisenhower Correspondence, 1955-1957*, Peter Boyle ed. (hereafter *Eden-Eisenhower Correspondence*) (Chapel Hill: University of North Carolina Press, 2005), 119; Eden to Eisenhower, 5 August 1956, *Eden-Eisenhower Correspondence*, 113; David Nichols, *Eisenhower 1956* (New York: Simon & Schuster, 2011), 164.

early March, "a policy of appeasement will bring us nothing in Egypt."[2] Eden was particularly convinced of the ineffectiveness of appeasement, as he had previously resigned as foreign secretary during the Neville Chamberlain government in 1938 due in part to growing dissatisfaction over British efforts to appease Nazi Germany in the lead up to World War II.

Resorting to force, however, had much deeper implications in the context of the larger battle between East and West during the Cold War. Eisenhower told Eden that he feared Nasser might work closely with the Soviets if Western powers pushed too aggressively in Egypt. "I share your current concerns over the current developments in the Middle East", Eisenhower wrote on 9 March, "we face a broad challenge to our position in the Near East […] [as] the Soviets have made it abundantly clear even in their public statements their intentions toward the Near East." He added that "some moves by Nasser have assisted the Soviets", and under these circumstances, "it may well be that [the United States and Britain] shall be driven to conclude that it is impossible to do business with Nasser. Yet for all of his concerns, Eisenhower was not willing to completely dismiss finding a peaceful solution with Nasser. "I do not think that we should close the door yet on the possibility of working with him", he argued in a letter to Eden.[3] Eisenhower, in short, wanted to explore all options to maintain the US position in the Middle East in order to stop Soviet expansionism in the region and protect American access to regional oil reserves.

Prelude to Crisis

By mid-1956, the prospect of finding a peaceful solution with Nasser evaporated quickly. On 19 July, Secretary of State John Foster Dulles announced that the United States was formally withdrawing aid for the Aswan Dam Project. In a meeting with Egyptian Ambassador in Washington Ahmed Hussein, Dulles suggested that there was "little goodwill toward Egypt on the part of the American public", so much so that Dulles doubted whether the Administration could obtain the funds from Congress. "For the time being", Dulles told Hussein, "the

---

2 Eden to Eisenhower, 6 March 1956, NARA, RG 59, 780.5/3-656.
3 Eisenhower to Eden, 9 March 1956, in *Eden-Eisenhower Correspondence*, 122.

Dam project should be put on the shelf while we try to develop a better atmosphere and better relations."[4]

One week later, Nasser announced Egyptian plans to nationalise the Suez Canal. Nasser declared that this was the "answer to American and British conspiracies against Egypt" and a response to "imperialistic efforts to thwart Egyptian independence."[5] Nasser's decision greatly concerned Eden, who immediately began plans to intervene militarily in Egypt. He believed that Nasser's action was not only a threat to Britain's economic interests but it was also a provocative attack on British power and authority. Eden immediately established an Egypt Committee (an inner circle of British Cabinet members that planned for a Suez operation) and warned Eisenhower that Britain was prepared to use force in Egypt. "My colleagues and I are convinced that we must be ready, in the last resort, to use force to bring Nasser to his senses", Eden told Eisenhower on 27 July.[6]

Figure 17. Egyptian Prime Minister Gamal Abdel Nasser cheered in Cairo after nationalising the Suez Canal. Photo by unknown (1956), Wikimedia, https://commons.wikimedia.org/wiki/File:Nasser_cheered_by_supporters_in_1956.jpg, public domain.

---

4   Memorandum of Conversation, 19 July 1956, FRUS 1955-1957 Vol. XV, 871.
5   Embassy in Egypt to the Department of State, 26 July 1956, FRUS 1955-1957 Vol. XVI, 1.
6   Eden to Eisenhower, 27 July 1956, in *Eden-Eisenhower Correspondence*, 153-155.

The surprising extent to which Eden was determined to retain control in Suez reveals much about his character and influence in British politics. After building an international name for himself as British foreign secretary during World War II, Eden worked largely in Churchill's shadow during the post-war years, first as deputy opposition leader between 1945 and 1951, and then as his deputy prime minister during Churchill's final term in office between 1951 to 1955. He did, however, exercise considerable influence over the conduct of British foreign policy—so much so that one biographer claimed he bullied Churchill into retreating on commitments regarding Europe and the Middle East that the Conservatives had made while in opposition.[7]

As prime minister, Suez became Eden's pivotal issue. He became fixated on Nasser and was determined not to let events in Egypt undermine British prestige. To be sure, while Eden did have some support for his actions in Suez, it was a far cry from what he told Eisenhower about his colleagues being convinced that force would be necessary as a last resort. In fact, his Egypt Committee excluded many top British policymakers and aimed to keep plans for an invasion secret. Indeed, most officials knew nothing about British plans and were astonished when they heard that Eden was potentially planning for an Anglo-French ultimatum and invasion. For one, Sir Evelyn Shuckburgh, who had been responsible for Middle Eastern policy, was not alone in the Foreign Office in thinking that Eden had "gone off his head."[8]

For their part, the Americans were not willing to consider the use of force. Instead, policymakers in Washington preferred a peaceful diplomatic approach. US Under Secretary of State Herbert Hoover Jr. urged Eisenhower not to consider military action as there were "grave dangers" in such a response. "While [a] strong position should be taken in order to preserve Western status in [the] Middle East", Hoover told Eisenhower on 28 July, the "confiscation of the Suez company was not sufficient reason for military intervention." Hoover added that "unless we (the United States) can introduce an element of restraint, Eden will tend to move much too rapidly and without adequate cause for armed

---

7   Richard Lamb, *The Failure of the Eden Government* (London: Sidgwick & Jackson, 1987).

8   G.C. Peden, "Suez and Britain's Decline as a World Power", *The Historical Journal* 55, no. 4 (2012), 1079, https://doi.org/10.1017/S0018246X12000246

intervention."[9] Eisenhower agreed with Hoover's assessment. "I cannot over-emphasise the strength of my conviction", Eisenhower wrote to Eden on 31 July, that all diplomatic routes must be explored "before action such as you contemplate should be undertaken."[10] Hoover and Eisenhower certainly held deep-seated concerns in Washington about Eden's temperament regarding the use of force in Suez, and needed to garner additional diplomatic support from American allies to persuade Eden not to use this course of action.

To this end, four days later Eisenhower met with Australian Prime Minister Robert Menzies and Australian Ambassador Percy Spender in Washington. Eisenhower hoped that the two Australians—both of whom had considerable experience in dealing with Eden—might assist US efforts in advising London against the use of force in the Middle East. As Eisenhower told Menzies, he "hoped that the United Kingdom and France would continue to exercise restraint." He added that London should be careful not to succumb to the "tyranny of the weak", a term he used to describe "the difficulty that arises when weak nations are in a position to challenge great powers by taking advantage of certain situations."[11]

Attempts to talk to Menzies about the repercussions of Eden's views on Egypt fell on deaf ears. Even though Australia had withdrawn from its defence commitments in the Middle East, Nasser's nationalisation of the canal prompted Menzies to pledge his support for British efforts in the region. On 30 July, Menzies suggested to the External Affairs Department that military action might be necessary in order to ensure that Nasser did not "get away with such an act of brigandage."[12] One day later, Menzies made similar comments in a meeting with British Ambassador in Washington Roger Makins and US Under Secretary of State Herbert Hoover. "I made it clear [to Makins and Hoover] that in my opinion Nasser's action was illegal", Menzies recalled, "and unless his prestige could be materially diminished, [the United States

---

9   Department of State to the Secretary of State, 28 July 1956, FRUS 1955-1957 Vol. XVI, 25.
10 Eisenhower to Eden, 31 July 1956, 31 July 1956, FRUS 1955-1957 Vol. XVI, 70.
11 Meeting between Eisenhower, Menzies and Spender, 3 August 1956, Ann Whitman File, International Series, Box 2, EL.
12 Menzies to Casey, Fadden and McBride, 29 July 1956, NAA, A1838, 163/4/7/3/3 Part 1.

and Britain] would be exposed to trouble after trouble in the Middle East."[13] Like Eden, Menzies saw developments in Egypt as an affront to British prestige and steadfastly urged the Commonwealth to defend its economic and strategic interests in the canal region. In this instance, Menzies's British "boot heels" were on clear display.

This view, however, was challenged by several policymakers in Canberra. Australian External Affairs Minister Richard Casey, Defence Minister Philip McBride and Deputy Prime Minister Arthur Fadden all urged Menzies against military action, suggesting that they all saw "substantial arguments against the use of force." If force was used, they claimed that trading vessels in the region would be in danger, the participating powers would be brought before the UN Security Council, and relations with Arab and Asian countries would be jeopardised.[14] Adding to these concerns was the complete lack of consultation between Australia and Britain especially in relation to the possibility of resorting to force. "We have had nothing from the UK about their intentions in respect of the use of force nor their appreciation of its military and political effects", Casey penned in his diary on 7 August.[15]

Although Casey, Fadden and McBride did not advocate the use of force to retain international control of the Canal, the military recommended that Canberra should support London if a decision was made to intervene. The Australian Defence Committee produced a report on 9 August that concluded that Western control of Suez was of "major importance" because Australia relied heavily on regional oil reserves and free access to the shipping route. The report also concluded that total Egyptian control of the canal would affect "the flow of reinforcements and supplies from the United Kingdom to the Far East in an emergency."[16] In this regard, Australian defence interests in the Middle East and the Asia-Pacific region became intertwined.

From a military standpoint, Australia fully supported British intervention despite its limited potential to contribute to military action. The "immediate military objective should be to seize and occupy the

---

13 Robert Menzies, *Afternoon Light* (London: Cassell, 1969), 149-150.
14 Casey, Fadden and McBride to Menzies, 1 August 1956, NAA, A4926, 14.
15 Casey Diary Entry, 7 August 1956, Casey's Diaries, 237.
16 Australian Strategic Interests in the Middle East, 9 August 1956, NAA, A5954, 1410/1.

canal", the Defence Committee report advised Menzies, even though it conceded that only a token Australian force might be available for deployment while most of its troops were stationed in Malaya. The report outlined that "if the situation was to deteriorate in Southeast Asia or the Far East, it may be necessary to bring back any Australian forces deployed in the Suez Canal area." In short, Australia was prepared to support Anglo-French military action in Suez. However, an Australian commitment to the region should "be small and limited to the navy and air force."[17]

New Zealand reached similar conclusions. Like Australia, Wellington was unable to proffer any significant number of defence forces in the event of an armed intervention (although a New Zealand warship aptly called the Royalist was stationed in the Mediterranean). Diplomatically, Wellington was fully behind any British action in the region to protect Commonwealth interests. As New Zealand Prime Minister Sidney Holland told British Foreign Minister Selwyn Lloyd on 30 July, "you may be assured that New Zealand will as always fully support any steps which the United Kingdom feels obliged to take to ensure that vital British rights are fully protected."[18] Holland's conviction that New Zealand should stand fully behind Britain was no secret. He made very similar comments in the New Zealand Parliament eight days later. "Where Britain stands, we stand; where she goes we go, in good times and bad", Holland announced on 7 August. In his estimation, that was the "mood of the New Zealand people" on the topic.[19] After Holland's speech, External Affairs Minister Thomas Macdonald made a similar speech that was particularly scathing of Egyptian action in the canal:

> The manner in which the Egyptian government has acted [...] has given Britain and other European countries no ground for comfort at all. Egypt has waged over the air against the United Kingdom a constant propaganda campaign which has at times been vicious and virulent. She has endeavoured to create trouble by turning neighbouring countries against the countries of Europe [...] Egypt gives us no reassurance at all concerning Egyptian intentions, and the unheralded and arbitrary

---

17 Defence Committee Report to Menzies, 9 August 1956, NAA, A5954, 1410/1.
18 Holland to Lloyd, 30 July 1956, Archives NZ, EA, 217/1/6 Part 1.
19 Holland Statement, 7 August 1956, New Zealand Parliamentary Debates (hereafter NZPD), 1956 Vol. 309, 885-894.

method of this latest seizure gives no promise of future harmony and can only be deplored.

For these reasons, Macdonald argued that New Zealand must stand wholeheartedly behind British action against Egypt, even with the potential use of force. "Britain has every justification for preparing to meet any eventuality", Macdonald declared. "As to mobilisation", he added, "I think it has been overlooked, and it should not be."[20] New Zealand support for the use of force, however, was not unanimous. Much as Casey, Fadden and McBride urged Menzies to renounce the use of force as a means to respond to Nasser's nationalisation, New Zealand High Commissioner in London Thomas Clifton Webb hoped Britain would not respond with military action. "Let us hope they have not committed themselves to something which [...] cannot be carried out", Webb wrote to Macdonald on 31 July, "either because of lack of support from [the] USA [...] or even from their own public here."[21]

While Britain and France contemplated the use of force in Egypt, an international conference was held in London during mid-August in the hope that a diplomatic solution might be found to return the canal to international control. Before the conference, Menzies made a television address to the British public on 13 August to outline his views toward the developing crisis. Menzies, in no uncertain terms, placed the blame for the crisis squarely on Nasser. "Nasser's actions in respect of the Suez Canal Company have created a crisis more grave [sic] than any since the Second World War", Menzies concluded. Menzies did not trust Nasser at all and was convinced that it would be "suicidal" to leave the Commonwealth's vital trading interests in Suez solely in his hands. Moreover, he stressed that Nasser's nationalisation of the canal was illegal under international law and would encourage further aggression if left unchecked. By nationalising the canal and rejecting the 1954 Anglo-Egyptian Treaty, Menzies argued that "Nasser violated the first principle of international law" and this grievance "will encourage other acts of lawlessness if not resisted."[22]

---

20 Macdonald Statement, 7 August 1956, NZPD 1956 Vol. 309, 904-908.
21 Webb to Macdonald, 31 July 1956, Archives NZ, EA, 217/1/6 Part 1.
22 Menzies Statement, 13 August 1956, Menzies Papers, Box 423, NLA.

At the conference, Menzies maintained that his country was unprepared to accept anything less than a return to international control of the Suez Canal. "Australia has a great interest in freedom of transit" in Suez, Menzies said in a speech in London. According to Menzies, the "essential factor" was the establishment of an efficient administrative body in the canal so that all nations could benefit from its free operation.[23] New Zealand External Affairs Minister Thomas Macdonald made a similar statement in London. The organisation of the Suez Canal, Macdonald argued, "must, in our view, be on an international basis [...] it should be able to assure free transit of the Canal, it should be efficient, and it should not be subject to financial instability."[24] In other words, both Australian and New Zealand representatives in London thought that international management of the canal was essential.

Even though Menzies announced that his government completely supported British action in Egypt, Australian External Affairs Minister Casey continued to urge him to renounce the use of force as an appropriate solution. "I recommended to Menzies that he should speak against the use of force to Anthony Eden, [as] it would put us completely in the wrong with public opinion in practically every part of the world", Casey penned in his diary on 17 August. He added that "I recommended that he should seek to get an appreciation from the UK of the military side, of which we were entirely in the dark. I failed to see what could be achieved by action of this sort."[25]

Casey's New Zealand counterpart, Thomas Macdonald, was suspicious that Australia and New Zealand were purposefully "left in the dark" at the conference in order to prepare for Anglo-French military action. Suspecting a secret invasion plot, Macdonald now thought that military action would be disastrous for Britain and Western interests in the region. Writing to the New Zealand Prime Minister on 23 August, Macdonald advised against supporting British military action. He suggested that the entire conference was designed to prepare an unacceptable proposal to offer to Nasser, which he would reject, in order to make the use of force appear more reasonable. This, in Macdonald's

---

23 Menzies Statement at Suez Conference in London, 18 August 1956, NAA, A1838, 163/4/7/3/3 Part 4.
24 Macdonald Statement, 17 August 1956, NZFP: SD, 444-448.
25 Casey Diary Entry, 17 August 1956, NAA, M1153, 38.

view, was "one of the main reasons for the conference."[26] Macdonald's suspicions proved to be correct. Eden had planned to take back the canal regardless of the outcome of negotiations. As one British Foreign Service Officer Anthony Nutting recalled later about the crisis, "Eden hoped that the conference would produce a solution unacceptable to Nasser."[27] In other words, the outcome of the Suez Conference was destined to fail. Eden had already authorised that French troops were to be stationed in Cyprus and asked British subjects to leave the Middle East area on 29 August, days before any diplomatic approach was made to Nasser.

Nonetheless a committee was appointed in London, comprised of representatives from Australia, Ethiopia, Iran, Sweden and the United States, in order to present a number of proposals to Nasser that were agreed upon by eighteen of the twenty-two participating powers at the conference. These proposals revolved around returning the canal to international control. On strong insistence from Dulles and Eden, Prime Minister Menzies agreed to lead this committee and present the agreed proposals to Nasser. Menzies surely felt it as a compliment that he might play an instrumental role in resolving a complex international situation. Unaware of Eden's actual plans, Menzies was especially enthusiastic about leading the committee because he was concerned that the outbreak of war in Egypt was "an even money chance." There was a "very distinct prospect", Menzies feared, that Britain and France would use military force should a diplomatic solution not be reached.[28]

Menzies and the Suez Committee met with Nasser in Cairo on 3 and 4 September to present the agreements reached in London. While making clear that there was "no spirit of hostility" about the agreements being proposed, Menzies emphasised to Nasser that the use of force was a realistic possibility should he choose to reject the proposals. As he warned Nasser, it would be "a mistake for you to exclude the possible use of force from your reckoning." Nasser, however, did not budge in the face of this possibility. "President Nasser took our proposals apart, tore them up, and metaphorically consigned them to the wastepaper basket",

---

26 Macdonald to Holland, 23 August 1956, NAA, A5462, 118/2/4 Part 2.
27 Anthony Nutting, *No End of a Lesson: The Story of Suez* (London: Constable, 1967), 53.
28 Menzies to Fadden, 22 August 1956, NAA, A4926, 13; Menzies Memorandum, 25 August 1956, Menzies Papers, Box 423, NLA.

Menzies recalled. Nasser then rejected the proposals formally on 9 September, claiming that they were a form of "collective colonialism."[29]

Menzies returned to Australia disappointed and frustrated by Nasser's stubbornness. Fending off media criticism that he had failed in his efforts to convince Nasser to agree to the committee's proposals, he stressed that Nasser was uncooperative and entirely to blame for the crisis. "This repudiation by the President of Egypt was committed without notice, without consent, and in fact, by force", Menzies said at a press conference in Sydney on 18 September, "those things are worth remembering." "It is quite true that I was appointed as chief spokesman for presenting these matters to the President of Egypt", Menzies added, but "I don't think anyone could challenge the fairness or indeed the generosity of one item in the proposals." He also rejected Nasser's claim that the Suez Committee's proposals were a form of collective colonialism. "I hope it will be remembered that under the proposals put forward Egypt's position as landlord was recognised completely", Menzies argued, stressing that "Egypt was to be the only nation deriving any profit from the Canal at all."[30]

Since it paved the way for military action, Eden was surely pleased by Nasser's rejection of the committee's proposals. Eden, however, placed the committee's failure squarely on Eisenhower, who during the conference told the media that he hoped for a peaceful solution to the crisis while the British were threatening Nasser with the use of force. This, in London's view, completely undermined their negotiating position with Egypt. "We must [...] show that Nasser is not going to get his way", Eden urged in a letter to Eisenhower on 6 September.[31] Meanwhile, Eisenhower continued to stress publicly that he would not use force in order to find a resolution to the crisis. "This country will not got go war ever while I am occupying my present post unless the Congress declares such a war", Eisenhower said at a press conference on 11 September. Dulles made similar remarks in a press conference the next day, suggesting that even if the United States had a right to

---

29 Menzies, *Afternoon Light*, 168. See also Menzies Memorandum, 4 September 1956, Menzies Papers, Box 423, NLA.
30 Menzies Statement, 18 September 1956, Menzies Papers, Box 423, NLA.
31 Eden to Eisenhower, 6 September 1956, in *Eden-Eisenhower Correspondence*, 164-167.

intervene militarily "we (the United States) did not intend to shoot our way through."[32]

Many policymakers in New Zealand, who continued to be very supportive of the British during negotiations over Suez, similarly placed blame on Eisenhower and the Americans for doing little to support British diplomatic efforts. As New Zealand External Affairs Secretary Alister McIntosh told his former Deputy Foss Shanahan on 24 August,

> How infuriating the British must find the Americans over Suez […] when it comes to ostriches I am sure that bigger birds never stuck their heads into a bigger expanse of sand than Dulles is now doing in the undignified spectacle they present near the Pyramids.[33]

In reality, there were no major differences with respect to US and British views about the threat Nasser posed. Anglo-American tensions were rather a result of differences about how they should respond to this threat. As Eisenhower described in a letter to Eden on 8 September, the United States and Britain had a "grave problem confronting Nasser's reckless adventure with the Canal" and did not differ in their "estimates of his intentions and purposes." The main point of Anglo-American disagreement, according to Eisenhower, was resorting to force and "the probable effects in the Arab world of the various possible reactions by the Western world." The possibility of a Western military response clearly concerned Eisenhower, which in his estimation would be a disaster and hurt US prestige in the Arab world. According to Eisenhower resorting to war "when the world believes there are other means available for resolving the dispute would set in motion forces that could lead, in the years to come, to the most distressing results."[34]

Eisenhower and Dulles were especially fearful that after the failed Menzies mission, Eden was even more likely to pursue military options in Egypt. On 6 September, Dulles held a Congressional meeting with Senators Hubert Humphrey, Mike Mansfield and William Langer to brief them on the Suez situation and gather bipartisan approval for renouncing the use of force in Egypt. Dulles warned that the British and the French thought that it was necessary to "begin military operations to

---

32 Dulles Press Statement, 12 September 1956, in Watry, Diplomacy at the Brink, 126.
33 McIntosh to Shanahan, 24 August 1956, in *Unofficial Channels*, 208.
34 Eisenhower to Eden, 8 September 1956, FRUS 1955-1957 Vol. XVI, 431-33.

curb Nasser." "The British feel that if Nasser gets away with it", Dulles said, "it will start a chain of events in the Near East that will reduce the UK to another Netherlands or Portugal in a very few years." Dulles told the Senators that he and Eisenhower were doing everything in their power to "strongly discourage" the use of force, as they felt it would be "disastrous for the French and the UK militarily to intervene at this point."[35] There were no criticisms or partisanship injected during the meeting. All three Senators agreed with Dulles's efforts to prevent the use of force in Egypt.

Meanwhile, Eisenhower sent several letters directly to Eden in the hope he might convince him to reconsider military action. Eden was, however, unconvinced by Eisenhower's reasoning. Instead, Eden argued that anything other than the use of force would be appeasement, a policy that could lead to catastrophic results. "There is no doubt in our minds that Nasser, whether he likes it or not, is now effectively in Russian hands, just as Mussolini was in Hitler's", Eden said to Eisenhower. He argued that "it would be as ineffective to show weakness to Nasser now in order to placate him as it was to show weakness to Mussolini [...] that is why we must do everything we can."[36] Seemingly out of touch with British thinking on the matter, Dulles also turned to Australia to express his concerns. "I am beginning to feel concerned", Dulles wrote to Menzies and Casey on 27 October, "I am not myself in close touch with recent British-French thinking but in view of [the] leading role Australia has played, I feel it appropriate to express my concern."[37]

Israel Invades Egypt

Eisenhower's and Dulles's messages to London and Canberra could not prevent the escalation of the crisis in the Suez Canal. Despite American efforts, Eden remained inclined to use military action to topple Nasser and re-internationalise the Suez Canal. Tensions in Suez reached a

---

35 Meeting between Dulles, Humphrey, Mansfield and Langer, 6 September 1956, John Foster Dulles Papers, Subject Series, Box 7, EL; Conversation between Eisenhower and Dulles, 7 September 1956, John Foster Dulles Papers, Subject Series, Box 7, EL.

36 Eden to Eisenhower, 1 October 1956, Ann Whitman File, International Series, Box 6, EL.

37 Dulles to Menzies and Casey, 27 October 1956, NARA, RG 59, 974.7301/10-2756.

climax on 29 October when Israeli forces, in collusion with Britain and France, invaded the Sinai Peninsula. None of the ANZUS powers, nor other Commonwealth countries, were informed beforehand of this secret Anglo-French plan. "For a long time the Middle East has been simmering", Eden said in a message to all Commonwealth Prime Ministers a day later, "now it is boiling over."[38] In the message, Eden detailed plans for an Anglo-French response, omitting entirely that London and Paris secretly supported the Israeli invasion in the first place. He explained that unless the Israelis and Egyptians withdrew within twelve hours, Anglo-French forces would seize the canal and overthrow Nasser. Nasser predictably rejected the ultimatum, which ultimately led to an Anglo-French invasion of Egypt on 5 November.

Figure 18. British Naval Carriers during the 1956 Suez Crisis. Photo by British Royal Navy official photographer (1956), Wikimedia, https://commons.wikimedia.org/wiki/File:British_carriers_during_Suez_Crisis_1956.jpg, public domain.

In Washington, the Eisenhower Administration was shocked and angered by Anglo-French action without American consultation. "I think the British made a bad error", Eisenhower told Senator William Knowland on 31 October, "I think it is the biggest error of our time." In a meeting with Dulles, Eisenhower said he was "astonished" that Eden avoided informing Washington of its decision. "They are our friends and allies [Britain and France]", Eisenhower said, "and suddenly they put us in a hole and expect us to rescue them."[39] At an NSC meeting on

---

38   Eden to Commonwealth Prime Ministers, 30 October 1956, Archives NZ, EA, 217/1/12 Part 1.

39   Eisenhower to Knowland, 30 October 1956, Ann Whitman File, DDE Diary Series, Box 18, EL; Eisenhower to Dulles, 30 October 1956, Ann Whitman File, DDE Diary

1 November, Eisenhower and Dulles argued that the United States must do all it could to push for a peaceful resolution by exerting the greatest possible pressure on Britain and France. "Recent events are close to marking a death knell for Britain and France", Dulles described, and the United States had to decide whether it would side with its oldest allies or the Arab world. Eisenhower made his choice clear: in his eyes, the action Eden had taken was "nothing short of disastrous." "How could we possibly support Britain and France if in so doing we lose the whole Arab world", Eisenhower asked rhetorically.[40]

In discussing the international reaction, Dulles specified that there was so far very little support for British-French action in Egypt. He stressed that the "verdict of the rest of the world [was] altogether unanimous" in its opposition to the use of force in Egypt. There were, however, two exceptions to this opposition to British-French action: as Secretary Dulles told the NSC, approval for the attacks had only come from Australia and New Zealand. However, as explained, there were extenuating factors in their cases. In Australia there was "much unhappiness" amongst the public about British action. Moreover, at the political level, Director of the Central Intelligence Agency Allen Dulles (John Foster Dulles's younger brother) suggested that there was "a wide split of opinion between Menzies and Casey." In New Zealand's case, John Foster Dulles simply suggested that "it was virtually a colony and almost invariably followed the lead of the United Kingdom."[41]

Meanwhile, angered by Eden's betrayal, Eisenhower wrote to the British Prime Minister to express his concern about the Anglo-French ultimatum. "I feel I must urgently express to you my deep concern at the prospect of this drastic action", he wrote, "even at the very time when the matter is under consideration in the United Nations Security Council."[42] Privately, Eisenhower followed the decisions reached at the NSC meeting on 1 November and put severe economic and military pressure on the British, hoping this would sway London to agree to a UN ceasefire and withdraw from the Canal area. The US Sixth Fleet harassed

---

Series, Box 18, EL.
40   NSC Meeting, 1 November 1956, Ann Whitman File, NSC Series, Box 8, EL.
41   Ibid.
42   Eisenhower to Eden, 30 October 1956, FRUS 1955-1957 Vol. XVI, 866.

the Anglo-French invasion fleet in the Mediterranean and delayed its arrival into Egypt, while in Washington, Eisenhower approved a series of economic sanctions against Britain to compel the British to withdraw.

Eisenhower likewise put diplomatic pressure on Britain and France through the introduction of a UN ceasefire resolution. After consultation with Dulles and the NSC, Eisenhower argued that the United States must present a ceasefire resolution to the United Nations as soon as possible. In his estimation, the United States must lead this ceasefire resolution before the Soviet Union presented its own resolution in order to prevent Moscow from "seizing a mantle of world leadership through a false but convincing exhibition of concern for smaller nations." Overall, in an effort not to embarrass the British and French by specifically naming them, US action in the UN aimed to avoid "singling out or condemning any one nation, but should serve to emphasise to the world our hope for a quick ceasefire."[43] An emergency United Nations session was then called on 1 November. Dulles introduced a ceasefire resolution that passed by a margin of 64-5. Along with Britain, France and Israel, Australia and New Zealand were the only other countries to oppose the resolution.

As Dulles predicted, then, Australia and New Zealand both publicly supported British action in the Suez Canal. While disturbed by conflict in the Middle East, New Zealand Prime Minister Holland believed that the British response protected Commonwealth interests and was necessary to preserve Britain's vital interests in the region. "We are naturally gravely concerned", Holland wrote to the New Zealand High Commission in London, yet he added that "there is no need for me to stress New Zealand's ties of blood and empire and our traditional attitude of standing by Britain in her difficulties. He added that "I can assure you of our deepest sympathy for the United Kingdom in the situation now confronting her. It is our desire, as always, to be of the most utmost assistance." Holland also shared these thoughts to the New Zealand public. In a statement on 1 November, Holland announced that "I have the full confidence in the United Kingdom's intentions in

---

43   Eisenhower Memorandum, 1 November 1956, Ann Whitman File, DDE Diary Series, Box 18, EL.

moving forces into the Canal area" and declared New Zealand would do all it could to assist Eden and the Britons in their hour of need.[44]

In Canberra, Menzies pledged similar public support for British action. Writing to Dulles, he stated that his government supported Anglo-French action. "Quite frankly I do not believe that it would be in the interests of any of us to have [the] Canal closed for weeks and possibly months", Menzies said; "from this point of view my colleagues and I see considerable merit in police action which is involved in the Anglo-French ultimatum."[45] He made a similar statement to the Australian public on 3 November, stressing his opinion that Anglo-French action was necessary. "The action taken by the United Kingdom and France was the only quick and practical means of separating the belligerents and protecting the Canal", Menzies announced. He also argued that it was "wrong and absurd" to consider Nasser, the "author of the Canal confiscation and promoter of anti-British activities in the Middle East", as an "innocent victim of unprovoked aggression."[46] Put another way, Menzies clearly thought that Nasser's actions had caused military action against Egypt and on some level Nasser deserved it.

Privately, however, policymakers in the Tasman countries expressed grave concerns about British action. Canberra and Wellington were also concerned that pledging public support for Britain compromised their security relationship with the United States. New Zealand reports from Washington confirmed these concerns shortly after the Israeli invasion on 29 October. As the crisis escalated, New Zealand Ambassador in Washington Leslie Munro met with US Assistant Secretary of State for Near Eastern Affairs William Rountree in Washington to discuss the American reaction to the crisis. He reported to Wellington on 31 October that the situation was of the "utmost gravity, both from [the] point of view of [an] Anglo-American breach and in terms of general security in the Middle East." Munro warned that the situation could develop to a point where the Western position in the Middle East

---

44 Holland to the NZ High Commission in London, 1 November 1956, Archives NZ, EA, 217/1/12 Part 1; Holland Statement, 1 November 1956, NZFP: SD, 452.
45 Menzies to Dulles, 1 November 1956, 1 November 1956, NAA, A1838, S170 Part 5.
46 Menzies Statement, 3 November 1956, Menzies Papers, Box 423, NLA.

became "irretrievable."⁴⁷ In a subsequent cablegram to Prime Minister Holland later that day, Munro stressed that Anglo-French action "put New Zealand in a difficult position vis-à-vis its ANZUS partner, the United States, and confronts us with a critical choice between British and American policies in the Middle East."⁴⁸

Australia was caught in a similarly difficult position. In Canberra, Menzies stressed that a rift in Anglo-American relations was deeply concerning to Australia. "I have myself urged upon both British and American leaders that consultations should speedily occur to reconcile any differences of opinion", Menzies said to the House of Representatives on 1 November. He added that "it is a great misfortune that there have been public differences between those great democracies whose friendly cooperation is so vital to us all." Nonetheless, despite this rift in Anglo-American relations, Menzies remained supportive of British action. Menzies echoed this belief in an address to Parliament on 3 November, stating that Anglo-French action was "the only quick and practical means of separating the belligerents and protecting the Canal."⁴⁹ He then wrote to Eden, reassuring the British Prime Minister that he had Australia's full support:

> You have indeed had a difficult decision to take but I am sure that you are right. Under these circumstances, an abandonment of operations by [Britain] and France would have left the Canal unprotected, would have given fresh heart to Egypt and would have meant a lot of destructive fighting around and over the Canal itself [...] our support remains undiminished and that we think that you were and are right. It is tragic at a time like this you should have to encounter such intemperate and stupid attack.⁵⁰

It is indeed telling that, even without any consultation from London, Australia chose to place its support behind British action. As far as Canberra was concerned, Britain's vital interests came before any

---

47   Munro to NZ Department of External Affairs, 31 October 1956, Archives NZ, EA, 217/1/12 Part 1.

48   Munro to Holland, 31 October 1956, Archives NZ, EA, 217/1/12 Part 1.

49   Menzies Address to the House of Representatives, 1 November 1956, NAA, A2908, S170 Part 5; Menzies Statement, 3 November 1956, 1 November 1956, NAA, A1838, S170 Part 5.

50   Menzies to Holland, 6 November 1956, NAA, A1838, S170 Part 5.

possible diplomatic backlash in Washington. "I believe that Anglo-French action was correct", Menzies later told Eisenhower, "in Australia I believe that approval of the British action is widespread."[51]

Even then, choosing sides between the United States and Britain was quite difficult for Australian policymakers. Casey, fearing the effect this crisis would have on Australian-American relations, did not stand completely beside Menzies in his support for British action. For Casey, it was greatly concerning that a rift in Anglo-American relations was so publicly exposed. During discussions for a ceasefire in the United Nations, Casey reported to Menzies that "I was greatly distressed by [the] atmosphere at [the] United Nations." He added that "the almost physical cleavage between United Kingdom and United States was one of the most distressing things I had [sic] ever experienced."[52]

Casey was not alone. Many Australian and New Zealand diplomats were privately concerned by an Anglo-American rift over Suez because it put Canberra and Wellington in a very difficult position between its two most important allies. To this end, Australian and New Zealand diplomats agreed that they faced the same dire situation. Writing about a meeting he had with New Zealand High Commissioner in London Clifton Webb as well as other British Ministers on 2 November, Casey recalled that:

> There is a great deal of doubt, to put it mildly, in most people's minds, about the wisdom of the enterprise on which the UK has launched. The fact is that I have met no-one (apart from senior Ministers) amongst the many friends with whom I have been in contact, who are in favour of it, and many of them are genuinely and greatly distressed. Their fears are not on account of the outcome of the military operation, but for the effect on the position and prestige of Britain and as to whether the operation will not have a longstanding effect the reverse of what is intended.[53]

In Wellington, the New Zealand External Affairs Department expressed deep concern about London's decision to intervene. In a letter to Foss Shanahan, External Affairs Secretary Alister McIntosh compared the

---

51 Menzies to Eisenhower, 20 November 1956, DDE Diary Papers, International Series, Box 2, EL.

52 Casey to Menzies, 22 November 1956, NAA, A1838, S170 Part 5.

53 Casey Diary Entry, 2 November 1956, NAA, M1153, 49D.

Suez Crisis to the outbreak of the Second World War. "The last few days have been all too reminiscent of 1939", McIntosh told Shanahan; "we in the Department have been horrified at the implications of British action, but Cabinet as a whole and the Prime Minister have been thoroughly in favour of backing the United Kingdom."[54]

McIntosh was particularly alarmed by British action. Writing to New Zealand's Deputy High Commissioner in London Frank Corner, McIntosh described Eden's decision to intervene in the Suez area as "criminal." "In my view", McIntosh concluded, "he [Eden] ought to be impeached." He was particularly concerned that the crisis had developed so suddenly and without any consultation with Wellington. In another letter to Corner, McIntosh wrote that "one of the features about this Middle East Crisis that has shaken me most is not only the lack of consultation between the United Kingdom and the Dominions but also the slackening flow of information as the crisis has proceeded." Corner agreed with McIntosh's grim assessment of the deteriorating situation and criticised the lack of information that came from London, suggesting that Eden must be quite mad. "It is said that the Arabs have enormous respect for madmen", Corner said memorably, "because Allah is supposed to reveal himself through them. If only the doctors would confirm the diagnosis of Whitehall and certify Eden."[55] Corner's comments were particularly intriguing because rumours about Eden's health and its impact on his decision-making had been circulating for quite some time. Many historical studies have also raised this concern in analyses of British policy during the Suez Crisis.[56]

In the end, enormous diplomatic, economic and military pressure eventually forced Britain and France to agree to another UN ceasefire and an emergency peacekeeping operation on 6 November, enabling an Anglo-French withdraw from the canal. London and Paris had nothing to show for all their efforts in Suez except failure and

---

54 McIntosh to Shanahan, 8 November 1956, in *Unofficial Channels*, 209.
55 Corner to McIntosh, 23 November 1956, in *Unofficial Channels*, 212-215.
56 See, for example, The Rt Hon Lord Owen CH, "The Effect of Prime Minister Anthony Eden's Illness on his Decision-making During the Suez Crisis", *QJM: An International Journal of Medicine* 98, No. 6 (2005), 387–402, https://doi.org/10.1093/qjmed/hci071; Eamon Hamilton, Sir Anthony Eden and the Suez Crisis of 1956: The Anatomy of a Flawed Personality, MA Thesis, University of Birmingham, 2015.

embarrassment. As the US Embassy in Cairo reported to Washington, the British and French "gained nothing except loss of prestige and increased hatred of Arabs."[57] Shouldering the brunt of the blame and embarrassment for the crisis—as well as struggling with several health issues—Eden resigned as Prime Minister on 9 January 1957. For all the shock and surprise surrounding events in Suez, his resignation was predicted. "Eden has had a physical breakdown and will have to go on vacation immediately [...] this will lead to his retirement", the US Embassy in London cabled Washington on 19 November. His replacement, Harold Macmillan, quickly asked the United States to provide a "fig leaf to cover our nakedness" in early January so that British troops could finally withdraw from Egypt.[58] As Anglo-French forces withdrew, even those in Australia and New Zealand who wholeheartedly supported British policy recognised that the crisis signalled the end of Britain's claim to major power status. As New Zealand External Affairs Officer Frank Corner told Secretary Alister McIntosh "the centre of effective power and decision has, I think, passed away from London. Washington and New York are likely to be the most interesting places from now on."[59]

Since the invasion of the Sinai Peninsula failed due to American diplomatic, economic and military pressure, the end of the 1956 Suez Crisis publicly exposed a bitter rift in Anglo-American relations and essentially confirmed the end of British world leadership. It also exposed noticeable differences between Australia, New Zealand and the United States over the control of the Suez Canal, defence policy in the region, and Britain's role in world affairs. While each of the ANZUS powers had defence interests in the Middle East, both the Australian and New Zealand prime ministers declared their support for British action during the 1956 Suez Crisis despite strong private reservations in their respective Cabinets and External Affairs Ministries. The United States, in contrast, bitterly opposed British action and forced their withdrawal from Egypt.

---

57 US Embassy in Cairo to the Department of State, 10 November 1956, Dulles-Herter Series, Box 8, EL.

58 US Ambassador in London to Eisenhower and Dulles 19 November 1956, Ann Whitman File, DDE Diary Series, Box 18, EL.

59 Corner to McIntosh, 10 November 1956, in *Unofficial Channels*, 210.

Defence interests in the Middle East and responses to the Suez Crisis demonstrated clear policy differences between the ANZUS powers that stemmed from trans-Tasman British ties and views surrounding US leadership. It also demonstrated a critical point in alliance diplomacy for both Canberra and Wellington. During the Suez Crisis, Australia and New Zealand held similar views and were not prepared to defer to US leadership when vital British interests were at stake. In short, five years after the conclusion of ANZUS, Australia and New Zealand were still prepared to pledge support for vital British interests instead of aligning all strategic policies with their chief protector, the United States. For Canberra and Wellington, Suez starkly exposed the limitations of British power when London's views were at odds with those in Washington.

Conclusion

The eleven years between the end of World War II and the end of the Suez Crisis wrought many changes in how Australia, New Zealand and the United States worked with one another in response to issues of mutual concern. After their wartime alliance during World War II, these countries shared common interests in defending themselves against Communist expansion, preventing a revival of Japanese aggression and broadly preserving the peace and security of the Asia-Pacific region. In practice, however, the ANZUS countries struggled to act in a united fashion during the early years of the Cold War.

For Australia, the alliance provided formal protection and was viewed as a necessary security measure to offset Britain's inability to meet Australian defence requirements. Policymakers in Canberra also hoped ANZUS would be a gateway to access information on US global strategic planning and influence world affairs. Across the Tasman, New Zealand also accepted that their country must rely on US protection but policymakers in Wellington wanted a less formal arrangement. A non-binding agreement with the United States, in short, was less likely to jeopardise New Zealand's relationship with Britain; a critical issue for policymakers in Wellington. For the United States, the conclusion of ANZUS was a trade-off to ensure Australian and New Zealand acquiescence to the Japanese Peace Treaty. It also served as further support for the American position in Northeast Asia.

After Eisenhower entered the White House, the alliance began to evolve into a more complex and meaningful relationship, despite continued strategic disagreement. The alliance became especially important once a series of crises broke out in the Asia-Pacific and Middle East regions, such as those in Indochina, the Taiwan Straits, and the Suez Canal. Each response by Australia, New Zealand and the US provides interesting insights into the contrasting views of the ANZUS powers as well as their differing ideas about Britain's post-war role in world affairs. The United States saw no major role for Britain without American cooperation, whereas Australia and New Zealand tended to favour the British position in these conflicts and erroneously thought that Britain was still capable of wielding enough influence to act without American support (particularly during the Suez Crisis). By 1956, events in Egypt ultimately demonstrated a critical point in alliance diplomacy in Canberra and Wellington: Australia and New Zealand were still prepared to pledge support for vital British interests instead of aligning all strategic policies with their chief protector, the United States.

As with any alliance, the extent to which a treaty such as ANZUS comes into fruition and works in practice often depends on the impact of individuals. Regardless of whether their impact was ultimately positive or negative, many diplomats played a critical role in the development of the ANZUS relationship. For instance, Australian External Affairs Minister Herbert Evatt loomed as a large yet divisive figure in trilateral relations during the late 1940s. Evatt caused more problems than he solved in regard to managing Australia's relationships with New Zealand and the United States, especially when it came to his abrasive and non-consultative diplomatic style about matters relating to the Japanese occupation and the post-war control of the Pacific islands. Percy Spender, Evatt's replacement as External Affairs Minister, then led the way in arguing for the conclusion of a mutual defence arrangement, despite pushback from his pro-British Prime Minister, Robert Menzies. Once Spender moved on to serve as Australian Ambassador in Washington, he and his replacement as External Affairs Minister, Richard Casey, charted a more active role for Australia during consultations with their US, New Zealand and British counterparts during the international crises of the 1950s.

Across the Tasman, Alister McIntosh—Head of the joint New Zealand Prime Minister's and External Affairs Departments—was instrumental in shaping New Zealand's post-war foreign policy with Commonwealth countries such as Australia and Britain, at the same time as steering a slow but noticeable movement toward establishing closer relations with the United States. In this endeavour, McIntosh was supported by other key New Zealand diplomats such as Carl Berendsen, Walter Nash, and Frank Corner, all of whom provided unique insights into their frequent distaste for Australian diplomats and their respective foreign policy agendas, the usefulness of ANZUS, and a continued affinity toward creating international policies through the lens of the British Commonwealth.

More well-known figures also played key roles, but not always to the benefit of establishing a closer trilateral relationship. John Foster Dulles, who served as chief US negotiator for the ANZUS Treaty in 1951, had a somewhat chequered record of dealing with the British Dominions. While he successfully negotiated an ANZUS Treaty draft that was acceptable for US plans in Japan and the wider region, he was unable to secure the inclusion of the Philippines to avoid negative perceptions of a "White Man's Club" in Asia. Then, during his term as Secretary of State in the Eisenhower Administration, he consulted frequently with the Australians and New Zealanders to garner multilateral support for US policy vis-à-vis Indochina, the Taiwan Straits and Suez. Despite his wealth of experience in international affairs, Dulles was largely unsuccessful in securing trans-Tasman support in the face of contrasting British and American views on the most appropriate course of action.

In an episode that epitomised the challenge Dulles faced in securing Australian and New Zealand support for US policies, Robert Menzies and his New Zealand counterpart Sidney Holland severely strained their countries' relations with the US when they both publicly declared support for British efforts in Suez despite widespread international condemnation (as well as private criticism from inside their respective Cabinets and External Affairs Departments). A mention must also go to British Prime Minister Anthony Eden, whose push for the use of force in Suez made him a chief instigator of frosty Anglo-American relations, and by extension, Australian-New Zealand-American-British relations.

The early Cold War period was certainly one of great change and consequence for the future of relations between Australia, New Zealand and the United States. For instance, Australia and New Zealand began to agree more consistently over defence and foreign policies in their region, highlighted by their joint participation in the Vietnam War during the 1960s and 1970s despite British non-participation. Later, after New Zealand formally adopted a nuclear-free policy in response to protestations over harbouring American nuclear vessels during the mid-1980s, the United States suspended its security guarantee to New

Zealand in 1985. There were complicated reasons for this suspension, yet it was perhaps fitting that New Zealand, the country that often questioned its close relationship with the United States during the early Cold War, was later suspended from the treaty that neither country had initially wanted. Meanwhile Australia, the country that had been most eager to conclude a security arrangement in the first place, became the first signatory to formally invoke ANZUS in the aftermath of the terrorist attacks on the World Trade Center in New York on 11 September 2001. Taking future developments into account, major strategic and diplomatic issues between Australia, New Zealand and the United States throughout the following decades can certainly be traced to the post-war period. The early ANZUS Alliance, in short, had a decisive impact on the future of the relationship between these countries and their interactions with the wider world.

Bibliography

Primary Sources

ARCHIVAL COLLECTIONS

Archives New Zealand, Wellington, http://archives.govt.nz/

Dwight D. Eisenhower Presidential Library, Abilene KS, https://www.eisenhower.archives.gov/

Harry S. Truman Presidential Library, Independence MO, https://www.trumanlibrary.org/

National Archives of Australia, Canberra, http://www.naa.gov.au/about-us/organisation/locations/canberra.aspx

National Library of Australia, Canberra, https://www.nla.gov.au/

US National Archives and Records Administration, Washington DC and College Park, MD, https://www.archives.gov/

MANUSCRIPTS AND PAPER COLLECTIONS

John Foster Dulles Papers, Dwight D. Eisenhower Presidential Library, Abilene KS.

Percy Spender Papers, National Library of Australia, Canberra.

Richard Gardiner Casey Papers, National Archives of Australia, Melbourne.

Robert G. Menzies Papers, National Library of Australia, Canberra.

PUBLISHED COLLECTIONS

Australian Department of Foreign Affairs. *Current Notes on International Affairs.* (Canberra: Department of Foreign Affairs, 1936-1972).

Australian House of Representatives Debates, https://www.aph.gov.au/Parliamentary_Business/Hansard/Hansreps_2011

Department of Internal Affairs. *Document on New Zealand's External Relations* (Wellington: Historical Publications Branch, 1972).

Foreign Relations of the United States Series, https://uwdc.library.wisc.edu/collections/frus/

New Zealand Parliamentary Debates, https://www.parliament.nz/en/pb/hansard-debates/historical-hansard/

NEWSPAPERS AND MAGAZINES

Daily Advertiser

Evening Post

Foreign Affairs

Newcastle Morning Herald

Sunday Times

The Advertiser

The Canberra Times

The Courier Mail

The Melbourne Herald

The Mercury

The New York Times

Time Magazine

PUBLISHED PAPERS, STATEMENTS AND CORRESPONDENCE

Boyle, Peter ed. *The Eden-Eisenhower Correspondence, 1955-1957* (Chapel Hill: University of North Carolina Press, 2005).

Doran, Stuart, and David Lee eds. *Documents on Australian Foreign Policy: Australia and Recognition of the People's Republic of China, 1949-1972* (Canberra: Department of Foreign Affairs and Trade, 2002).

Ferrell, Robert ed. *Off the Record: The Private Papers of Harry S. Truman* (New York: Harper & Row, 1980).

Holdich, Roger, Vivianne Johnson, and Pamela Andree eds. *Documents on Australian Foreign Policy: The ANZUS Treaty, 1951* (Canberra: Department of Foreign Affairs and Trade, 2001).

Hudson, W. J., and Wendy Way eds. *Documents on Australian Foreign Policy, 1947-1949 Volume XII 1947* (Canberra: Australian Government Publishing Service, 1995).

Lowe, David, and Daniel Oakman eds. *Documents on Australian Foreign Policy: Australia and the Colombo Plan, 1949-1957* (Canberra: Department of Foreign Affairs and Trade, 2004).

McGibbon, Ian ed. *Unofficial Channels: Letters Between Alister McIntosh and Foss Shanahan, George Laking and Frank Corner, 1946-1966* (Wellington: Victoria University Press, 1999).

—. *Undiplomatic Dialogue: Letters Between Carl Berendsen and Alister McIntosh, 1943-1952* (Auckland: Auckland University Press, 1993).

Millar, T.B. ed. *Australian Foreign Minister: The Diaries of R.G. Casey, 1951-1960* (London: Collins, 1972).

Mills, Walter ed. *The Forrestal Diaries* (New York: The Viking Press, 1951).

Neale, Robert ed. *Documents on Australian Foreign Policy: Vol. XV Indonesia and the Transfer of Sovereignty* (Canberra: Australian Government Publishing Service, 1998).

Reynolds, Wayne, and David Lee eds. *Documents on Australian Foreign Policy: Australia and the Nuclear Non-Proliferation Treaty, 1945-1974* (Canberra: Australian Department of Foreign Affairs and Trade, 2013), https://dfat.gov.au/about-us/publications/historical-documents/Documents/australia-and-the-nuclear-non-proliferation-treaty.pdf

Shearer, A.R. ed. *New Zealand Foreign Policy: Statements and Documents, 1943-1957* (Wellington: New Zealand Ministry of Foreign Affairs, 1972).

MEMOIRS, BOOKS AND ARTICLES

Acheson, Dean. *Present at the Creation: My Years in the State Department* (New York: W.W. Norton & Co., 1987).

Allison, John. *Ambassador from the Prairie or Allison Wonderland* (Boston: Houghton Miffin, 1973).

Casey, Richard. *Friends and Neighbours: Australia and the World* (Melbourne: F.W. Cheshire, 1954).

Eisenhower, Dwight. *Mandate for Change, 1953-1956* (New York: Doubleday & Co., 1963).

—. *Waging Peace 1956-1961* (New York: Doubleday & Co., 1965).

Kennan, George. *Memoirs, 1925-1950* (New York: Bantam Books, 1967).

Larson, Arthur. *Eisenhower: The President Nobody Knew* (London: Leslie Frewin, 1968).

Menzies, Robert. *Afternoon Light* (London: Cassell, 1969).

—. *The Measure of the Years* (London: Cassell, 1970).

Nutting, Anthony. *No End of a Lesson: The Story of Suez* (London: C.N. Potter, 1967).

Spender, Jean. *Ambassador's Wife: A Woman's View of Life in Politics, Diplomacy and International Law* (Sydney: Angus & Robertson, 1968).

Spender, Percy. *Exercises in Diplomacy: The ANZUS Treaty and the Colombo Plan* (Sydney: Sydney University Press, 1969).

Tange, Arthur. *Defence Policy-Making: A Close-Up View, 1950-1980. A Personal Memoir* Peter Edwards ed. (Canberra: ANU Press, 2008), http://press.anu.edu.au?p=101541

Truman, Harry. *1945: Year of Decision* (New York: Doubleday & Co., 1955).

Watt, Alan. *The Evolution of Australian Foreign Policy, 1938-1965* (London: Cambridge University Press, 1968).

—. *Australian Diplomat: Memoirs of Sir Alan Watt* (Sydney: Angus & Robertson, 1972).

—. "The ANZUS Treaty: Past, Present and Future", *Australian Outlook* 24, no. 1 (1972), 17-36, https://doi.org/10.1080/10357717008444363

Secondary Sources

BOOKS

Adams, Valerie. *Eisenhower's Fine Group of Fellows: Crafting a National Security Strategy to Uphold the Great Equation* (Lanham: Lexington Books, 2006).

Albinski, Henry. *Politics and Foreign Policy in Australia: The Impact of Vietnam and Conscription* (Durham: Duke University Press, 1970).

—. *Australian Policies and Attitudes Toward China* (Princeton: Princeton University Press, 1965).

Ambrose, Stephen. *Eisenhower: Soldier and President* (New York: Pocket Books, 2003).

Arnold, Lorna, and Katherine Pyne. *Britain and the H-Bomb* (London: Palgrave, 2001).

Arnold, Lorna. *A Very Special Relationship: British Atomic Weapons Trials in Australia* (London: Her Majesty's Stationery Office, 1987).

Barclay, Glen St. John. *Friend in High Places: Australian-American Diplomatic Relations Since 1945* (Melbourne: Oxford University Press, 1985).

Bell, Coral. *Dependent Ally: A Study in Australian Foreign Policy* (Melbourne: Oxford University Press, 1988).

Blake, Kristen. *The US-Soviet Confrontation in Iran, 1945-1962: A Case in the Annals of the Cold War* (Lanham: University Press of America, 2009).

Blum, Robert. *Drawing the Line: The Origin of the American Containment Policy in South Asia* (New York: W.W. Norton & Co., 1982).

Bridoux, Jeff. *American Foreign Policy and Postwar Reconstruction* (New York: Routledge, 2011).

Buckley, Roger. *The United States in the Asia-Pacific Since 1945* (New York: Cambridge University Press, 2002).

Camilleri, Joseph. *Australian-American Relations: The Web of Dependence* (Melbourne: Macmillan, 1980).

Cohen, Warren. *The Cambridge History of American Foreign Relations, Volume IV: America in the Age of Soviet Power, 1945-1991* (New York: Cambridge University Press, 1993).

Cohen, Warren, and Akira Iriye eds. *The Great Powers in East Asia: 1953-1960* (New York: Columbia University Press, 1990).

Costigliola, Frank, and Michael Hogan eds. *America in the World: The Historiography of American Foreign Relations since 1941*, 2nd edn. (New York: Cambridge University Press, 2014).

Craig, Campbell, and Fredrik Logevall. *America's Cold War: The Politics of Insecurity* (Cambridge: The Belknap Press of Harvard University Press, 2009).

Davies, George. *The Occupation of Japan: The Rhetoric and Reality of Anglo-Australasian Relations, 1939-1952* (Brisbane: University of Queensland Press, 2001).

Dimitrakis, Panagiotis. *Failed Alliances of the Cold War: Britain's Strategy and Ambitions in Asia and the Middle East* (London: I.B. Tauris, 2011).

Edwards, Peter. *Australia and the Vietnam War* (Sydney: University of New South Wales Press, 2014).

—. *Arthur Tange: Last of the Mandarins* (Sydney: Allen & Unwin, 2006).

Etzold, Thomas, and John Lewis Gaddis eds. *Containment: Documents on American Policy and Strategy, 1945-1950* (New York: Columbia University Press, 1978).

Fain, W. Taylor. *American Ascendance and British Retreat in the Persian Gulf Region* (London: Palgrave, 2008).

Fraser, T.G., and Donette Murray. *America and the World Since 1945* (New York: Palgrave Macmillan, 2002).

Fenton, Damien. *To Cage the Red Dragon: SEATO and the Defence of Southeast Asia, 1955-1965* (Singapore: National University of Singapore Press, 2012).

Gaddis, John Lewis. *The Cold War: A New History* (New York: Penguin Books, 2005).

—. *Strategies of Containment: A Critical Appraisal of American National Security Policy During the Cold War* (New York: Oxford University Press, 2005).

—. *George F. Kennan: An American Life* (New York: Penguin, 2011).

Goldsworthy, David. *Losing the Blanket: Australia and the End of Britain's Empire* (Melbourne: Melbourne University Press, 2002).

Gurman, Hannah. *The Dissent Papers: The Voices of Diplomats in the Cold War and Beyond* (New York: Columbia University Press, 2012).

Harper, Norman. *A Great and Powerful Friend: A Study of Australian-American Relations Between 1900-1975* (Brisbane: University of Queensland Press, 1986).

Hogan, Ashley. *Moving in the Open Daylight: Doc Evatt, an Australian at the United Nations* (Sydney: Sydney University Press, 2008).

Horner, David. *The Spy Catchers: The Official History of ASIO, 1949-1963* (Sydney: Allen & Unwin, 2014).

Hudson, W.J. *Blind Loyalty: Australia and the Suez Crisis, 1956* (Melbourne: Melbourne University Press, 1989).

—. *Casey: A Bibliography* (London: Oxford University Press, 1986).

Jupp, James. *From White Australia to Woomera: The Story of Australian Immigration* (Cambridge: Cambridge University Press, 2002).

Kaufman, Victor. *Confronting Communism: US and British Policies toward China* (Columbia: University of Missouri Press, 2001).

Kobayashi, Ai. *W. MacMahon Ball: Politics for the People* (Melbourne: Australian Scholarly Publishing, 2013).

Lamb, Richard. *The Failure of the Eden Government* (London: Sidgwick & Jackson, 1987).

Leffler, Melvyn. *A Preponderance of Power: National Security, the Truman Administration, and the Cold War* (Palo Alto: Stanford University Press, 1994).

Lowe, David. *Australia Between Empires: The Life of Percy Spender* (London: Pickering & Chatto, 2010).

—. *Menzies and the Great World Struggle: Australia's Cold War, 1948-1954* (Sydney: University of New South Wales Press, 1999).

Lowe, Peter. *Containing the Cold War in East Asia: British Policies Towards Japan, China and Korea* (Manchester: Manchester University Press, 1997).

—. *Contending with Nationalism and Communism: British Policy Towards Southeast Asia, 1945-1965* (London: Palgrave, 2009).

Manne, Robert. *The Petrov Affair* (Melbourne: Text Publishing, 2004).

McNamara, Robert. *Britain, Nasser and the Balance of Power in the Middle East, 1952-1967* (London: Frank Cass Publishers, 2003).

Meaney, Neville. *Australia and the World: A Documentary History from the 1870s to the 1970s* (Melbourne: Longman Cheshire, 1985).

McClenahan, William. *Eisenhower and the Cold War Economy* (Baltimore: John Hopkins University Press, 2011).

McIntyre, W. David. *Background to the ANZUS Pact: Policy-making, Strategy and Diplomacy, 1945-1955* (Christchurch: Canterbury University Press, 1994).

—. *Winding up the British Empire in the Pacific Islands* (New York: Oxford University Press, 2014).

McKinnon, Malcolm. *Independence and Foreign Policy: New Zealand in the World Since 1935* (Auckland: Auckland University Press, 1993).

Millar, T.B. *Australia's Foreign Policy* (Sydney: Angus & Robertson, 1968).

Miscamble, Wilson. *From Roosevelt to Truman: Potsdam, Hiroshima and the Cold War* (New York: Cambridge University Press, 2008).

Morton, Peter. *Fire across the Desert: Woomera and the Anglo-Australian Joint Project, 1946-1980* (Canberra: Australian Government Publishing Service, 1989).

Mosley, Leonard. *Dulles: A Biography of Eleanor, Allen, and John Foster Dulles and their Family Network* (New York: The Dial Press, 1978).

Millar, T.B. *Australia's Foreign Policy* (Sydney: Angus and Robertson, 1968).

Newton, Jim. *Eisenhower: The White House Years* (Melbourne: Anchor Books, 2012).

Nichols, David. *Eisenhower 1956: The President's Year of Crisis* (New York: Simon & Schuster, 2011).

Oakman, Daniel. *Facing Asia: A History of the Colombo Plan* (Canberra: Australian National University Press, 2010).

O'Neill, Robert. *Australia in the Korean War: Volume 1, Strategy and Diplomacy* (Canberra: Australian Government Publishing Service, 1981).

Rabel, Roberto. *New Zealand and the Vietnam War: Politics and Diplomacy* (Auckland: Auckland University Press, 2013).

Reese, Trevor. *Australia, New Zealand and the United States, 1941-1968* (London: Oxford University Press, 1969).

Renouf, Alan. *The Frightened Country* (Melbourne: Macmillan, 1979).

Reynolds, Wayne. *Australia's Bid for the Atomic Bomb* (Melbourne: Melbourne University Press, 2000).

Schaller, Michael. *The American Occupation of Japan: The Origins of the Cold War in Asia* (New York: Oxford University Press, 1985).

Self, Robert. *British Foreign and Defence Policy since 1945: Challenges and Dilemmas in a Changing World* (New York: Palgrave, 2010).

Siracusa, Joseph, and David Coleman. *Australia Looks to America: Australian-American Relations Since Pearl Harbour* (Claremont: Regina Books, 2006).

Smith, Anthony. *Southeast Asia and New Zealand: A History of Regional and Bilateral Relations* (Wellington: Institute of Southeast Asian Studies, 2005).

Takemae, Eiji. *Inside GHQ: The Allied Occupation of Japan and its Legacy* (New York: Continuum, 2002).

Templeton, Malcolm. *Ties of Blood and Empire: New Zealand's Involvement in Middle East Defence and the Suez Crisis, 1947-1957* (Auckland: Auckland University Press, 1994).

Thorpe, D.R. *Eden: The Life and Times of Anthony Eden, First Earl of Avon, 1897-1977* (New York: Random House, 2004).

Trotter, Ann. *New Zealand and Japan, 1945-1952: The Occupation and the Peace Treaty* (London: The Athlone Press, 1990).

Tucker, Nancy Bernkopf. *The China Threat: Memories, Myths, and Realities in the 1950s* (New York: Columbia University Press, 2012).

—. *Strait Talk: United States-Taiwan Relations and the Crisis with China* (Cambridge: Harvard University Press, 2009).

Verbeek, Bertjan. *Decision Making in Britain during the Suez Crisis: Small Groups and a Persistent Leader* (Farnham: Ashgate, 2003).

Wang, Yi. *Australia-China Relations Post-1949: Sixty Years of Trade and Politics* (New York: Routledge, 2012).

Waters, Christopher. *The Empire Fractures: Anglo-Australian Conflict in the 1940s* (Melbourne: Australian Scholarly Publishing, 1995).

Watry, David M. *Diplomacy at the Brink: Eisenhower, Churchill and Eden in the Cold War* (Baton Rouge: Louisiana State University Press, 2014).

Williamson, Daniel. *Separate Agendas: Churchill, Eisenhower and Anglo-American Relations, 1953-1955* (Lanham: Lexington Books, 2006).

BOOK CHAPTERS

Beaumont, Joan. "Not the Cinderella it Once Seemed: The Historiography of Australian Foreign Policy", in Joan Beaumont, and Matthew Jordan eds. *Australia and the World: A Festschrift to Neville Meaney* (Sydney: Sydney University Press, 2013), 3-14.

—. "Making Australian Foreign Policy, 1941-1969", in Joan Beaumont, Christopher Waters, David Lowe, and Gary Woodard eds. *Ministers, Mandarins and Diplomats: Australian Foreign Policy Making, 1941-1969* (Melbourne: Melbourne University Press, 2003), 1-18.

Bongiorno, Frank. "John Beasley and the Postwar World", in Carl Bridge, Frank Biongiorno and David Lee eds. *The High Commissioners: Australia's Representatives in the United Kingdom, 1910-2010* (Canberra: Australian Department of Foreign Affairs and Trade, 2010), 111-126, https://dfat.gov.au/about-us/publications/historical-documents/Documents/high-commissioners.pdf

—. "Norman Makin and Post-War Diplomacy, 1946-1951", in David Lowe, David Lee and Carl Bridge eds. *Australia Goes to Washington: 75 Years of Australian Representation in the United States, 1940-2015* (Canberra: ANU Press, 2016), 39-56, https://press.anu.edu.au/publications/australia-goes-washington

Cotton, James. "R. G. Casey's Writings on Australia's Place in the World", in Melissa Conley Tyler, John Robbins, and Adrian March eds. *R.G. Casey: Minister for External Affairs, 1951-1960* (Australian Institute of International Affairs, 2012), http://www.internationalaffairs.org.au/wp-content/uploads/2014/01/casey-book-final-revised.pdf

Day, David. "27th December 1941: Prime Minister Curtin's New Year Message, Australia Looks to America", in Martin Crotty and David Roberts eds. *Turning Points in Australian History* (Sydney: University of New South Wales Press, 2009), 129-142.

Goh, Evelyn, and Rosemary Foot. "From Containment to Containment? Understanding US Relations with China since 1949", in Robert Schulzinger ed. *A Companion to American Foreign Relations* (Hoboken: Wiley-Blackwell, 2003), 255-274.

Holloway, David. "Nuclear Weapons and the escalation of the Cold War, 1945-1962", in Melvyn Leffler, and Odd Arne Westad eds. *The Cambridge History of the Cold War: Vol. I, Origins* (London: Cambridge University Press, 2010), 376-297, https://doi.org/10.1017/CHOL9780521837194.019

Hybel, Roberto Alex. "Harry Truman and the Decision to Intervene in the Korean War and to Cross the 39th Parallel", in Alex Roberto Hybel ed. *US Foreign Policy Decision-Making from Truman to Kennedy: Responses to International Challenges* (London: Palgrave, 2014), 55-85.

Immerman, Richard. "Foreign Relations in the 1950s", in Robert Schulzinger ed. *A Companion to American Foreign Relations* (Hoboken, Wiley-Blackwell, 2003), 292-308.

Leffler, Melvyn. "The emergence of an American grand strategy, 1945-1952", in Melvyn Leffler, and Odd Arne Westad eds. *The Cambridge History of the Cold War: Vol. I, Origins* (London: Cambridge University Press, 2010), 67-89, https://doi.org/10.1017/CHOL9780521837194.005

Lowe, David. "Percy Spender, Minister and Ambassador", in Joan Beaumont, Christopher Waters, David Lowe, and Gary Woodard eds. *Ministers, Mandarins and Diplomats: Australian Foreign Policy Making, 1941-1969* (Melbourne: Melbourne University Press, 2003), 62-87.

Macmahon, Robert. "US National Security Policy From Eisenhower to Kennedy", in Melvyn Leffler and Odd Arne Westad eds. *The Cambridge History of the Cold War: Vol. I, Origins* (Cambridge: Cambridge University Press, 2010), 288-311, https://doi.org/10.1017/CHOL9780521837194.015

McIntyre, W. David. "From Dual Dependence to Nuclear Free", in Geoffrey Rice, W. H. Oliver and B. R. Williams eds. *The Oxford History of New Zealand*, 2nd edn. (Melbourne: Oxford University Press, 1993), 520-527.

Stueck, William. "The Korean War", in Melvin Leffler, and Odd Arne Westad eds. *The Cambridge History of the Cold War: Vol. I, Origins* (Cambridge: Cambridge University Press, 2010), 266-287, https://doi.org/10.1017/CHOL9780521837194.014

Ward, Stuart. "The 'New Nationalism' in Australia, Canada and New Zealand: Civic Culture in the wake of the British World", in Joan Beaumont and Matthew Jordan eds. *Australia and the World: A Festschrift to Neville Meaney* (Sydney: Sydney University Press, 2013), 191-214.

Waters, Christopher. "Cold War Liberals: Richard Casey and the Department of External Affairs, 1951-1960", in Joan Beaumont, Christopher Waters, David Lowe, and Gary Woodard eds. *Ministers, Mandarins and Diplomats: Australian Foreign Policy Making, 1941-1969* (Melbourne: Melbourne University Press, 2003), 88-105.

—. "The Great Debates: H.V. Evatt and the Department of External Affairs, 1941-49", in Joan Beaumont, Christopher Waters, David Lowe, and Gary Woodard eds. *Ministers, Mandarins and Diplomats: Australian Foreign Policy Making, 1941-1969* (Melbourne University Press, 2003), 45-61.

JOURNAL ARTICLES

Albinski, Henry. "Australia and the Chinese Strategic Embargo", *Australian Outlook* 19, no. 2 (1965), 117-128, https://doi.org/10.1080/10357716508444200

Braddick, C.W. "Britain, the Commonwealth, and the Post-war Japanese Revival, 1945–70", *The Round Table* 99, no. 409 (2010), 371-389, https://doi.org/10.1080/00358533.2010.498975

Cotton, James. "R.G. Casey and Australian International Thought: Empire, Nation, Community", *The International History Review* 33, no. 1 (2011), 95-113, https://doi.org/10.1080/07075332.2011.555380

De Matos, Christine. "Diplomacy Interrupted?: Macmahon Ball, Evatt and Labor's Policies in Occupied Japan", *Australian Journal of History and Politics* 52, no. 2 (2006), 188-201, https://doi.org/10.1111/j.1467-8497.2005.00414.x

Jones, Matthew. "Great Britain, The United States, and Consultation over Use of the Atomic Bomb", *The Historical Journal* 54, no. 3 (2011), 797-828, https://doi.org/10.1017/S0018246X11000240

Kaufman, Victor. "Operation Oracle: The United States, Great Britain, New Zealand and the Offshore Island Crisis of 1954-55", *Journal of Imperial and Commonwealth History* 32, no. 3 (2004), 106-124, https://doi.org/10.1080/0308653042000279687

Lee, David. "Australia, the British Commonwealth, and the United States, 1950-1953", *The Journal of Imperial and Commonwealth History* 30, no. 3 (1992), 445-469, https://doi.org/10.1080/03086539208582880

—. "Australia and Anglo-American Disagreement over the Quemoy-Matsu Crisis, 1954-55." *The Journal of Imperial and Commonwealth History* 23, no. 1 (January 1995), 105-128, https://doi.org/10.1080/03086539508582946

—. "The National Security Planning and Defence Preparations of the Menzies Government, 1950-1953", *War & Society* 10, no. 2 (1992), https://doi.org/10.1179/072924792791198913

Lin, Hsiao-ting. "US-Taiwan Military Diplomacy Revisited: Chiang Kai-shek, Baituan, and the 1954 Mutual Defense Pact", *Diplomatic History* 37, no. 5 (2013), 971-994, https://doi.org/10.1093/dh/dht047

Mann, Jatinder. "The End of the British World and the Redefinition of Citizenship in Aotearoa New Zealand, 1950s–1970s", *National Identities* (2017), 1-20, https://doi.org/10.1080/14608944.2017.1369019

Meaney, Neville. "Looking Back in Fear: Percy Spender, the Japanese Peace Treaty and the ANZUS Pact", *Japan Forum* 15, no. 3 (2003), 399-410, https://doi.org/10.1080/0955580032000124790

—. "Britishness and Australian Identity: The Problem of Nationalism in Australian History and Historiography", *Australian Historical Studies* 32, no. 116 (2001), 76-90, https://doi.org/10.1080/10314610108596148

McLean, David. "Anzus Origins: A Reassessment", *Australian Historical Studies* 24, no. 94 (1990), 64-82, https://doi.org/10.1080/10314619008595832

McGibbon, Ian. "New Zealand's Intervention in the Korean War: June-July 1950", *International History Review* 11, no. 1 (1989), 272-290.

Peden, George. "Recognising and Responding to Relative Decline: The Case of Post-War Britain", *Diplomacy and Statecraft* 24, no. 1 (2013), 59-76, https://doi.org/10.1017/S0018246X12000246

—. "Suez and Britain's Decline as a World Power", *The Historical Journal* 55, no. 4 (2012), 1073-1096, https://doi.org/10.1017/S0018246X12000246

Pfeiffer, Rolf. "New Zealand and the Suez Crisis of 1956", *Journal of Imperial and Commonwealth History* 21, no. 1 (1993), https://doi.org/10.1080/03086539308582888

Robb, Thomas K. and David James Gill. "The ANZUS Treaty during the Cold War: A Reinterpretation of U.S. Diplomacy in the Southwest Pacific", *Journal of Cold War Studies* 17, no. 4 (2015), 109-157, https://doi.org/10.1162/JCWS_a_00599

Smith, Tony. "New Bottles for New Wine: A Pericentric Framework for the Study of the Cold War", *Diplomatic History* 24, no. 4 (2000), 567–591, https://doi.org/10.1111/0145-2096.00237

The Rt Hon Lord Owen CH. "The Effect of Prime Minister Anthony Eden's Illness on his Decision-making During the Suez Crisis", *QJM: An International Journal of Medicine* 98, no. 6 (2005), 387–402, https://doi.org/10.1093/qjmed/hci071

Umetsu, Hiroyuki. "Australia's Response to the Indochina Crisis of 1954 Amidst Anglo-American Confrontation", *Australian Journal of Politics and History* 52, no. 3 (2006), 398-416, https://doi.org/10.1111/j.1467-8497.2006.00426.x

—. "The Origins of the British Commonwealth Strategic Reserve: The UK Proposal to Revitalise ANZAM and the Increased Australian Defence Commitment to Malaya", *Australian Journal of Politics and History* 50, no. 4 (2004), 509-525, https://doi.org/10.1111/j.1467-8497.2004.00350.x

Waite, James. "Contesting 'the Right of Decision': New Zealand, the Commonwealth, and the New Look", *Diplomatic History* 30, no. 5 (2006), 893-917, https://doi.org/10.1111/j.1467-7709.2006.00583.x

THESES

Hamilton, Eamon. *Sir Anthony Eden and the Suez Crisis of 1956: The Anatomy of a Flawed Personality*. MA Thesis, University of Birmingham, 2015, http://etheses.bham.ac.uk/6445/

Hardy, Travis. *The Consanguinity of Ideas: Race and Anti-Communism in the US-Australian Relationship, 1933-1953*. PhD Thesis, University of Tennessee, 2010.

McLean, Craig. *R.G. Casey and Australian Foreign Policy: Engaging with China and Southeast Asia, 1951-1960*. PhD Thesis, Victoria University, 2008, http://vuir.vu.edu.au/15200/

Umetsu, Hiroyuki. *From ANZUS to SEATO: A Study of Australian Foreign Policy. 1950-54*. PhD Thesis, University of Sydney, 1996.

List of Illustrations

1. US General Douglas MacArthur signs as Supreme Allied Commander for the formal surrender of Japan during WWII, September 1945. Photo by US Navy (1945), US National Archives Catalog, https://catalog.archives.gov/id/520694, unrestricted use.   14

2. Australian Prime Minister Ben Chifley, Australian External Affairs Minister Herbert Evatt and British Prime Minister Clement Attlee meet at the 1946 Commonwealth Conference. Photo by unknown (1946), Flickr, https://www.flickr.com/photos/chifleyresearch/14483884882, CC BY 2.0.   17

3. Delegates to the British Commonwealth Conference on the Japanese Peace Treaty in Canberra, August 1947. Photo by unknown (1947), Flickr, https://www.flickr.com/photos/archivesnz/28950147372, CC BY 2.0.   40

4. Chairman Mao Zedong proclaiming the founding of the People's Republic of China (PRC), 1 October 1949. Photo by Hou Bo (1949), Wikimedia, https://commons.wikimedia.org/wiki/File:PRCFounding.jpg, public domain.   53

5. New Zealand Prime Minister Sidney Holland (1949-1957). Photo taken by Crown Studies of Wellington (1951), Wikimedia, https://commons.wikimedia.org/wiki/File:Sidney_George_Holland_(1951).jpg, public domain.   56

6. Australian Prime Minister Robert Menzies (1939-1941, 1949-1966). Photo by unknown (1950), National Library of Australia, https://catalogue.nla.gov.au/Record/3307904, copyright expired.   57

7. A Soviet-made North Korean T-34 tank knocked out during the UN led intervention on the Korean Peninsula. Photo by Curtis A. Ulz (1950), Wikimedia, https://commons.wikimedia.org/wiki/File:T-34_knocked_out_September_1950.jpg, public domain. ... 64

8. President Truman meeting with US Secretary of Defence George Marshall, Secretary of State Dean Acheson and Secretary of the Treasury John Snyder, October 1950. Photo by Abbie Rowe (1950), US National Archives Catalog, https://catalog.archives.gov/id/200235, unrestricted use. ... 73

9. John Foster Dulles, US Negotiator to the ANZUS Treaty and US Secretary of State (1953-1959). Photo by US Department of State (n. d.), Flickr, https://www.flickr.com/photos/statephotos/2358513061/, unrestricted use. ... 77

10. ANZUS logo. Archives New Zealand (n. d.), Flickr, https://www.flickr.com/photos/archivesnz/20921987801/, CC BY 2.0. ... 89

11. Australian External Affairs Minister Richard Casey (1951-1960). Photo by Australian News and Information Bureau (1951), Wikimedia, https://commons.wikimedia.org/wiki/File:Richard_Casey_1951.jpg, Crown Copyright. ... 95

12. Eisenhower during the US Election Campaign in Baltimore, MD, September 1952. Credit: Dwight D. Eisenhower Presidential Library, Wikimedia, https://commons.wikimedia.org/wiki/File:I_like_Ike.jpg, public domain. ... 110

13. US President Dwight Eisenhower (1953-1961). Photo by Fabian Bachrach (1952), US Library of Congress, https://www.loc.gov/resource/cph.3c17123/, public domain. ... 111

14. Viet Minh soldiers capture French troops and escort them to a prisoner-of-war camp, 1954. Photo by unknown (1954), Wikimedia, https://commons.wikimedia.org/wiki/File:Dien_Bien_Phu_1954_French_prisoners.jpg, public domain. ... 119

15. French Foreign Minister Georges Bidault, British Foreign Secretary Anthony Eden, US Secretary of State John Foster Dulles. Photo by unknown (n. d.), Wikimedia, https://commons.wikimedia.org/wiki/File:Georges_Bidault,_Anthony_Eden_and_John_Foster_Dulles.jpg, CC BY 3.0. ... 129

List of Illustrations   199

16. Map of the Taiwan Strait. Created by Andrew Kelly, adapted from map by NordNordWest (2008), Wikimedia, https://commons.wikimedia.org/wiki/File:Taiwan_location_map.svg, CC BY 3.0.   137

17. Egyptian Prime Minister Gamal Abdel Nasser cheered in Cairo after nationalising the Suez Canal. Photo by unknown (1956), Wikimedia, https://commons.wikimedia.org/wiki/File:Nasser_cheered_by_supporters_in_1956.jpg, public domain.   159

18. British Naval Carriers during the 1956 Suez Crisis. Photo by British Royal Navy official photographer (1956), Wikimedia, https://commons.wikimedia.org/wiki/File:British_carriers_during_Suez_Crisis_1956.jpg, public domain.   170

Index

Acheson, Dean 52, 96, 104
Anglo-American relations. *See* United States; Britain
ANZAM 43, 106, 109
ANZUS 1–4, 6, 8, 10, 55, 60, 82, 85–86, 89–90, 93–97, 102, 104, 113, 120, 134, 137, 146, 151, 174, 178–179
  British membership 100
  machinery 94, 114
  origins 13
Atomic weapons 45–46, 113–114, 142
Attlee, Clement 18, 44
Australia 1, 5–6, 8, 13, 18, 20, 26, 35, 52, 59, 72, 114, 123, 126, 133, 149–150, 162, 181
  Australian views on Pacific Pact 60, 83
  defence policy 13, 17–20, 35, 44, 87, 113, 123–124, 154, 179
  domestic politics 123
  domestic views on China 144, 152
  Indochina 124
  Japanese occupation 29–32, 34–35, 78, 83
  Korean War 65, 71
  Quemoy-Matsu Crisis 137–138, 146, 148–149
  recognition of China 54, 67, 143, 154–155
  relations with Britain 3, 5–6, 16–17, 19–20, 32, 45, 59–60, 101, 103, 162, 173–174
  relations with New Zealand. *See* trans-Tasman relations
  relations with the United States 3, 5, 13, 24–25, 36, 45, 47–48, 52, 57, 59–61, 64, 66, 72, 97–98, 114–115, 123, 126, 141, 149–151, 161–162
Australian-New Zealand relations. *See* trans-Tasman relations

Ball, William Macmahon 31–32
Beasley, John 37
Berendsen, Carl 21, 24, 26, 31, 33, 46, 58, 60–61, 66
Britain 2, 5, 18, 170
  British views on ANZUS 83–86, 93, 100
  defence policy 19
  Indochina 128
  Invasion of Egypt 170
  post-war situation 18, 43
  Quemoy-Matsu Crisis 138, 147–148, 151
  relations with Australia and New Zealand 3, 44, 100, 104–106, 174
  relations with the United States 128, 142, 151, 158, 169
  SEATO 132
Byrnes, James 16, 23, 29

Cairo Conference 22
Canberra Pact 22
Casey, Richard 8, 94–95, 97, 101–104, 107, 110, 114–115, 123–125, 127, 132, 137–138, 140, 143–144, 146, 151–152, 154–155, 162, 165, 169, 171, 175, 180, 193

125

Chifley, Ben 17–18, 44–45, 51
China, People's Republic of 9, 51, 53–55, 67–68, 97, 110–111, 135, 138–139, 141–144, 146–149, 153–155
China, Republic of 53, 138, 144, 150, 152
Churchill, Winston 100, 105, 121, 128, 160
Cold War 63
   containment 4, 15, 34, 71. *See also* Communism
   East-West conflict 53, 158, 172
   nuclear deterrence 113–114
Colombo Conference 55
Colombo Plan 58
Communism 4, 8, 34, 53, 55–56, 71, 82, 119. *See also* Cold War
Corner, Frank 7, 17, 96, 106, 113, 117–118, 176, 180
Curtin, John 13

Dien Bien Phu 117–118, 124, 130
Doidge, Frederick 51, 55, 58, 62, 74–76, 79, 81–84, 90
Domino Theory 120. *See also* Communism; Cold War
Dulles, John Foster 8, 62–63, 72, 74, 76–77, 79–89, 105, 108–109, 112, 114, 119–123, 125, 128, 131–133, 135–136, 138–142, 145, 147–154, 158, 166–172, 177, 181

Eden, Anthony 18, 121, 138, 142, 157, 160, 167, 176–177, 181
Eggleston, Frederic 41
Egypt. *See* Suez Canal
Eisenhower, Dwight vii, 7–8, 15, 94, 107, 109–110, 112–115, 117, 119–120, 122, 124, 128, 130–131, 135, 141–142, 144, 148, 154, 157–161, 168–172, 181
   1952 election 109
Enlai, Zhou 147, 153
Europe 3, 87, 160
   post-war reconstruction 18

Evatt, Herbert 8, 18, 22–23, 27, 31, 35–38, 40, 43, 46, 48, 51, 54, 180

Far Eastern Commission 30. *See also* Japan
Five-Power Staff Agency 105
France 117, 126, 128, 164
   Indochina 128
Fraser, Peter 14, 25–26, 36, 52

Geneva Conference, 1954 130

Holland, Sidney 55, 78, 106, 139, 148, 163, 172

Indochina 1, 52, 67, 106, 108, 115, 117–118, 120–130, 132, 134, 181
   United Action 122, 124–128, 130
Israel 169

Japan 29, 34, 62, 72, 83
   Commonwealth Conference 39
   occupation 29, 32
   Peace treaty 3, 40, 62–63, 72, 76, 78–80, 83, 88–89, 93, 179, 197
   World War II 13

Kai-shek, Chiang 53, 141, 149, 152
Kennan, George 29, 34
Korean War 3, 51, 63, 65, 71, 76, 110

Laking, George 96

MacArthur, Douglas 33, 42
Macdonald, Thomas 139–140, 146, 163–165
MacKintosh, Elizabeth. *See* Tey, Josephine
Makin, Norman 37
Malaya 1, 43–45, 52, 85, 100, 106, 108, 118, 128, 132, 148, 151, 163
Malaysia. *See* Malaya
Manus Island 22, 25, 43
Marshall, George 36, 40, 88
McCarthy, Joseph 119
McIntosh, Alister 2, 8, 17, 25, 27, 31, 33–34, 37, 46, 54–55, 58, 62, 66–68,

83, 85–86, 96, 99, 103–104, 106–107, 111, 115, 118, 126, 168, 175, 180
Menzies, Robert 6, 56, 60, 64, 101, 148, 151–152, 161, 165–167, 173–174
Middle East 18, 87, 99, 112–113, 160
Munro, Leslie 111, 120, 126, 140, 147

Nasser, Gamal Abdel 112, 157–159, 164, 167, 170
NATO. *See* North Atlantic Treaty Organisation
New Zealand 2, 6, 8, 14, 18, 27, 52, 74, 78, 84, 163, 181
   defence policy 13, 20–21, 61, 81, 84, 113, 179
   Indochina 126–127
   Japanese occupation 29–30, 33–34, 40, 78, 83
   Korean War 66
   New Zealand views on ANZUS 93, 96
   New Zealand views on Pacific Pact 60, 81, 84
   Quemoy-Matsu Crisis 139, 146, 148
   recognition of China 55, 111
   relations with Australia. *See* trans-Tasman relations
   relations with Britain 6–7, 17, 46, 87, 103, 126, 163–164, 168, 172–173, 175
   relations with the United States 6–7, 14, 21, 52, 58, 61, 96, 111, 115, 126, 147
   SEATO 133
North Atlantic Treaty Organisation 3, 79, 81, 97, 133
Nuclear weapons. *See also* Atomic weapons

Operation Oracle. *See* Quemoy-Matsu Crisis

Pacific Pact 2, 23–24, 52, 60–62, 64–65, 71–78, 81, 84, 86, 97. *See* also ANZUS
Pearl Harbor 14

Petrov Affair 123
PRC. *See* China, People's Republic of

Quemoy-Matsu Crisis
   Defence Treaty 141
   Operation Oracle 140, 142, 146, 153

Radford, Arthur 98, 113, 118, 121, 131, 136

SEATO. *See* Southeast Asia Treaty Organisation
Southeast Asia Treaty Organisation 130, 133–134
South Pacific 22
Soviet Union 16, 34, 51, 63, 135
Spender, Percy 1, 8, 51, 56–60, 64–65, 67–68, 71–76, 78, 80–84, 87, 89–90, 94, 97–98, 101–102, 107, 114, 117, 120, 122–123, 140–141, 149–150, 153, 161, 180
Suez Canal 6, 87, 160
   1956 Crisis 157
   Aswan Dam Project 158
   Suez Committee 166

Taiwan. *See* China, Republic
Taiwan Straits Crisis. *See* Quemoy-Matsu Crisis
Tange, Arthur 65
trans-Tasman relations 4, 22, 26–27, 34, 45, 54, 58, 66–68, 80, 112, 118, 140, 181
Truman, Harry 4, 7, 23–24, 30, 62, 67, 72–73, 79, 94, 107, 109, 113, 117, 192

United Kingdom. *See* Britain
United Nations 26, 64, 68, 138–139, 172, 176
United States 2, 7–8, 62, 130, 181 4
   American views on ANZUS 88, 93, 96, 98
   American views on Pacific Pact 76
   defence policy 15–16, 22–23, 25, 52, 113–114, 131, 136, 141, 179

domestic politics 119–120, 168
domestic views on China 145
Indochina 128, 130
Japanese occupation 29, 33–34, 41–42, 63, 74
Korean War 71
Quemoy-Matsu Crisis 136, 145, 150
recognition of China 54, 110
relations with Australia and New Zealand 4, 13, 16, 21, 24–25, 36, 42, 47, 63, 76, 79–80, 96, 98, 114, 120–122, 132, 139, 141, 150, 161
relations with Britain 128, 142, 148, 158, 168–171

Vietnam. *See* Indochina

Webb, Thomas Clifton 103–104, 107, 111–112, 126, 164, 175
White Australia 125
World War II 13

Zedong, Mao 53, 144

This book need not end here...

Share

All our books—including the one you have just read—are free to access online so that students, researchers and members of the public who can't afford a printed edition will have access to the same ideas. This title will be accessed online by hundreds of readers each month across the globe: why not share the link so that someone you know is one of them?
This book and additional content is available at:
https://www.openbookpublishers.com/product/781

Customise

Personalise your copy of this book or design new books using OBP and third-party material. Take chapters or whole books from our published list and make a special edition, a new anthology or an illuminating coursepack. Each customised edition will be produced as a paperback and a downloadable PDF. Find out more at:
https://www.openbookpublishers.com/section/59/1

Like Open Book Publishers
Follow @OpenBookPublish
Read more at the Open Book Publishers BLOG

www.ingramcontent.com/pod-product-compliance
Lightning Source LLC
Chambersburg PA
CBHW050525170426
43201CB00013B/2091